1,234 -see green sheres

LOOKING FORWARD

LOOKING FORWARD

Comparative Perspectives on Cuba's Transition

edited by

MARIFELI PÉREZ-STABLE

Foreword by Fernando Henrique Cardoso

University of Notre Dame Press

Notre Dame, Indiana

Copyright © 2007 by University of Notre Dame
Notre Dame, Indiana 46556
www.undpress.nd.edu
All Rights Reserved

Designed by Wendy McMillen
Set in 10.6/14 Minion by BookComp, Inc.
Printed on 55# Nature's Natural paper in the U.S.A. by Sheridan Books, Inc.

Library of Congress Cataloging-in-Publication Data

Looking forward : comparative perspectives on Cuba's transition / edited by
Marifeli Pérez-Stable.
p.   cm.
Includes bibliographical references and index.
ISBN-13: 978-0-268-03891-5 (pbk. : alk. paper)
ISBN-10: 0-268-03891-0 (pbk. : alk. paper)
1. Cuba—Forecasting.   2. Cuba—History—1990–
I. Pérez-Stable, Marifeli, 1949–
F1788.L576   2007
972.9106'40112—dc22   2007019520

 *This book printed on recycled paper.*

In memory of my father,

Eliseo Pérez-Stable (1921 – 2005)

Contents

Foreword

Few countries have been the subject of so much controversy, debate, and probing in the past four decades as much as Cuba. Some forty-six years after the Revolution, Cuba continues to be a symbolic force far beyond its small size and weak economy.

Interest in Cuban affairs is once again rising, yet the reason is no longer the Revolution as a role model for building new societies under the nose of the world's largest capitalist power. The issue now is the question posed by the approaching demise of the principal leader of a regime that will not survive him: Where is Cuba headed after Fidel?

To answer this question, Marifeli Pérez-Stable, the Cuban-born author of *The Cuban Revolution: Origins, Course, and Legacy*—an essential reference on the topic—has organized a collection of essays that attempt to interpret the social, political, and economic transformations noted or foreseen in Cuba as it enters a likely transition.

The traditional free hand of the essay writer is firmly in evidence here. All authors start from a common point—Cuba's domestic and foreign affairs, mainly since the fall of the Soviet Union. And as they search for support for their perception of future trends, they employ comparisons with political or economic transitions observed within the past twenty years in Latin America, the former Soviet bloc, and East Asia.

The result is an all-inclusive, orderly review of all the possible *futures* of Cuba. It ranges from classical transition studies (i.e., the role of the military, the emergence of civil society, relations between émigrés and the internal opposition, the role of outside actors) to issues closer to the microphysics of power, such as race and gender relations and the ideological and cultural dimensions of politics, which is essential to understanding a regime that made a vast symbolic investment to consolidate its power.

By treating three normally unconnected perspectives—institutions, social relations, and ideology—as complementary, this book makes an especially interesting contribution to the debate on Cuba after Fidel. Will it be a market democracy, or perhaps a hybrid—a mixed economy with a freer society still controlled by the heirs to the regime? If the former, will change be abrupt or gradual? Will a transition necessarily do away with the social gains made by the Cuban people, or will it be an opportunity to augment them after years of economic crisis?

These questions elicit both hope and concern in those who have been fighting for democracy, equality, and peace in Latin America and the Caribbean because in that long march Cuba stands as a special chapter whose fate makes a great difference for the entire region.

By surviving the fall of the Soviet Union, Cuba shifted this transition to an era no longer ruled by the exultant liberal certainties of the late 1980s. We know now that transitioning to any kind of market economy requires not the destruction but the reform of existing institutions, lest the transition end in economic collapse and social breakdown. We also know that building democracy is a gradual, rather uncertain collective undertaking whose success depends on the old regime's institutional legacy and the ability of political actors to build institutions capable of ensuring effective citizenship.

For domestic and foreign actors, the lessons of the last two decades advise a negotiated transition along with measures designed to build economic confidence and political tolerance. Absent gradual confidence-building measures, attempts to build a regime of increased freedoms will make no progress. Instead, they may trigger a repressive backlash or the emergence of criminal groups whose actions can turn a democratic state into an utter impossibility and a market economy into a stage for mafia-style warfare.

Paving the way for a successful transition in Cuba is an immense responsibility. I am frankly skeptical of the chances here of an Asian-style transition such as Vietnam's, with capitalism moving ahead under a one-party system with a tight rein on society. For good or ill, Cuba is part of the Western world. Therefore, I am of the view that demands for greater economic freedom will rise in tandem with increased demands for greater political and civil liberties.

Both by act or omission, the United States is in a position to make the outside winds blow for or against an orderly transition conducted from within, which is why the increasingly unilateral stance of U.S. foreign policy, particularly on issues regarded as part of the domestic agenda, is of so much concern. Cuba fits the bill, with a twist: in addition to being on the security agenda, the presence of a highly politicized émigré community in the crucial state of Florida also makes it part of the electoral scenario. Thus, the type of smooth cooperation from both sides of the Atlantic that proved so useful to the transition in Eastern Europe would in this case appear to be that much more difficult.

Though difficult, cooperation is not impossible. As is to be expected in a pluralistic society, many in the United States are now actively questioning unilateralism and the notion that freedom and democracy—values to which this great nation does not hold title—could or should be imposed at gunpoint. It remains to be seen whether this new attitude will translate into concrete action by the current and future administrations.

Cooperating with Cuba is also Latin America's responsibility. We share with it our Iberian heritage, the language of the former Spanish colonies, the presence of blacks and natives in our social and cultural makeup, the mixing of many different races. Ever since the return to democratic rule, this common background has provided a basis for dialogue and exchange—not always easy, yet never broken—with Cuba. The political capital earned in these exchanges may prove to be a valuable asset for a Cuban transition, provided it is expended within the principles of democracy and noninterference enshrined in the Inter-American Democratic Charter of 2001.

However important the external players may be, the fate of Cuba will be primarily decided within Cuba. No formula concocted abroad will ever provide a lasting solution. Cuban socialism, it must be understood, is a variant of Cuban nationalism—the reverse of the experience of Eastern Europeans, who had socialism imposed on them from abroad. In Cuba, socialism stood on the shoulders of nationalist sentiment, and it has endured by laying deep roots in it, especially once the Soviet Union fell and took Cuba's umbilical cord with it.

In a Cuba after Fidel, nationalist sentiment will help maintain cohesion. Its challenge, then, is to build on the notion that Cuba belongs to all Cubans—a formidable challenge for a bitterly divided people who question each other's legitimacy. Émigrés blame the regime for taking away their right to live at home, while its supporters charge émigrés with being agents of their biggest foreign foe—a role that the United States took on with disastrous results, bolstering rather than thwarting the regime it purported to fight.

Thus, in a Cuban transition, national reconciliation will be no mere goal—it will be a prime imperative. Without it, no institutional framework will ever stand. Allowing, promoting, and facilitating reconciliation will be a responsibility second to none for all directly or indirectly involved at this crucial stage of Cuban history.

The cornerstone of Cuba's national reconciliation is the internal opposition that arose in the 1990s as the harbinger of good news among so much bad. This opposition, which resides within Cuba, stands against the regime rather than against the Revolution as a whole. It emerged by using the right of petition entrenched in the Constitution—a device whose legitimacy the regime could not question. Initiatives such as the Varela Project were used to confront the regime, successfully mobilizing thousands of Cubans for human rights and political freedom. Operating under more adverse conditions, they did what we so often did under the Brazilian military dictatorship: use every venue allowed by the regime to challenge it and sow the seeds of democratic ferment to bring about its downfall. This allowed us to steer clear of the deadly dilemma of either joining the regime or rising up in arms against it.

The emergence of an internal opposition, thus, makes it possible to break free of the unyielding in-country Cubans versus overseas Cubans dichotomy. This can pave the way for a transition that is free from civil strife and outside intervention and lay the basis for a broadening of the civil, political, and social rights and freedoms of the people of Cuba. The force of such an option will depend on whether the elites of the regime and émigré communities can build leaderships—such as that of Oswaldo Payá Sardiñas in the Varela Project—that are driven more by their hopes for a better future than by a compulsion to settle old scores.

Leadership such as that will be required, especially because a new institutional framework will have fragile underpinnings. Unlike in Eastern Europe, socialism in Cuba was built less on institutions than on regimentation of the masses around a charismatic leader. True, as an essay points out, Cuba is not entirely inexpert in the functioning of liberal constitutional institutions. Yet its experience is more limited than that of Hungary, Poland, or Czechoslovakia prior to the "velvet revolutions," during which—truth be told—transitions had begun long before, under socialism. The economic and political reforms introduced in Cuba in the early '90s were tepid, then neutralized, then downright repealed soon after.

This recognition should not be interpreted as gloomy prophecy. To paraphrase a well-known dictum by the older Marx, people make their own history but they do not make it under circumstances they choose. Even so, it is they who make it. Cuban society has long been demonstrating that despite the curtailment of freedoms life under the crusty old regime remains vibrant. This means that there will be life after it. It is to be hoped that Cubans' zest for life translates into a renewal of the Cuban Revolution's selfless dream, turned into a nightmare by the deliberate smothering of freedoms. If freedom can move forward by nourishing rather than razing what is commendable about the Revolution—universal access to public services and goods—Cuba will have finally fulfilled the high hopes first raised in now-distant 1959.

That, I believe, is the aspiration of the authors in this book. It certainly is mine.

Fernando Henrique Cardoso
Translated by Patricio Mason

Acknowledgments

"Always say thank you," my grandmother used to say. Politeness aside, in this case, it is essential to acknowledge the institutions and many individuals who made the publication of *Looking Forward* possible.

This collection has four institutional sponsors: the Kellogg Institute for International Studies at the University of Norte Dame, the Foundation for International Relations and External Dialogue (FRIDE) in Madrid, the Inter-American Dialogue in Washington, DC, and the Latin American and Caribbean Center and the Cuban Research Institute at Florida International University (FIU). At FRIDE, I am especially grateful to Fernando Espada, José Luis Herrero, and Diego Hidalgo. At the Inter-American Dialogue, to Peter Hakim, Christina Nielsen, and, especially, Ivana Rossi and Jaclyn Shull-González for the intelligence with which they read the essays. Christian Gómez and Nathan Doyel diligently worked on the manuscript's final stages. At FIU, I am not sure what I would have done without the tireless help of Julissa Castellanos and Alma DeRojas. Finally, Patricio Mason did an impeccable translation of President Cardoso's preface, which Sergio Fausto at the Instituto Fernando Henrique Cardoso in Sao Paulo facilitated. Alisa Newman finely translated Rafael Rojas's chapter.

The Kellogg Institute and FRIDE defrayed the costs of the meetings that we held to discuss the texts. The first was at the University of Notre Dame in September 2003 in order to coincide with my stay at the intellectual retreat that the institute generously offers to outside researchers. Discussants there were Gilberto Cárdenas, Michael Coppedge, Teresa Ghilarducci, Frances Hagopian, Scott Mainwaring, Juan Méndez, George López, A. James MacAdams, Anthony Messina, María-Rosa

Olivera-Williams, Christopher Welna, and Christina Wolbrecht. When we met at FIU, in May 2004, Eduardo Gamarra, Guillermo Grenier, Ivelaw Griffith, Tony Maingot, Timothy Power, Elisabeth Prugl, Jean Rahier, and Rick Tardanico commented on the texts, along with Bruce Bagley of the University of Miami and Carlos Manuel de la Cruz. The authors of *Looking Forward* greatly appreciated your input. To my colleagues: I apologize for having mercilessly insisted you follow the template that I created for the essays.

The Ford Foundation awarded FIU's Latin American and Caribbean Center a generous grant that made *Looking Forward* possible and allowed me the time to bring it to fruition. As always, Cristina Eguizábal was an excellent interlocutor and a keen observer of Cuban affairs. Thanks as well to Barbara J. Hanrahan and Lowell A. Francis at the University of Notre Dame Press.

As the book inched closer to reality, I thought about its dedication. My dear friends and colleagues, Jorge I. Dominguez and Carmelo Mesa-Lago, immediately came to mind. Dedicating the book to them might be somewhat inappropriate, I told myself, considering that both are contributors to *Looking Forward,* but other authors—and not a few readers—are well aware of how much the field of Cuban studies owes to Jorge and Carmelo.

Then the life course of my father, Eliseo C. Pérez-Stable (1921–2005) made me change my mind.

Papi left Cuba when he was forty years old with only his family and his extraordinary talent in medicine. We went from living a rather idyllic life in Havana to one that truly tested our mettle. In Pittsburgh, Papi learned English, though he never lost his heavy Cuban accent. He also never shed his mustache, which American men didn't wear then. He revalidated his medical credentials and embraced academic medicine. And he quickly came to understand the United States through his patients at the Veterans' Administration Hospital who had fought in World War II and Korea; through football, which he loved passionately for the rest of his life, and through *60 Minutes,* which he watched faithfully every Sunday night. Papi called our years in Pittsburgh "the heroic era."

In the early 1990s, Papi wholeheartedly embraced a second vocation: politics, especially regarding Cuba and Cubans everywhere. In 1993, after a forty-two-year absence, he traveled to Cuba. In an op-ed piece published in *El Nuevo Herald,* he expressed what had become a new mission: reconciliation among Cubans. He saw himself as a bridge between old and new friends on the island, his friends here—especially his high school classmates from La Salle and those from medical school at the University of Havana—and, always, his family, here and there. My heart breaks because he won't share with us the day that we Cubans can finally live in peace. Still, I am full of pride and joy that Papi did his part to make that day possible. And for that and so much more, I offer *Looking Forward* in his memory.

Marifeli Pérez-Stable
Miami
January 2007

Acronyms

AECI	Spanish Agency for International Cooperation
ALBA	Bolivarian Alternative for the Americas
CAFTA	Central American Free Trade Agreement
CANF	Cuban American National Foundation
CCD	Cuban Committee for Democracy
CEAP	Center for Alternative Political Studies
CEELI	Central European and Eurasian Legal Institute
CIA	Central Intelligence Agency
CIS	Commonwealth of Independent States
CPE	Centrally Planned Economy
CRI	Cuban Research Institute
CRRP	Cuban Refugee Resettlement Program
ENEC	Cuban National Ecclesial Encounter
EU	European Union
FAR	Revolutionary Armed Forces
FATF	Financial Action Task Force
FCSC	Former and Current Socialist Countries
FDI	foreign direct investment
FTAA	Free Trade Area of the Americas
GDP	gross domestic product

GDR	German Democratic Republic
IADB	Inter-American Development Bank
IFC	International Finance Corporation
IFI	international financial institution
IMF	International Monetary Fund
IUD	intrauterine device
KKKK	Ku Klux Klan Kubano
MIR	Movement of Racial Integration
MNU	United Black Movement
NAFTA	North American Free Trade Agreement
NATO	North Atlantic Treaty Organization
NED	National Endowment for Democracy
NGO	nongovernmental organization
OAS	Organization of American States
OECD	Organization for Economic Cooperation and Development
PAN	National Action Party
PCC	Cuban Communist Party
PIC	Independent Party of Color
POW–MIA	Prisoners of War–Missing in Action
PRD	Party of the Democratic Revolution
PRI	Revolutionary Institutional Party
UBPC	basic unit of cooperative production
UN	United Nations
UNESCO	United Nations Educational, Scientific and Cultural Organization
USAID	United States Agency for International Development

Introduction

MARIFELI PÉREZ-STABLE

*The world still awaits. After the fall of the Berlin Wall, many ob-*servers expected a political transformation in Cuba as well. The Cuban regime might have collapsed as did those of Central and Eastern Europe after Mikhail Gorbachev announced that Soviet troops would never again be used to keep Communist regimes in power. In Central and Eastern Europe, citizens took to the streets, and communist leaders simply failed to summon the will for massive repression. But there was no such outcry from civil society in Cuba, nor did Fidel Castro embrace the profound reforms-from-above that China began putting in place in 1979 and Vietnam in 1986. Though they are still dictatorships, these two Asian countries have embarked on radical economic transformations well beyond what Hungary—the most innovative among the former Soviet bloc countries—ever attained under communism. Cuba has not changed.

Why Cubans have remained politically quiescent is a nagging question that has no easy answers. That the revolution was autonomous and at one point engaged the Cuban people as no other event in the island's history is certainly a factor. Unlike Central and Eastern European communism, Cuba's has reaped the benefit of nationalism. The U.S. embargo has, indeed, bolstered the David-Goliath imagery that serves Castro well. That for most of its lengthy tenure the regime did not bear the stigma of illegitimacy in the eyes of most Cubans—and the rest of the world—is also a consideration. Only in the past fifteen years has its legitimacy been questioned on the island and abroad. So the Cuban regime carries anachronistically on. Fear also plays its part in keeping ordinary Cubans quiet. Repression—which had been fierce in the 1960s—has largely evolved into the "low-intensity" variety: a climate that instills fear and encourages a *doble moral,* where people say one thing in public while believing another in private. Ordinary Cubans resist official Cuba in myriad but politically unthreatening ways—for example, engaging in illegal economic activities, stealing from the state, pretending support while tuning out, planning to leave. Monsignor Pedro Meurice, archbishop of Santiago de Cuba, has aptly characterized Cubans as suffering from "an anthropological lesion" that has, thus far, kept them from being actors for change in the public arena. Long gone are the days when the revolution thrived on the will, energy, and passion of the Cuban people. Largely gone as well is the willingness of broad sectors of the population to listen to official appeals. Fear, apathy, and a sense of impotence are widespread, but those sentiments have, in fact, contributed to the stability of the regime. Human rights activists, a small independent civil society, and other peaceful opponents of the regime are a symbolic, courageous presence but, for the time being, not much more.

At the Iberoamerican summits of the early 1990s, Spanish Prime Minister Felipe González, Mexican President Carlos Salinas, and Colombian President César Gaviria pressed upon Castro the need to, at a minimum, open the economy to engage the post–Cold War world. In response, Cuba loosened the centralized control over the economy, allowed foreign investors to establish joint ventures with the state, and accepted the U.S. dollar as legal tender. Castro gave these reforms his grudging support but flatly refused to deepen their reach in mid-decade. Cuba would not bring the China-Vietnam model to the Caribbean. Had full-throttle reforms happened, the leadership would surely have caught people's ears once again. Beginning in 2003, moreover, the regime imposed curbs on self-employment, foreign investments, and the use of the U.S. dollar, which constitute outright regression from the timid openings of the last decade. The concessions that had been made to the market after the disappearance of Soviet subsidies were no longer necessary, the Comandante announced. The income derived from a growing tourism industry, the remittances sent by exiles to relatives on the island, the availability of Venezuelan oil, and new economic agreements with China have served as a lifeline of sorts for Castro.

Unlike Central and Eastern Europe before 1989 or contemporary China and Vietnam, Cuba's leadership has never come to terms with the imperatives of daily life. It has never embraced markets as integral and irrevocable elements of its rule. Castro prefers to mobilize the masses under the banners of socialism and anti-imperialism over allowing citizens the right to open their own businesses. Yet while registering notable advancements in education, health care, and other social indicators, Cuba has mostly fallen short of meeting the basic expectations of its citizens. A popular joke asks: What are the Revolution's three successes? Education, health care, and social security. The three failures? Breakfast, lunch, and dinner.

Still, Cuba has survived. At the 1999 Iberoamerican summit in Havana, Castro expressed smug satisfaction in his welcoming remarks. When Cuba was selected as the host country years earlier, no one, he implied, had expected him to be in power. He had, moreover, remained at the helm on his own terms. In Giuseppe di Lampedusa's *The Leopard,* a young Italian aristocrat-turned-revolutionary comments: "If we want things to stay as they are, things will have to change." And so it has been for the Cuban regime: Castro deflected the calls—from within the elite and the citizenry—for broader market reforms in the manner of China and Vietnam and rejected all talk of even a minimal political loosening. The United States has not wavered from a policy of isolation while the European Union, Canada, and Latin America have wagered on a policy of engagement. Havana has stood defiant. Neither approach has worked to prompt a radical economic restructuring, let alone the democratic transition that is the common objective. While other factors may yet intervene, Cuba will not likely engage in true transformation until Fidel Castro passes from the scene.

Ironically, the regime has endured under the Comandante's terms long enough that today it finds itself in more favorable international circumstances than could have ever been imagined in the early 1990s. Back then, democracy and capitalism stood triumphant worldwide, and hopes ran high that Latin America would, at last, emerge from poverty and consolidate democracy. By the end of the decade, antiglobalization movements were gaining ground everywhere, and Latin Americans were growing increasingly frustrated at the shortcomings of their democratic regimes, particularly regarding living standards and physical security. More recently, a resurgent anti-Americanism worldwide—fueled by the Iraq war, the wave of elected center-left governments in South America, and the rise of Hugo Chávez's Bolivarian revolution—are stirring winds favorable to the Cuban government. The Castro-Chávez alliance has, indeed, challenged the paradigm of representative democracy and market reforms that held back the left during the 1990s. The two leaders are gathering support, especially through their opposition to free trade and U.S. policies. Fellow travelers Evo Morales, Daniel Ortega, and Rafael Correa moreover, won presidential elections in Bolivia (2005), Nicaragua (2006), and Ecuador (2006). In Peru, however, Ollanta Humala did not fare well. Today, it is democrats of all stripes who seem to be falling short of accomplishing their goals of relieving popular frustrations through economic growth, job creation, and human-capital investments while upholding democratic institutions and civil liberties. State-centered, populist policies—even if historically the source of some social mobility—had run amok by the late 1970s, and Latin American economies imploded. There is no reason to believe that contemporary populism will yield a different outcome. Yet many Latin Americans are angry enough to be swayed by its promises. Cuba after Castro may well have to contend with similar currents.

The direction Cuba will take after Castro's death is difficult to predict and so is the life span of the present regime without his leadership. On July 31, 2006, Raúl Castro—Fidel's brother, the Armed Forces Minister and First Vice President of the Council of State—assumed temporary charge of Cuba. Intestinal bleeding had forced the elder Castro to undergo emergency surgery. Though alive as of this writing, the Comandante looked stunningly deteriorated in the video images released by Havana. His illness and Raúl's interim command offered the regime a dress rehearsal of sorts. From his sick bed, Fidel had reason to be gratified by how smoothly the temporary transfer had gone. In anticipation of his passing, questions still abound. Is a democratic transition likely sooner rather than later? Do Cuban elites have the wherewithal to consolidate a successor regime? Will ordinary Cubans continue to be quiescent? Can Castro's successors engage them in a new national project? Four plausible scenarios come to mind.

1. A successor regime consolidates. Cuban elites skillfully manage Castro's passing, retain their cohesion, and start moving on economic reforms. The economy heads toward a Caribbean variant of the China-Vietnam model, and living standards improve at a reasonable pace. Breakfast, lunch, and dinner become less of a chore. Ordinary Cubans give the government a chance to deliver on promises long forsaken. While the Cuban Communist Party continues to have a monopoly on power, the pressures of daily life for ordinary Cubans slowly ease. Civil liberties may not be restored, but many economic freedoms are. The succession that official Cuba had heralded since the late 1990s as the inevitable outcome after the Comandante's passing becomes a reality.

2. A successor regime gives way to a democratic transition. Initially, Cuban elites succeed in maintaining political stability and launch an economic reform process. In this scenario, however, forces within the regime itself and from civil society push for a political loosening and are not quieted by improving living standards. The successors do not muster the will to repress on a massive scale and thus agree to unleash a process of negotiations. Some political openings happen in the short term, and a transition to democracy follows in the medium term.

3. A successor regime is confronted with poor or slow economic results. Economic restructuring is either halfhearted or takes longer in producing results, so that ordinary Cubans become impatient and

regime reformers nervous when protests erupt in several major cities. Hardliners lose their case for using force against the demonstrators, and reformers call a national dialogue that rather quickly results in a democratic transition.

4. A successor regime wobbles from the start. Cuban elites are too cautious and merely restore the pre-2003 economic status quo while remaining intransigent at any hint of political loosening. Castro is buried, but his ideas are not as his successors do little for fear of losing control. Yet that's exactly what happens: things simply cannot stay as they were, and real change becomes unavoidable. The advice of Lampedusa's young aristocrat-revolutionary could serve Cuban elites only once. Popular protests spread throughout the island, state security cannot contain them, violence escalates. The army is called to act, but some generals refuse to give the order to shoot and those that do are faced with soldiers that shoot into the air. Chaos reigns, and more rafters begin to head across the Straits of Florida on a daily basis. A U.S. intervention or a multinational peacekeeping force is a real possibility.

While improbable as long as the Middle East looms so large in international politics, a unilateral intervention by the United States cannot be entirely dismissed. Some in the United States government surely contemplate it as do certain sectors of Cuban Miami. If Castro's successors cannot maintain order and chaos takes over Cuba as it did Haiti in 1994 and 2004, the United States might be drawn in, either on its own or in conjunction with regional allies. A post-Castro Cuba in turmoil would test Washington like no other Cuban event since the Missile Crisis of 1962. Beyond the fact that unilateral intervention would be catastrophic for Cuba's future political stability and further fuel the flames of anti-Americanism everywhere, there are two reasons why this doomsday scenario seems far-fetched. One has already been mentioned: the United States is embroiled in Iraq without a clear exit strategy, the U.S. military is overstretched, and tensions can quickly increase to the flash point elsewhere in the Middle East or in North Korea. The other is that a chaotic Cuba is also the nightmare of Cuban elites. Indeed, the desire to avert chaos and outside interference may just be as strong a cohesion factor among them as Castro himself has been for decades. Cuban elites are likely to do their mightiest to consolidate a successor regime and, if not, to seek a way out that keeps violence in check. Defending Cuban sovereignty is certainly a motivation but so is self-interest: while Cuban elites would be best served under the China-Vietnam model, they would do better in scenarios two and three than under U.S. or even multilateral intervention. Absent the China-Vietnam scenario, negotiations to cede power may well be preferable. For that, the deep-seated polarization that has existed among Cubans for nearly five decades must be eased through dialogue and compromise. To succeed, Cubans—first and foremost, those on the island—must occupy center stage in a transition from the current regime.

Looking Forward: Comparative Perspectives on Cuba's Transition is a reader that imagines the island's future after the "poof moment"—Jorge I. Domínguez's vivid phrase—when the current regime will no longer be or, at least, will not have the profile it has today. *Looking Forward* does not try to predict when and how the "poof" will happen.

The book is divided into twelve topics—politics, the military, the legal system, civil society, gender, race, economic transition strategies, social policy and social welfare, corruption, the diaspora, memory, ideology and culture, and U.S.-Cuba relations. I asked each author to think along the lines of three questions:

1. What are the experiences of new democracies regarding your topic?
2. How might the Cuba of the 1990s and early twenty-first century condition the transition regarding your topic?
3. In view of the first two questions, what might be plausible and/or desirable alternatives in your topic for a Cuba in transition?

The reader is far from comprehensive. Important topics such as relations between Cuba and the European Union or the play of regional differences in Cuba in either a transition or a succession are missing. I had to make choices; resources were generous but not infinite. The questions carry an obvious bias in favor of a democratic transition. Still, I also asked the authors to consider a scenario that follows the paths opened by China and Vietnam, which, I believe, would be the best option for consolidating a successor regime. Some of us did that, others did not. Though each author chose the countries or regions he or she deemed appropriate, comparisons were integral to all the chapters. For the sake of readability, I asked authors not to include references, end- or footnotes, or literature reviews. For the most part, the only people named are either current actors or of historical significance. Essays are what I aimed for and, happily, that is what I got in the end. While all of us would be gratified if academic experts find *Looking Forward* of interest, our aim is to reach a public beyond the professoriate: students, journalists, analysts, policy makers, and others in the United States, Europe, Latin America, and, of course, Cuba. In 2006, Editorial Colibrí, a Madrid-based publisher of titles about Cuba in the humanities and social sciences, issued the reader in Spanish, *Cuba en el siglo XXI: Ensayos sobre la transición.*

Looking Forward opens with my chapter, which is on politics. Two codependent facts lie at the heart of the Cuban political system: Fidel Castro and the leadership's inability to come to terms with the normalization of state socialism as Eastern European communists were able to do—or as the Chinese and the Vietnamese are doing. Markets and institutions are anathema to the Fidelista style of governance. Instead, the Comandante relies on mass mobilizations and an intimate network of unconditional loyalists to promote his agenda. Though he was crucial to the survival of the regime in the early 1990s, Castro may now have become a liability for his successors. No one else can govern the way he has, and his heirs might be left in a stronger position if normalization started before his departure. I offer points of comparison with Latin America and the eight formerly communist countries in Central and Eastern Europe that joined the European Union in 2004. I also make comparisons to contemporary China and Vietnam. The first set consists of largely contrasting experiences of democratic transition and market transformation; the second represents a viable alternative that retains Communist Party control while opening the economy. In any case, Cuba is unlikely to emerge immediately as a full, consolidated democracy. A hybrid regime that combines liberalization and authoritarianism may well settle in, as it has in most new democracies.

Jorge I. Domínguez looks ahead at civil-military relations in a post-Castro Cuba. The armed forces today are not only professional but have an excellent record winning wars in Angola and Ethiopia. In that sense, the Cuban military is unlike its counterparts in Latin America and Central and Eastern Europe at their respective moments of change in political regime. Military successes abroad have had significant effects on Cuban society. As a result, the claims veterans make on the state and the residues of the social prestige of the armed forces are likely to linger after a transition. This would be a mixed blessing, to be sure, as a democratic regime will face multiple demands from various sources and will need to establish civilian control over the military. Domínguez offers an overview of civil-military relations worldwide and underscores three facts: successful coups have been rare, unsuccessful coups a bit less so, and civilian supremacy—even if incomplete—is intrinsic to the logic of democratic politics. He is less optimistic regarding the capacity of democratic civilian institutions to set policy and oversee the military's internal affairs. So the cutbacks in Cuba's military budget and in the size of the armed forces are two developments since 1990 that augur well for a democratic Cuba. Less auspicious are the continuing confrontation with the United States and the military's expanded importance in politics and the economy, both of which undermine civilian imperatives. Domínguez posits four scenarios: (1) a successor regime that resembles China led by Raúl Castro, the head of the armed forces; (2) a transition to a Costa Rica–like regime where the armed forces are abolished; (3) a transition gone astray with high levels of crime, armed protests, and social unrest; (4) and a democratic Cuba with a small, professional military that becomes an active participant in international peacekeeping operations.

Gustavo Arnavat focuses on the legal reforms necessary to support a transition to representative democracy and a market economy. He cites Poland and Hungary as successful cases where constitutional amendments bolstered political pluralism, protected civil liberties, and guaranteed the right to private property. In no small part thanks to their judicial independence, constitutional courts in those two countries have played critical roles in upholding the rule of law. In the early stages of the transition, Polish and Hungarian civil societies effectively pressured for constitutional changes and have remained a significant check on those in power. Arnavat then discusses two Cuban constitutions—that of 1940 and the 1976 charter, which draws considerably from the earlier one in terms of the social and economic rights extended to the citizenry. The fundamental difference between the two lies in the limited or non-existent autonomy for the political and judicial systems and the submission of individual rights to the greater socialist good that the 1976 constitution calls for. After the end of the Cold War, the 1976 constitution was amended to include the recognition of some property rights that, in turn, led to the modest economic openings of the 1990s. In 2002, the constitution was again amended to consecrate the irrevocableness of socialism in Cuba, a fact that further complicates the future process of constitutional reforms. By way of conclusion, Arnavat proposes the need to legitimize the rule of law by a representative body and to hold a plebiscite or referendum on constitutional amendments or to create a new text altogether if Cuba is to follow the successful countries in Central and Eastern Europe.

The good, the bad, and the ugly—that is the story of civil society in new democracies told by Damián Fernández. Democratic transitions have opened up spaces for autonomous organizations and thus for opportunities that strengthen civil society. Civil society, in turn, nurtures democracy. That is the good news. The bad and the ugly, however, quickly surfaced throughout Central and Eastern Europe, the Commonwealth of Independent States, and Latin America. The deflation of expectations, the spread of pessimism, and the disengagement of citizens from the civic sphere resulted in social fragmentation. Incivility is a common condition in post-communist and post-authoritarian societies. Fernández presents a ten-point summary of the lessons that these experiences offer regarding civil society. He emphasizes that historical legacies, the role of external actors, and the acceptance of democratic rules are more central to democratic consolidation than the vitality of civil society. He then sets the Cuban stage after 1990, where a proto–civil society has emerged in the form of human-rights organizations, opposition groups, and other associations. The Catholic Church is the only independent, nationwide institution but, the author argues, one that has perhaps been overly cautious in fully claiming its space. Fernández also examines the youth sector as a civil-society actor. And he posits three scenarios: (1) succession with limited economic and political change, (2) a democratic transition, and (3) a radical economic transformation as in China.

Cuba's government has enacted some of the world's most progressive policies for gender equality. If a transition toward democracy and a market economy begins on the island, what will happen to this progressive approach? Mala Htun makes the useful distinction between regimes that promote positive freedoms, as do Cuba and other socialist countries—which stress the material conditions enabling people to exercise certain rights—and negative freedoms, as do liberal regimes that build hedges to defend individuals from state intrusion. Both regime types have made advances on gender equality. In Central and Eastern Europe and Latin America, democratization has resulted in contradictory outcomes. In Central and Eastern Europe, liberal abortion and reproductive rights were sometimes rolled back and women's representation in politics plummeted as resurgent patriarchal and nationalist discourses often crowded out feminist movements. In Latin America, liberal politics created opportunities for debate and change that military governments had repressed. Democracy also opened space for conservative movements and generated a stalemate on the important policy issue of abortion. While Cuba has made notable advances in gender equality, its experience highlights several disadvantages. Progress hinges on the will of the state and the Communist Party, which posit gender emancipation as solely dependent on participation in the labor force and the public sphere, disregarding the role of culture and ideology. And men and women did not benefit equally from the modest market reforms put in place after 1990: women, particularly, suffered the consequences of the so-called Special Period. Continuing economic crisis will seriously undermine the capacity of a transition state to compensate for market inequities and even its ability to enforce the gender equality laws that remain on the books.

Alejandro de la Fuente notes the deterioration of race relations in Cuba since the early 1990s. Blacks and mulattos are underrepresented in positions of power, the media, and the most desirable jobs, such as those in the tourist sector, while they are overrepresented in the informal economy. Over the past decade, surveys indicate that many Cubans associate blackness with degrading attributes and despicable behaviors. Virulent racist remarks come too quickly and frequently to the mouths of whites. Cuba, nonetheless, has made considerable progress in reducing racial inequality in areas where the government places high priority, such as education and health care. Since blacks and mulattos have fewer relatives abroad than whites do, they have had a far smaller share of the remittances and therefore have borne a greater burden during the economic crisis. De la Fuente uses two comparative contexts to situate Cuba's prospective transition: the Cuban past and Brazil. In earlier political transitions on the island—the founding of the republic in 1902, the downfall of dictator Gerardo Machado in 1933, and the revolution of 1959—race was as central as it now appears to be to many Cubans. In all three transitions, the outcome was mixed. In the case of Brazil, which shares with Cuba a history of slavery, racism, and racial mobilization, the idea of nationhood and racial democracy are closely knit. That is also the case in Cuba. Under military dictators, Brazilian authorities were—as Cuban authorities are—intolerant to public debate on race. Since the return of democracy, Brazilian governments have implemented rather impressive policies of reparation and affirmative action. Whatever forms a democratic Cuba adopts in race relations, state-directed efforts against discrimination will be needed. Building on post-1959 achievements and addressing the regime's shortcomings are imperative for black and mulatto Cubans to wield their citizenship fully.

The Cuban economic collapse of the early 1990s did not compel the Cuban government to enact a radical program of economic restructuring or commit to political liberalization. It is, however, only a matter of time before the island embarks on a path toward markets and democracy. Jorge F. Pérez-López outlines the main elements of a plausible transition strategy from the experiences of Central and Eastern Europe and the former Soviet Union. Macroeconomic stabilization (i.e., cutting fiscal deficits and inflation) and microeconomic restructuring (i.e., liberalizing prices) were both necessary first steps, though the timing and strategy for enterprise and institutional reforms differed in the individual countries. The existing conditions at the beginning of the transitions also influenced the pace and results of reforms. Institutions are, finally, central in promoting economic growth; legally protected property rights, banking and investment codes, and a fair and efficient tax system are imperative. Pérez-López offers a succinct overview of the key reforms of the 1990s in Cuba, including dollarization, self-employment, agricultural cooperatives, the tax code, peasant markets, foreign investment, and the banking sector. He concludes that the reforms were piecemeal, tardy, limited, and shallowly implemented. Since 2003, an ongoing regression on reforms does not augur well for the economy. Finally, he sketches the macro- and microeconomic policies a transition or successor regime would need to follow for a full transformation in the Central and Eastern European model or a less complete but still significant restructuring as those taking place in China and Vietnam.

Carmelo Mesa-Lago offers readers a careful overview of social policy and social welfare in Cuba during the crisis of 1990–2002 and explores what could happen under a transition or a succession. In former and current socialist countries, reforms have resulted in increased unemployment, deteriorated social services, increased poverty, and greater inequality. Though its reforms in the 1990s were modest, Cuba suffered similar consequences. Furthermore, Cuba has not implemented the macroeconomic policies necessary to increase GDP, output, jobs, real wages, and fiscal revenue. Without these, social policy is more about sharing poverty than enjoying a modicum of wealth. Fiscally responsible social policies, for which sustained economic growth is imperative, are the best purveyors of social welfare. Mesa-Lago explores three scenarios. Under the first, the regime remains in power and resumes the reforms of the 1990s. Even a modest resumption would bolster political legitimacy by showing a commitment to improving living standards. A socialist-market scenario—possible only after Castro's passing—is the best road map for a successor regime. The third is a full democratic and market transition. Whatever the scenario, balancing growth and equity need to be at the heart of economic transformation. Adequate economic incentives are indispensable for savings, growth, and employment. Tax policy is a crucial tool in promoting a fair balance.

Corruption has played a crucial role in Cuba's past and will remain a feature of the island's landscape whatever happens. That is Daniel P. Erikson's central premise. The question is not whether corruption can be quickly eliminated but rather how to secure a democratic transition that is not severely hampered by the breakdown of existing institutions, the explosion of theft of state assets, and a surge in organized crime. New democracies struggle with corruption. Large power disparities, ineffective institutions, weak civil societies, and low levels of social capital all contribute to the high incidence of corruption in the developing world. Though in theory democracy is a corrective for these conditions, in practice it has not made significant enough gains to curb corruption. The crisis of the 1990s highlighted the avenues for corruption in Cuba, namely abuse of power, state capture, the theft of public goods, and a thriving black market. Meeting daily needs requires most Cubans to step outside the law. Erikson suggests that a managed succession, as in China and Vietnam or a democratic transition as in Central and Eastern Europe and Latin America would present different types of corruption problems. In any case, a transition that results in a weak or failed state would compound the dangers of the island becoming the Caribbean hub for drug trafficking and money laundering. Ultimately, the only hope of containing corruption depends on steady progress on improving the quality of democracy once the transition happens.

Will the émigré community play a role in the island's future? What is the historical tradition of Cuban émigré communities in the United States regarding the destiny of their homeland? How well is the post-1959 diaspora positioned to play a role in the island's future? Do post-socialist experiences offer valuable insights for the Cuban case? What are the experiences of other countries, especially in Latin America, regarding diasporas? What are the likely and desirable alternatives for émigré involvement in Cuba's transition? These are the questions that Lisandro Pérez addresses in his essay. Since the nineteenth century, Cuban émigrés have been central to political developments on the island. Cuban independence from Spain would have been impossible without them. Fidel Castro himself planned his revolution in Mexico and the United States. The current Cuban diaspora draws from that long-entrenched tradition. Exile politics have been closely aligned with ten U.S. administrations, most particularly with the current one, that of George W. Bush. For hard-liners who have long dominated the discourse, a policy of confrontation and embargo are the only acceptable means to combat Castro. Over the past fifteen years, currents of moderation as well as exile contacts with the island have been on the rise. These moderates, however, have yet to translate opinions into power. Pérez draws upon the German re-unification experience, the role of diasporas in the Chinese and Vietnamese transformations, post-Franco Spain, post-Sandinista Nicaragua, and, more currently, Afghanistan and Iraq. In his conclusion, he presents a useful table of possible levels of Cuban émigré involvement in a transition along with various scenarios ranging from conflictive to peaceful.

Rafael Rojas speaks to the symbolic dilemmas of the Cuban transition. For five decades, Cuba has been polarized by a civil war—at first armed and violent, and then political, ideological, and cultural—that has torn the nation, its communities, and its families. Confrontations over memories such as the centennial anniversaries of José Martí's death in 1995, the U.S. intervention in Cuba's independence war in 1998, and the founding of the republic in 2002, as well as the legacies of historical and literary figures rage on between the heirs of the revolution and the opposition. In 2000, the regime launched a "battle of ideas" on ideological, educational, and cultural fronts, emphasizing the revolution's national roots, which permits a certain openness within national traditions as long as the legitimacy of the status quo is not questioned. There have also been some displays of national reconciliation, including the conferences on nation and emigration held in 1993 and 1995, the thirtieth (1992) and fortieth anniversaries (2002) of the Missile Crisis, and, especially, the fortieth anniversary of the Bay of Pigs invasion (2001). The existing polarization must make way for the political competition and pluralism needed in a democracy. Reconciliation will be difficult and, in fact, will not be achieved until the fear of exclusion and annihilation many Cubans feel is forever banished. Rojas refers to the experiences in former totalitarian states such as the Soviet Union and Poland as well as former authoritarian regimes such as post-1958 Spain under Francisco Franco and Mexico under the Institutional Revolutionary Party.

William M. LeoGrande deals with Cuba's future relations with the United States. As the Cold War ended, the island's foreign relations changed dramatically but not with Washington. The administrations of George H. W. Bush, William J. Clinton, and George W. Bush hardened sanctions against Havana. LeoGrande examines the models presented by the succession regimes in China and Vietnam and the democratic transitions of Central and Eastern Europe, and asks how Cuba's relationship with the United States would emerge under these alternative scenarios. He also looks at Nicaragua, where a pro–United States electoral coalition defeated the Sandinistas in 1990, and where the issues to be resolved in the slow easing of tensions fell into the familiar economic, political, security, and humanitarian categories. The knotted U.S.-Cuba relationship poses similar challenges: the embargo and compensation for U.S. properties, democracy and human rights, security issues such as migration, the U.S. Naval base at Guantanamo Bay, the trafficking of narcotics, and humanitarian concerns, particularly in relation with Cuban Americans. Compensation issues—for properties confiscated from U.S. citizens and Cuban nationals who are now U.S. citizens or residents— are likely to be the most entangled and could turn into a serious crisis after a transition takes place. LeoGrande notes that Havana and Washington have grown used to their "minuet of acrimony." Nonetheless, the inevitable embrace will ultimately occur, even if new challenges and conflicts are sure to arise.

ONE

Looking Forward

Democracy in Cuba?

MARIFELI PÉREZ-STABLE

A democratic Cuba is not yet in the offing, and conditions favoring a transition may not emerge for the foreseeable future. Yet only democracy can be a credible conduit for the island's citizens to express their diversity and thus promote the greater good. How democratization might come about in Cuba after Fidel Castro passes from the scene is the great unknown.

The Comandante lies at the center of the Cuban regime. He has ruled for nearly fifty years and seems intent upon remaining on the job until—as he said in March 2003—his "last breath." Gone are the days when many on the island and abroad hoped Castro would take the initiative to renew and transform Cuban socialism. In the early 1990s, he grudgingly supported modest economic reforms, but he flatly refused to deepen their reach in mid-decade and has led a partial reversal since 2003. Political changes have been minor and cosmetic, unflinchingly reaffirming one-party rule. Unlike most of Central and Eastern Europe before 1989 or China and Vietnam today, Cuba has never come to terms with the normalization of state socialism. Castro has always valued ideology over economics, and as a result Cuban socialism has been driven by mobilizational authoritarianism, a politics rooted in the Revolution's heyday of the 1960s. The Comandante's incontestable leadership, the mobilization of the masses, and the defense of *la patria* (the homeland) are its ideological tenets; the Cuban Communist Party (PCC) and, especially, the Revolutionary Armed Forces (FAR) have been its primary institutions. Though heavy handed, mobilizational authoritarianism also has drawn on the willingness of the majority—or of critical sectors—to second the leadership's callings. The regime's latent political crisis, in fact, lies in Castro's inability to govern differently—that is, putting full-throttle market reforms at the political center—which ever deepens the chasm with the citizenry. What used to resonate with patriotism now rings hollow and stubborn as ordinary Cubans strain to meet their daily needs.

At the beginning of the twenty-first century, Cuba must choose between continued regression on economic reforms, resumption of the modest pace Castro halted in the mid-1990s, or a true economic restructuring. The choice carries great political consequences. True economic restructuring would take Cuba down the paths cleared by China and Vietnam, but that is an impossibility under the Comandante. Still, Castro is indelibly intertwined with the regime's survival. How Cuban elites manage him as he continues to age—that is, their success or failure in moving toward some form of normalization—could be decisive in determining the fate of the regime after his passing. Would a successor regime contend favorably with a transition by restoring modest economic reforms? Might it do a turnabout on Fidelismo and launch an aggressive economic restructuring? Would either of these options enable the permanent succession, so heralded by Cuban elites, to take root or instead unleash a spiral of democratization? One thing is certain: mobilizational authoritarianism is plainly not an option for Castro's successors. Even before temporarily assuming the reins of power in July 2006, Raúl Castro had taken steps away from his brother's leadership style, most notably by reinvigorating the machinery of the Cuban Communist Party.

It is this author's normative assumption that a medium-term democratic transition is likely in Cuba, though not certain. Under that assumption, the transitions in Central and Eastern Europe, the Baltics, and Latin America offer experiences that may be pertinent to the future of Cuba. With the former communist bloc, the Cuban regime shares the institutions, practices, and dynamics of state socialism, even if in Cuba these are still marked by tensions between mobilization and normalization, between ideology and the economy. With Latin America, Cuba shares a history, cultural traditions, and the contemporary context of the Western Hemisphere, even if the island—like all countries in the region—bears its own distinctiveness.

DEMOCRACY'S THIRD WAVE

During the 1980s and early 1990s, military dictatorships in Latin America and communist regimes in Central and Eastern Europe fell by the wayside. The new democracies that followed joined the so-called third wave of democratic transitions that began with Spain, Portugal, and Greece. Bereft of political competitors, liberal democracy seemed to be the inevitable endpoint of these transitions. It was assumed that democratization would move in stages toward full, well-functioning political systems as had been the experience in the West: universal suffrage; free, fair, and periodic elections; and duly protected civil liberties under the rule of law would eventually take root. There was a great deal of optimism in Latin America and Central and Eastern Europe.

Since then, however, a sober realism has settled in, as new democracies have produced a decidedly mixed record. Most are hybrid regimes that linger in the gray zones where authoritarianism and democracy coexist. Of nearly one hundred post-transition regimes, no more than twenty are on track to consolidate democracy along the familiar Western patterns. Central Europe and the Baltic countries have provided the most fertile ground: Poland, Hungary, the Czech Republic, Estonia, and Slovenia lead the group. In Latin America, Chile, Uruguay, Brazil, Mexico, and Argentina are—in varying ways and degrees—on or near a path of consolidation. Costa Rica—an established democracy since 1948—never succumbed to military coups or suffered from the civil wars that plagued Central America in the 1970s and 1980s. Venezuela—solid until the early 1980s—is a prime example of democratic decay and involution.

A substantial majority of post-authoritarian regimes, therefore, lie along the continuum between dictatorship and democracy. As Cuba moves away from authoritarianism, it would more likely emerge as a hybrid regime than one more or less clearly tracked toward full democratization.

Experts on transitions agree that for these regimes, how and when a break in favor of consolidation takes place are crucial questions that cannot yet be answered. Hybridity may already be sufficiently established in a number of countries—most of the former Soviet republics, for example—to warrant considering it a distinct type of government that responds to its own dynamics rather than just a stop on the road to full democracy. If so, the sequence-bound transition template—first, a period of political openings under the dictatorial regime; then the regime's collapse followed by a democratically elected government; and finally, a slow but sure-footed democratic consolidation—needs substantial revisions. At the same time, post-authoritarian societies should not be gauged by abstract constructions that emerged from the experience of select cases. The contradictory tendencies of hybrid regimes—those that trend toward greater openness and accountability versus those that entrench unchecked powers—need to be better understood. Permanent hybridity need not be destiny, but democratic consolidation is far from inevitable.

Universal suffrage, sound elections, and civil liberties are the proverbial necessary conditions of well-grounded democratic governments, but they alone are insufficient. Vigorous political parties, majority rule and minority rights, a vibrant civil society, institutional checks and balances, a functioning state bureaucracy, an independent judiciary, and a reasonable representation of citizen interests are all needed to create a synergy of accountability, trust, and participation. In the United States and Western Europe, the responsiveness of the early democracies—either through conventional, institutional means or by unconventional movements—allowed for consolidation. In these countries, excluded groups engaged in contentious struggles for the right to share in the promises of a democratic system. As a result, confrontation, responsiveness, and resilience drew a virtuous circle that made democracy the inevitable political choice. Honest, fair, and periodic elections, when combined with progressive inclusion, trustworthy institutional recourses, a political culture that values compromise, and an economy that affords improvements in living standards, yielded the requisite synergy of consolidation.

Nonetheless, even long-standing consolidated democracies fall or have fallen short of the promise of full participation for all their citizens. The United States only became a full democracy in the mid-1960s when the civil and voting rights of African Americans were finally secured. And since then, U.S. voter turnout—except in 2000 and 2004—has dangerously declined, a sign of a fraying democratic fabric. Additionally, electoral supervision in the United States, unlike in most well-functioning democracies, is in partisan hands rather than independent commissions. In the United States and other well-established democracies, money is distorting the character of elections and representative institutions. Western European democracies—where parliamentarism results in larger voter turnouts and more inclusive representation across the political spectrum—are struggling to properly tend to the rights of immigrant and ethnic minorities. In 2005, French and Dutch voters rejected the Europe-wide constitution, in part out of concern about the growing Muslim communities in their midst and Turkey's possible membership in the European Union.

Most countries in Central and Eastern Europe, the Baltic region, and Latin America already conduct legitimate elections, which shifts the discussion to the quality of their democracies and to the trends that point toward consolidation, stagnation, or reversal. In contrast, most of the republics that integrated the Soviet Union—especially in Central Asia—have not established fair and competitive procedures for giving citizens a choice in freely selecting their political leaders. Closed, hegemonic groups dominate their political systems, and citizens lack the means to hold those in positions of power accountable. A Cuba in transition could steer in a similar direction. The Western Hemisphere, however, has the institutional and experiential wherewithal to prod a post-authoritarian Cuba to establish minimally sound electoral mechanics. Cuba would need to comply with these minimum standards for it to be fully integrated into the hemisphere. If a democratic transition begins, geography is likely to encourage electoral accountability in Cuba, which it did not in most former Soviet republics.

Central and Eastern Europe and the Baltic Region in the European Union

Geography divides the countries that constituted the old Soviet bloc. As one travels east, politics become less open, economies poorer and more closed, inequalities wider, corruption more entrenched, and life more insecure. In May 2004, the Czech Republic, Estonia, Hungary, Latvia, Lithuania, Poland, Slovakia, and Slovenia entered the European Union, a step that attests to their relatively successful transitions. Since 1989, these eight countries have moved in the right direction regarding democratic consolidation and the rule of law. Free and fair elections in multiparty parliamentary systems with relatively high rates of voter turnout are the norm. In general, their civil societies have flourished and their media freedoms have been protected. Their state bureaucracies have implemented more or less effective policies to bring about a market transition, and judicial independence has been largely established. These transitions underscore the fact that liberalization in politics and economics have worked in tandem.

Still, the countries of Central and Eastern Europe have not made uniform progress. Overall, Poland's is the most complete transition; Slovenia and the Baltics are not far behind. In some cases, they have experienced reversals. In the Czech Republic, the judiciary is particularly weak: law enforcement is lax, sentences are light, and wrongdoing by public officials often goes unpunished. Organized crime originating in the former Soviet Union and the Balkans has gained a foothold, hardening the Czech citizenry's perception that the state cannot uphold public safety. In Hungary, the system of checks and balances between the legislative and executive branches has somewhat eroded. Until 1999, parliament freely exercised the power to question the executive branch and establish committees to investigate its activities. Since then, the ruling party coalition has limited the frequency of plenary sessions, which has weakened the legislature's oversight powers and taken a toll on accountability. In both the Czech Republic and Hungary, the government has sometimes tried to force inquisitive journalists to reveal their sources or has curtailed the independence of state-owned media. None of the countries in Central and Eastern Europe has fully met the legal protection needs of ethnic minorities. Though most serious in the Czech Republic, Latvia, and Slovakia, corruption is also a problem in the other five countries, largely the result of privatizations, conflicts of interest, and state bureaucracies that are often bribe rather than service driven. Still, Transparency International ranks the region's three countries where corruption is most problematic in the middle range of its continuum.

The non-Baltic former Soviet republics provide the true gauge of the progress that countries in Central and Eastern Europe and the Baltics have made. There, the outlook for democratization, the rule of law, and economic liberalization is quite different. In states that have barely shed the centralized practices of the past, limited or aborted democratization and erratic marketization are prevalent. So are uncompetitive or rigged elections, hegemonic parties, concentration of powers, limited press freedoms, weak civil societies, rampant cronyism, and pervasive corruption. After an initial period of economic contraction in Central and Eastern Europe and the Baltics, living standards have since improved, if unequally by region and social sector. The social and economic conditions of ordinary citizens in the former Soviet republics have, in contrast, markedly deteriorated. How can these disparities be explained?

The difference in historical legacies is central. In Central and Eastern Europe and the Baltics, communism lasted five decades, as opposed to more than seven in Russia and the other Soviet republics. Even before 1989, civil societies were less restricted in Central and Eastern Europe, which influenced the way communism collapsed: mostly by way of nonviolent civic movements led by noncommunists against unpopular regimes. In the Baltics, noncommunist nationalists ushered in statehood. In some of these countries, former high-ranking communist officials were banned from holding public office. In the other Soviet republics, however, coalitions of civil society and communist party reformers or the communist parties themselves guided the change, and communists and ex-communists largely assumed power after independence in executive-centered political systems. Whether in or out of power, these communist parties have retained most of their old trappings and are, therefore, retrograde forces. In Central and Eastern Europe and the Baltics, after the first round of elections noncommunists took the reins of parliamentary governments, although some communist successor parties—now social democratic—have made a comeback, most notably in Poland and Hungary. In these two cases, however, skilled elites modernized the parties, which, in turn, have generally been a positive force in consolidating democracy.

The two regions of the old Soviet bloc offer a telling contrast. The countries of Central and Eastern Europe and the Baltics are advancing democracy. Even countries like Albania, Bulgaria, and Croatia—which are not yet in the European Union—are making progress toward democratization, the rule of law, and economic liberalization. The non-Baltic former Soviet republics cannot be said to be transiting anywhere; rather they are either hybrid, without meaningful movement toward democratization, or—in cases like Belarus, Turkmenistan, and Uzbekistan,—outright autocracies. Ukraine's democratic revolution in late 2004 may be the exception that proves the rule.

Some 73.5 million people live in the eight countries that entered the European Union in May 2004. After the fall of communism, formally joining Europe has been the most signal collective event in their lives. In the fall of 2004, a Eurobarometer survey drew a profile of their public mood. Solid majorities expressed satisfaction with their lives, ranging from 77 percent in the Czech Republic to 50 percent in Hungary; in the mid to late 1990s, less than half said they were satisfied. Unsurprisingly, younger, better educated people, managers, and entrepreneurs are the most satisfied and feel most optimistic about the future. Among them, there was no nostalgia for the past, in contrast to those—generally older and with lower educational levels—who were most affected by the loss of the basic safety net that state socialism afforded them. Unemployment, other issues regarding living standards, and crime remained the three most pressing concerns, while the mass media uniformly ranked at the top or near the top of the most trusted institutions. The military, the European Union, and the United Nations also received strong approval and trust. The least trusted institutions were political parties, parliament, trade unions, and large corporations. Nonetheless, citizens said they trusted the "climate" of democracy and, especially, the European Union's salutary influence in their countries' politics. Finally, the survey asked these citizens to rate their satisfaction with democracy. On average, in 2004 almost 40 percent were satisfied with democracy, ranging from 57 percent in Slovenia to 25 percent in Slovakia; in the mid to late 1990s, the average was 29 percent. Overall, Europeans registered 57 percent satisfaction with democracy in 2004. If the ten new members (eight former communist countries plus Cyprus and Malta) are excluded, the figure rises to 68 percent, with France, Italy, and Portugal being at or below the expanded European Union average.

Latin America

According to Latinobarómetro, Latin Americans are growing disillusioned with democracy. Fifty-five percent agreed in 1996 that democracy was preferable to any other kind of government, but only 50 percent did in 2004. In the 2004 poll, the three countries where the citizenry held democracy in highest esteem were Uruguay (78 percent), Venezuela (74 percent), and Costa Rica (67 percent); the three weakest were Guatemala (35 percent), Nicaragua, and Paraguay (each at 39 percent). At the same time, the minority (20 percent or below) that viewed an authoritarian government as sometimes preferable declined everywhere except in Paraguay, Ecuador, Argentina, Bolivia, and Peru. At least 50 percent of those polled—and more than 60 percent in most countries—expressed dissatisfaction with how democracy works. Peru, Paraguay, and Ecuador registered the highest levels of dissatisfaction (80–90 percent), and Uruguay, Venezuela, and Chile the lowest (a still high level of 50–60 percent). Sixty-three percent of Latin Americans said that they would never support a military government, though in Paraguay, Honduras, El Salvador, and Peru more than half would. Institutions were largely deemed untrustworthy. The Catholic Church ranked the highest in trust (80 percent); the military and the president rated a distant second (40 percent), followed by the police and the judiciary (each at 35 percent). Political parties and congress were at the bottom (20 percent).

Democracy is but a system of rules that allows for peaceful conciliation of interests in plural societies. Latin American countries are now governed by freely elected leaders, and the political rights of citizens are more universal and protected than ever before. Given Latin America's past, these are no small achievements. Yet Latin Americans are dissatisfied, in large measure because their expectations regarding their living standards have not been met. During the 1980s and 1990s, Latin America embraced privatization of state-owned enterprises and liberalization of foreign trade, which gave market forces unprecedented play. While these reforms curbed hyperinflation, restored fiscal discipline, and brought macroeconomic stability, Latin American economies have not sustained solid growth, vigorous job creation, or significant poverty reduction, or yielded lasting improvements in the well-being of average citizens. By the end of the 1990s, many Latin Americans had turned against neoliberal policies—the so-called Washington consensus—that had disproportionately benefited the wealthy. The Argentine crisis of 2001 symbolized the frustrations felt by many Latin Americans, particularly since Argentina under President Carlos Menem had been an aggressive reformer.

The rise of populism is contesting the premises of economic liberalization and representative democracy. This is occurring primarily with Hugo Chávez in Venezuela and Evo Morales in Bolivia, but also elsewhere, with the Movement of Landless Rural Workers in Brazil, some sectors of Mexican society supportive of Andrés Manuel López Obrador's presidential candidacy, and the indigenous movements in Ecuador and Peru. Though popular exasperation is well founded, the populist alternatives— nationalizations, open-ended social spending, and protected markets— hark back to an earlier era that concluded with the economic implosion of the 1980s. It is safe to say that contemporary populism will not sustain growth, job creation, poverty reduction, and improvements in living standards. There is, nonetheless, no gainsaying the enormous political challenge that populism poses to the region's committed, pro-market democrats. To expand the general well-being of the population, steady doses of new liberal reforms are imperative. These, in turn, require concerted action by the political class, the private sector, and civil society, especially the trade unions. Promoting new export activities to lessen dependence on agricultural products and raw materials is of the essence. In the late 1980s, Ireland followed that model and turned itself from an economic basket case into a "Celtic tiger" with living standards higher than Great Britain's. Contrary to populism, public opinion in Latin America favors the market economy and the democratic system as the twin engines of development: in the Latinobarómetro poll, an average 72 percent of those polled viewed democracy as the bearer of development while between 50 and 70 percent thought the same of the market economy. At heart, then, the matter is about politics—having the leadership and the will to call forth governing coalitions that continue the reform process, bolster popular well-being, and, consequently, reinforce the standing of democracy with the citizenry.

Chile and Mexico are cases in point. Chile is Latin America's only clear success story, one wrought by sound economic policies and good democratic governance. Best known for its neoliberal economics, which weakened the state's centrality as an economic agent, Chile should stand out just as much for having strengthened the state's capacity to foster development. Chile was able to increase social spending between 1990 and 2001 from 19.9 percent of GDP to 26.6 percent as a result of its expansion of the weight of the private sector. While total spending increased 33 percent, private social investment grew faster (50 percent) than the state's (24 percent). Said differently, the state's share of social spending declined from 60 percent to 55 percent and the private sector's increased from 40 percent to 45 percent. Though still marked by jarring inequalities, Chile is closest to the synergy of inclusion that democratic and capitalist countries—such as Canada, the United States, and the countries of Western Europe—historically struck to establish political legitimacy and citizen welfare. Unlike in the rest of Latin America, Chile's economic reforms are solidly enthroned as state policy. Securing an economic consensus that can weather changing political winds is an overarching task that the rest of the region's democracies have still to meet.

In Mexico, the economic and political opening has, no doubt, been remarkable. Under President Miguel de la Madrid, the country took the path of economic liberalization and eventually joined the North American Free Trade Agreement (NAFTA). Along the way, the Revolutionary Institutional Party (PRI), the rest of the political class, and civil society managed a process of democratization that allowed Vicente Fox and the National Action Party (PAN) to win the presidency in 2000. Over the course of fifteen years, the old consensus of state-led development, protected markets, and one-party rule came apart. While the PRI remained in power, the contour of a new consensus—based on liberal economics and democratic politics—was being drawn and filled in, though the 1994 crisis slowed market reforms. With the PRI's loss of the Chamber of Deputies in 1997 and, especially, the presidency in 2000, the political class—particularly, the three major parties, PRI, PAN, and the Party of the Democratic Revolution (PRD)—is still looking for ways to govern effectively.

In no small part, proposals for fiscal, labor, and energy reforms have stalled due to Fox's poor management of executive-legislative relations and the PRI's unwillingness to compromise. But these reforms aim to advance a still emerging consensus among a political class largely skeptical of pro-market policies, so opposition would have been staunch even under a PRI president, although strong leadership might have prodded it along. The reforms might still take hold if the PAN's Felipe Calderón—the winner of the hotly contested 2006 presidential election—applies ability and will to the exercise of executive power, and if the political class as a whole meets its responsibility to establish common ground, bit by bit. The costs of failure would be steep. Would Mexico be able to keep up in a world where China, India, the nations of Central and Eastern Europe, and the Baltics continue to develop? Without palpable improvement in the dire conditions under which nearly half of all citizens live, would Mexico face a populist challenge to its still struggling democratic order, as Venezuela and Bolivia have?

Unmet economic expectations are not the only reason Latin Americans are frustrated with democracy. In hybrid or unconsolidated democracies, citizens do not have sufficient or strong means to hold politicians and functionaries accountable. As a result, the exercise of citizenship is not satisfactorily established, even when the right to vote is solidly established in elections that are responsibly supervised. The reelection of officeholders is an important factor of accountability. Legislators can be reelected everywhere but Mexico and Costa Rica, where no reelection means that senators and deputies are more beholden to party machineries that to their constituents. This is particularly unfortunate in a young democracy such as Mexico's. Easy-access technology—in the form of recorded votes, published reports, and live coverage—has rendered legislatures more transparent than ever and potentially emboldens citizen scrutiny. Similarly, ready access to government information—which Mexico, Colombia, Chile, Peru, Ecuador, Panama, and Venezuela have instituted by law—is a powerful tool for citizens and civil-society organizations. Unlike the reelection of legislators, presidential reelection is not widespread in Latin America, an understandable measure in a region where dictatorships and *caudillos* (military chiefs) have flourished. During the 1990s, however, several countries—Argentina, Brazil, and Peru among them—allowed presidents to be reelected. In Colombia, the Constitutional Court favorably decided on the legality of Álvaro Uribe's bid for a second term, which he won handily in 2006. Reelection gives presidents and legislators a longer time span to learn on the job and to carry out their programs; it also gives the citizenry the opportunity to reward effective performers and turn out ineffective ones.

Mexico and Nicaragua offer examples of opposite experiences in citizen empowerment. Though dampened by the 2006 election, the Mexican Federal Electoral Institute is still a model institution that enjoys broad-based legitimacy and heartfelt popular support. The institute has ensured the integrity of voter registration lists and created a massive civic education program. In the PRI-dominated system, voting was a ritual of affirmation in which the party machinery mobilized the base to go to the polls. Citizens complied, with the expectation of benefiting from PRI largesse. As the PRI began to lose state and then federal elections, more citizens exercised their suffrage freely. Enough of them did in 1997 to deny the PRI control of the Chamber of Deputies and in 2000 to put Fox in Los Pinos, Mexico's White House. In 2000, the Electoral Institute organized a network of citizens throughout the country to supervise the balloting, an unprecedented feat. The Electoral Institute has, no doubt, made an unimpeachable contribution to promoting citizenship and weakening clientelism.

Nicaragua offers a marked contrast. Neither the Somozas nor the Sandinistas placed citizens at the heart of Nicaraguan politics. The first ruled despotically and kleptomaniacally; the second instituted an authoritarian regime that mobilized the "masses" in revolutionary pursuits. In 1990, however, Nicaraguans did behave like citizens when they voted the

Sandinistas out of power. Still, the way democracy has worked in their country has far from empowered them. In 2000, the notorious Liberal-Sandinista pact between Arnoldo Alemán and Daniel Ortega ensured that most political matters would be settled among the elites of the two parties. By controlling all major institutions, Alemán and Ortega eviscerated the separation of powers and prevented any semblance of citizen accountability. In November 2006, Ortega won the presidency with less than 38 percent of the vote—his lowest share ever—thanks to a lowered threshold for avoiding a second round negotiated with Alemán and the division among Liberals, which split the anti-Sandinista vote.

The ability of citizens to exercise their rights within democratic institutions and processes is a vital imperative for Latin American democracies. Failure to allow full citizen participation increases the opportunities for alternate forms of empowerment, such as that expressed in the streets by Bolivia's indigenous people or embodied by Chávez for the poorest Venezuelan.

CUBA AFTER 1990

Had the wave that brought down the Berlin Wall also washed away Castro's government, Cuba would have faced the painful onset of capitalism and democracy together with the old Soviet bloc. Latin America, too, was already—or would soon be—on the paths to democratization and economic liberalization. And Cuba would have partaken of both the hopes and the frustrations that third-wave democracies generated. In lieu of a transition, however, Cuba managed a reconstitution that secured the regime against all expectations. Castro called the new era the "special period in time of peace" and set in motion a program to stem the economic collapse and preempt a political implosion. Modest reforms loosened state control over the economy, citizens were allowed to engage in limited private enterprise, and the Constitution was modified to permit multiple forms of property. But no similar political concessions to a limited pluralism were ever made; uncontested one-party rule has remained burned at the core of official Cuba. While limited economic reforms have permitted the citizenry to become well versed in some market practices, comparable legal spaces for political diversity have not been sanctioned. In short, the crisis weakened the state's control over economic activity, but the state retained—or attempted to retain—a stranglehold on politics.

During the 1990s, the dissonance between rhetoric and reality that had been piercing the polity for decades reached unprecedented levels. The Communist Party itself recognized as nefarious the pervasive *doble moral*—the practice of saying one thing in public but believing another— but has proved unable or unwilling to eliminate it. While citizens are doggedly fixated on their daily livelihood, the leadership has refused to engage in a full economic restructuring, conducting instead *la batalla de ideas* (battle of ideas), a shrill ideological battle with real and imagined enemies at home and abroad. Still, the regime's reconstitution stands as the most significant political fact after 1990. In the 1960s, when the island was awash in revolution, or even after 1970, when the leadership tried to establish a state-socialist normality of sorts, the government stood on platforms that engaged important sectors of the population. The twin goals of survival and reconstitution, in contrast, have magnified the dissonance between official Cuba and the overwhelming majority of its citizens—including regime members and supporters—who clamor for substantive economic reforms. Instead of reform, however, Castro is leading his government in retrogression. In October 2004, for example, the government pared back licenses for some forty private gainful activities, among them clowns, magicians, masseurs/masseuses, and seller-producers of sundries like soap, mousetraps, and funeral wreaths. The state, it was argued, could once again better provide these services.

The Cuban government could have turned to an alternate model of state socialism: the radical economic restructuring that the communist parties of China and Vietnam have successfully effected. But the Cuban leadership could not—or would not—fully assume the political consequences of earnest, steady, and encompassing economic reforms. Normalization has always required that communist parties switch their focus from ideology, mobilizations, and historical callings to economics and the everyday concerns of ordinary citizens. Once having reached a consensus on market reforms, these ruling parties also transform their style of governance. That is what happened in Hungary after the 1956 revolution and what has been happening in China and Vietnam. But just as Castro looked askance at Hungary in the 1970s, so has he dismissed the ways of his Asian counterparts after 1990, though admiring their ability to maintain one-party rule. Market socialism is almost as much of an anathema to him as full-blown capitalism. The Comandante simply cannot envision summoning the Cuban people around a platform of "getting rich" as Deng Xiaoping did in China in the early 1990s.

In Cuba, economic reforms have been half-hearted—sometimes even rolled back—because of the leadership's inability or unwillingness to put the living standards of ordinary Cubans at the center of the political system. Politics work against the grain of economics, something that is unlikely to change until Castro's physical or mental passing. An overview of two established institutions, the Cuban Communist Party and the National Assembly of Popular Power, and of the more recently created Association of Combatants of the Cuban Revolution illustrates the viselike grip that mobilizational authoritarianism has over Cuban politics.

The Cuban Communist Party

The Communist Party and the armed forces are the institutional foundations of mobilizational authoritarianism in Cuba. Even so, the military is clearly the primal institution: armed struggle led to the victory of the Revolution, and Castro has a praetorian understanding of politics. There is, moreover, only one way to run an army: through a command structure that enforces strict and unyielding discipline. Over decades, officers and soldiers have borne the defense of *la patria* and engaged in the pursuit of regime goals abroad as well as taken up many civilian tasks at home. The boundaries between civilian and military matters are blurred one way: from the military to civilian life; the opposite is unthinkable. Unlike the Soviet Union, Central and Eastern Europe, and China, where the military tended to be under civilian control, Cuba's Communist Party simply does not supervise the armed forces. That, indeed, is a key measure of the party's relative weakness or, said differently, an indication that it has never fully functioned as communist parties traditionally did when they were in power.

During the 1990s, two party congresses were convened (1991 and 1997), regular assemblies were held at all levels, and the party ranks expanded. More than 700,000 Cubans are now members, 51 percent of whom joined in the 1990s. The congresses offered pointed contrasts. The one in 1991 took place amid uncertainties regarding the regime's survival. In 1990, the Communist Party had called an unprecedented series of island-wide meetings for citizens to express their views on the country's problems. By most accounts, people spoke, if not freely, at least without the usual strictures. Calls for reopening peasant markets and holding direct elections of National Assembly deputies were repeatedly registered. (The congress, however, only authorized the elections; the markets were not sanctioned until 1994.) The Central Committee integrated younger and better educated individuals, a more numerous cohort from the provinces, an increased representation of Communist Party cadres, and a marked addition of ordinary citizens.

More important than the congress itself was the debate over the authorization of Cuban-owned private enterprise that took place over the subsequent years, a debate that was joined by the Communist Party, the National Assembly, the media, trade unions, and the island's intellectuals. Had that authorization been approved, economic liberalization would have been thrust to the forefront of the Communist Party's agenda. Discreetly, some senior officials and mid-level cadres also proposed innovative political ideas such as changing the name of the Communist Party—to Partido de la Nación Cubana (Party of the Cuban Nation), which suggested a Mexican PRI-like governing institution—and dividing the government's executive functions among the prime minister, the party secretary general, and the president, with the goal of giving official Cuba faces other than Castro's. Easing tensions with the United States also figured prominently in these reform proposals and, indeed, their implementation may have prodded Bill Clinton's administration to respond with what then-Secretary of State Warren Christopher called "calibrated measures." By mid-decade, unfortunately, the window of reform was closed: "All openings have brought us risks," Castro affirmed then. "If we have to open up some more, we will. For the time being, it's not necessary." Reforms were held in abeyance until 2003, when partial retrenchment was started.

By 1995–1996, the leadership had regained its footing. The Communist Party turned inward, and the composition of the Central Committee reflected the new orientation: cadres increased their share by a third while ordinary citizens saw theirs reduced by nearly two-thirds. While ordinary citizens were nicely symbolic, they were jettisoned in favor of the *ejército político* (political "army"), that is, the party and its cadre of trustworthy officers. In the second half of the 1990s, the Communist Party rotated the elite within its ranks as well as in the ministries and other institutions. For the most part, staffing alterations were routinized, thus virtually eliminating the stigma of persona non grata historically associated with communist regimes. Elite rotation without stigma had begun in the 1980s when no one imagined the tsunamic changes of 1989 that would end the Cold War. That the Communist Party found its bearings and resumed politics as usual under such trying circumstances no doubt demonstrated a certain resilience.

Nonetheless, it has been Castro, not the party, who has propelled all crucial policy shifts since the 1960s, and it was no different in the 1990s. Under his leadership, the party survived when, without him, it may have imploded. The Comandante, however, has wielded an impregnable veto over the economic transformations that, if implemented, might leave the Communist Party in a stronger position after his passing. He not only has obstructed further economic reforms, but has also shifted to high-intensity mobilizational politics. During the Elián González crisis in 2000, Castro raised his politics-centered vision to levels unseen since the Revolution's halcyon years. Mass demonstrations, televised round-table discussions of the issue of the day in *la batalla de ideas,* weekly open forums in a selected city or town, and brigades of revolutionary vigilance culminated in a 2002 referendum that declared socialism irrevocable and led the National Assembly to amend the constitution accordingly. The referendum and constitutional amendments were an overstated, hyperactive, and theatrical response to Oswaldo Payá Sardiñas and the Varela Project, which had presented the National Assembly with more than 11,000 signatures petitioning a referendum on political and economic changes in accordance with Article 88 of the Cuban Constitution, which stipulated a minimum of 10,000. In May 2002, former President Jimmy Carter paid tribute to the Varela Project in a speech broadcast live at the University of Havana. Between 1999 and 2004, the Varela Project collected more than 25,000 signatures.

The Cuban Communist Party should have called a congress in 2002 or 2003. Though not specified in its statutes, party congresses have been customarily held every five or six years. A Communist Youth meeting—which is usually followed sometime later by the party's—was held in December 2004. Castro has resisted the unavoidable discussion on the economy that a party congress would necessarily entail, and therein lies the paralysis that afflicts official Cuba. Yet even prior to Castro's emergency intestinal operation in July 2006 and the temporary transfer of power to his brother Raúl, signs of life—or what passes as such in a one-party regime—were evident in the Communist Party. At the end of 2005, the elder Castro himself noted the centrality of the Communist Party as guarantor of the Revolution and socialism. In the spring of 2006, the younger Castro affirmed the party as the only heir to Fidel's authority. The party secretariat—an executive body within the Central Committee that had been disbanded in 1991—was restored, which, presumably, will enhance the leadership's ability to supervise and control implementation of its policies. In early July 2006, Raúl Castro presided over a plenary meeting of the Central Committee that reinforced the charge to bolster the party at the heart of the political system. He knows he needs more than his generals to govern Cuba. The year 2007 could finally see the long-postponed congress of the Communist Party.

On July 31, 2006, Fidel Castro's proclamation of the temporary transfer of power revealed a lot about how he has wielded power, extraordinary and unchecked. Raúl assumed his charges as party leader, commander-in-chief of the armed forces, and president of Cuba; four other men have been assigned his duties in the health, education, and energy programs; three more are now handling the transfer of funds—which he had personally overseen—to these key programs. Micromanaging was his trademark until his health forced him to cede power. He simply could not live by the insight he expressed to journalist Lee Lockwood in 1965: "All of us ought to retire relatively young." Also of interest in the proclamation was the absence of the economy and the living standards of ordinary Cubans, another trademark of his long reign.

The National Assembly of Popular Power

In the early 1990s, the government did open opportunities for freer discussions about how Cuba should change within socialism and under
Castro's leadership. Popular Power assemblies became the object of intense public discussion. Created in the mid-1970s, these assemblies
were protolegislatures that were never meant to have check and balance
functions in a political system led by the Communist Party. All communist regimes have had these protolegislatures. In Cuba, Popular Power
assemblies were integral to the process of institutionalization after the
convulsive decade of the 1960s. Though lacking independence from the
Communist Party, the National Assembly—which meets briefly twice a
year—did witness some meaningful deliberations of national matters,
and local assemblies provided citizens with a regular forum for engaging
local officials.

By 1990, Popular Power had lost its early impetus, which was duly
noted in the public exchanges that suggested ways to revitalize the assemblies. Several proposals were discussed, among them empowering
local assemblies to address national as well as local matters, convening
the National Assembly more frequently and for longer periods, and
limiting the number of deputies who are high government officials (an
implicit call for separation of powers). Nonetheless, except for direct
elections at the national and provincial levels, significant changes of
Popular Power assemblies have not ensued. An incident in December
1993 sheds light on the difficulties of bringing about change. The National Assembly was engaged in a lively discussion of broader economic
reforms when Castro intervened: "Every time something is said here, we
have to wait for 55 people to talk before we even have a chance to at least
explain some ideas. I ask myself if I will have to wait until the 56th
deputy speaks to explain that is not the purpose of this meeting." The
discussion ended, and the National Assembly has not addressed the matter of further economic reforms since.

The direct election of National Assembly deputies, approved by the
Communist Party in 1991, afforded the leadership an opportunity to involve the citizenry in new ways. By all accounts, some elite sectors gave

serious consideration to sanctioning some measure of real electoral competition and political diversity in the National Assembly. In March 1992,
Carlos Aldana, who was the party's ideological secretary at the time, held
out the prospect of some pluralism of "ideas and points of view" when
he suggested that dissidents, as individuals, might be nominated. The
suggestion proved short-lived, as did Aldana's tenure; he suffered a pre-
cipitous fall from power the following September. In October 1992, the
electoral law was modified to allow direct elections for national deputies.
Castro himself welcomed the change: "The decision should be up to each
individual's conscience. If we say that people should vote for all the candidates, it might give credence to the idea that the outcome of these elections is foreordained. It is not, precisely because people have the choice
to vote for the candidates they want or for none at all." Elections for local
Popular Power assemblies—which had been routine since 1976—were
held in December 1992; the first direct election of national deputies followed in February 1993.

The two-step electoral process resulted in distinctively different outcomes. In December, various sources estimated that up to one-third of
the voters cast blank or defaced ballots, an act tantamount to an anti-
government vote in politically uncompetitive elections. Initially, the government neither refuted these estimates nor gave its own figure. Two
months later, it admitted to less than 15 percent null or void votes and
eventually offered a final, official figure of 10 percent. Cuban leaders
were obviously surprised: up to one-third of the electorate had sent them
a strong and unexpected message. At a minimum, the government's
delay in publishing ultimately conflicting figures raises questions about
the actual number of invalid ballots cast in December. Truly gauging the
popular will was, indeed, risky business, and extraordinary measures
were taken to obtain more certain results in February.

First, Castro made a patriotic appeal to vote in favor of all the candidates: *la patria* demanded a demonstration of unity rather than a
selective vote, which contradicted what he himself had stated months
earlier. Second, the government exerted pressure to bring the stray one-
third back into the fold and to dissuade other citizens from invalidating
their ballots or voting selectively. It updated voter registration lists,

increased the number of polling places, and sent block-committee activists to visit every home to instruct the citizenry on the allegedly complex voting procedures. On February 24, 1993, 88.5 percent voted the straight ticket and 7.2 percent cast invalid ballots; in Havana, nullified ballots totaled 14.3 percent. No deputy received less than 87 percent of the votes. About 18 percent of the voters did not do what the government had asked them to do: vote for the entire slate. The late Carlos Rafael Rodríguez—a high-ranking Communist Party member and government official—once characterized the Cuban people in the late 1960s as manifesting a resigned support. In 1993, they perhaps expressed a resignation to vote for all. Since then, Popular Power elections have followed the constitutionally mandated schedule (local assemblies every two-and-a-half years, national and provincial assemblies every five). The leadership saw the 1992–1993 round as foundational in the new era but returned to the electoral routine established in the 1970s.

The Association of Combatants of the Cuban Revolution

Founded in 1993, the Association of Combatants of the Cuban Revolution has nearly 340,000 members and more than 12,000 chapters in neighborhoods throughout the island. Fifty percent of the members are Communist Party or Communist Youth affiliates and only 6 percent are women. Membership is voluntary and open to veterans of the Rebel Army and the urban-based armed struggle against Fulgencio Batista in the 1950s, the various campaigns against the Revolution's opponents in the 1960s, internationalist missions like the guerrilla movements of the 1960s and the wars in Angola (1975–1989) and Ethiopia (1977–1978), as well as active armed forces and Interior Ministry members with at least fifteen years of service. The Association's main charge is to defend the Revolution unconditionally. Members are the trusted bearers of the revolutionary legacy and thus considered the best role models of patriotism in their communities, particularly among the young. Besides conducting civic-education programs in schools, they train young people in the handling of weapons by holding frequent target-shooting practice. Members are also involved in a host of other activities from "getting out the vote" in Popular Power elections to combating crime and corruption. The association emphasizes that combatants—not veterans—populate its ranks.

Though not much is known about the Association of Combatants, its very creation highlights the leadership's praetorian understanding of politics and the emphasis placed on ideology. Veterans/combatants are the most trusted vanguard, the keepers of the flame, even if only half belong to the Communist Party or the Communist Youth. In the event of U.S. military action against Cuba, they would form a neighborhood-based line of defense to repel the invaders, block by block. Absent an invasion, their task is to guard the revolutionary legacy and transmit it to young people so that they can raise the torch on their own when the time comes. Armed with correct ideas and military skills, the next generations would be ready to advance the Revolution.

Though many of its members might well welcome a China or Vietnam transition scenario, the Association of Combatants might never have been founded had Cuba emulated Asian communists in the early 1990s. Its creation was part of a series of measures taken in the 1990s that underscore the fact that official Cuba is more attuned to military imperatives—whether they have to do with warding off the United States or preempting the growth of an organized internal opposition—than to the daily needs of civilian life. Never shy about its resolve to remain in power, the Cuban leadership in the early 1990s began making its battle for permanence the central element of the survival strategy. In 1991, the Communist Party congress took the first step when it passed a resolution empowering the Central Committee to take all necessary steps to uphold the government, including the suspension of civilian institutions. In 1992, when the Constitution was modified, three new security-related articles were included: (1) the declaration of a state of emergency, (2) the establishment of a National Defense Council, (3) and the recognition of the "people's" right to resort to armed struggle in defense of the Revolution. In 1994, the National Assembly passed a defense and national security law. A year earlier, General Sixto Batista had tersely summarized the official will by affirming that the public arena is for revolutionaries only: "We are going to crack heads." In other words, a situation like Tiananmen Square would never be tolerated in Cuba.

CUBA AFTER FIDEL CASTRO

While other factors may yet intervene, the regime's likely watershed will be Castro's passing. Without him, mobilizational authoritarianism is simply not sustainable. Full-throttle economic restructuring requires pragmatic appeals to the citizenry such as "a pork sandwich for all" or "all will have sweets." Under Castro, such a turnabout is impossible. So when the Comandante departs, Cuban elites will step on virgin ground: they will govern on their own, which means they will have to establish new rules of engagement to reach consensus and manage conflict among themselves.

Most among the governing elite surely know their hold on power is not eternal and may well be developing a new outlook: a resignation to assume the role of an opposition. Economic reforms have already provided a soft-landing for many—particularly members of the armed forces and the Interior Ministry—who have stakes in joint ventures with foreign capital, or whose offspring do. In the early 1990s, some elite sectors seemed ready to embrace economic restructuring and even a cautious political opening. A PRI-like path toward openness might have ensued had the Communist Party been renamed Party of the Cuban Nation, had some opponents been incorporated to the National Assembly, and had a separation of functions of the party, the state, and the government been enforced. But that opening did not take place, and more than a decade later the old revolutionary truths are even more frayed. So it is reasonable to suppose that in the absence of Fidel Castro the disposition for profound change will be even more widespread.

The key question is whether a successor regime would manage to stabilize a new status quo resembling China's or Vietnam's. A lot of time has been wasted in Cuba, especially during the 1990s, which may have irretrievably undermined this scenario. China and Vietnam similarly wasted time, that is, both had also resisted the normalization of state socialism: China particularly during the Cultural Revolution, Vietnam from the time the war ended in 1975 until the launching of reforms in the mid-1980s. Before the Cultural Revolution, the Chinese Communist Party had been adding institutional girth since the late 1920s, Mao Tse-Tung truly being first among equals. The Cultural Revolution nearly destroyed the party, but the defeated factions rose not long after Chairman Mao's death and made economic transformation their mandate. In Vietnam, Ho Chi Minh died before the war was over and thus a collective leadership has steered the Vietnamese Communist Party since the North-South reunification of 1975. While it may yet prove to be resilient and resourceful, the Cuban Communist Party has been so dependent on the Comandante for direction and so incapable of taming him—even to convene a congress and address the economy seriously—that its fate as a governing party without him is in question. Historical time, moreover, may not complement the Cuban Communist Party's inflection point as it did China's and Vietnam's: the early twenty-first century provides Cuba an entirely different international context than the 1970s and 1980s did for the two Asian countries. A unipolar world, the Democratic Charter of the Organization of American States (OAS) and the Cuban Communist Party's untested character combine for a less than auspicious setting for Cuba's "moment of truth."

Nonetheless, a market-Leninist scenario could stabilize if the elites reach a consensus on economic restructuring and learn to govern on their own, if the citizenry gives their platform a chance and remains relatively quiescent, and if reforms work quickly enough for the new rulers to gain a foothold of legitimacy. The Communist Party, the National Assembly, and the Association of Combatants of the Cuban Revolution could each play a part in securing the new order. The party could, at last, fully place improving living standards at the heart of its platform, and it could welcome the self-employed and newly legalized entrepreneurs into its ranks. The National Assembly could move toward becoming a legislature, meeting more often and for longer periods and allowing provincial and local assemblies more authority. Even the Association of Combatants could be useful in the sense that its members have the credentials to campaign for economic transformation as a revolutionary mandate, much as the Chinese have—contortedly, it is true—included Mao in the new China.

If a successor regime stabilizes and moves in the right economic direction, the United States, the rest of the Western Hemisphere, and the Cuban diaspora would be duly challenged. Would realpolitik lead the OAS to bypass its Democratic Charter and the United States to lift the

embargo to help a new Cuban government land softly? Since the nineteenth century, the United States has placed a premium on Cuban political stability. Indeed, recent U.S. administrations may have been partly
thankful for the delay in Castro's passing and the inevitable day of reck-
oning: a successor regime or a democratic government may not be able
to control migration and curtail the use of the island as a passage for
drugs. A stable Cuba moving in the direction of China and Vietnam may
suffice for the United States and the OAS to devise a policy of special
treatment that could ease the island back into the fold while economic
reforms take hold and, perhaps, political openings emerge. Cuba could
even be invited to join NAFTA, the Central American Free Trade Agreement (CAFTA), or the Free Trade Area of the Americas (FTAA), when
and if the latter is enacted.

If Castro's successors cannot stabilize a new order, they may be
forced to engage in some form of political opening. One of the possible
scenarios for a transition in Cuba is an unwilling and violent change
forced from below that could carry some form of U.S. or OAS intervention. Given that, a peaceful transition from above would be a pragmatic
move: the governing elites would choose truly free and fair elections
over mass repression against popular upheavals that might prompt an
external intervention. Competitive elections are, of course, risky: there
are no guarantees of victory, and they cannot be orchestrated, as those of
1992 and 1993 were. But opting for meaningful change from above would
also entail a will for hemispheric reintegration and thus an acceptance of
the OAS minimum standard for democracy. Taking the electoral route
would, consequently, make sense only if done for real, with fair electoral
procedures and internationally supervised elections. "There's life after
losing an election," former President Jimmy Carter reportedly told Daniel
Ortega after the Sandinistas were defeated in 1990. Cuban elites should
heed him since both Carter and the Sandinistas have had long political
lives after losing power. After actually winning an election, Ortega has
even returned to the presidency of Nicaragua.

Another possible scenario, then, is that Cuban elites—out of their
own self-interest—commit to the rule of law, civil liberties, and free
elections. After all, they do not want a government that does to them what
they have done to the opposition over decades. They would, moreover,

find support for this new political will among the vast so-called gray zones of the Cuban intelligentsia and society at large, neither of which truly supports the regime. The open opposition is numerically small and, after the March–April 2003 repression, battered. Still, as in Central and Eastern Europe before 1989, the opposition's platform of human rights, democracy, and economic reform—in short, freedom—will likely be embraced by a substantial majority of Cubans once there is a political opening. The gray-zone intelligentsia constitutes the human capital necessary for establishing a coherent state bureaucracy. Society at large is exhausted and would welcome the opportunity to live in peace. If this commitment happens, it would be a crucial step toward putting Cuba on a track bound for democratization and institution building. One of the biggest challenges for governing elites in this case would be to get ordinary Cubans to listen and become engaged in the foundation of a new Cuba. The *doble moral* and a widespread disenchantment with politics will be high hurdles for a new political class to overcome. The China-Vietnam scenario would also face similar stumbling blocks, except a Cuba in transition would do so under the airing of freedom, which renders the relationship between government and citizenry all the more involved and open. Unlike dictatorships, democracies are bound by elections and transparency.

The Communist Party, the National Assembly, and the Association of Combatants could likewise abet an incipient democratization. The party would, perhaps, split into social-democratic and nationalist-populist organizations or movements. Ex-communists who become social democrats—like those of Hungary and Poland—could well be salutary for a fledgling Cuban democracy, first by learning to live in the opposition, then by possibly getting, at last, a chance to govern: Communist Party reformers, after all, have never had many opportunities to implement their policies. In this scenario, the National Assembly could be transformed into a full-fledged legislature, and one of its first tasks might be to draft a new constitution or call a convention that does. The Association of Combatants could metamorphose into a veterans' organization that joins civil society, standing up for its members' interests. As in the China-Vietnam scenario, many old *combatientes*—out of conviction or opportunism—could press their imprimatur on the new Cuba.

Others would second the nationalist-populist wing of the divided Communist Party and run against the current of political and economic liberalization, as similar movements are doing in the ex-Soviet republics or Hugo Chávez's Bolivarian revolution and Evo Morales's Movement toward Socialism in Bolivia.

Realism, however, is in order. Even if a transition happens and progresses relatively smoothly, an elite commitment to democratization is not going to vaporize the political culture of nearly fifty years, which, moreover, has deep roots in pre-1959 Cuba. Castro has governed through networks of loyalty as much as through institutions that, in any case, have never functioned like those in Central and Eastern Europe before 1989 or China and Vietnam today. Concentric circles of fealty down the hierarchy have, likewise, been as important as institutions—that is, the (mostly) men in the Comandante's immediate entourage nurture their own networks, and so on down the chain of command. Castro has socialized generations of Cubans with a vocation for a clientelistic, patrimonial kind of politics that is certain to endure, no matter what happens. If it remains the dominant mode during the transition, citizenship would be limited, the autonomy of civil society impinged upon, and hegemonic elites would lord over the masses instead of governing.

Unlike Central and Eastern Europe before 1989, there are enough believers in national sovereignty and social justice among elites and ordinary Cubans to support populist movements during and after a transition. Building checks and balances to consolidate democracy would then be an uphill battle, and hybridity may settle over Cuban politics. The present circumstances would seem to be tilting the balance toward that type of outcome.

The central question regarding the military is its disposition to submit to civilian control. The armed forces are a paradox: they are the most professional and the most political military in Cuba's history. Several questions come to mind. Would the presence of enough "civic soldiers" in positions of authority (public or private) be sufficient guarantee for the generals to return to the barracks? Is it reasonable to assume that the armed forces' unified command translates into unified positions about the present and future of Cuba? Are there hard-liners, reformers, and in-betweens in the armed forces as there are in the Communist Party?

Could diagonal alliances develop? One way or another, the scenario of a violent transition involves the armed forces. Yet there are powerful incentives for the military (and civilian elites) to avoid the type of chaos that might bring U.S. or OAS intervention. The armed forces may well be willing to entertain scenarios that preserve the military's professional and institutional integrity.

Both the China-Vietnam and the democratization scenarios unavoidably imply a politics of depolarization. Economic restructuring without political liberalization would force the Communist Party to shed mobilizational authoritarianism once and for all and to put the economy and ordinary Cubans front and center. A democratic transition would be more complex because liberalization would be extended to the political system. Polarization entails a great divide between extremes, and democratization would require allowing new and unexpected political coalitions to gather at the center of the political spectrum. Though differently, both scenarios would mobilize actors and propel coalitions among them: current political elites, the armed forces, the so-called *tronados* (party members and government officials who have been purged), the new economic sectors, the intelligentsia, civil society, the opposition, and the diaspora. It bears mentioning here that, whatever the scenario, the diaspora—especially Cubans in Miami—will have a role in Cuba's future, if probably not a dominant one. Nearness, history, and the ties that already exist point in that direction. The diaspora is, moreover, crucial for the inevitable normalization of relations with the United States.

What kind of political class will emerge in Cuba? In the China-Vietnam scenario, would the Communist Party put forward a Deng Xiaoping? If a democratic transition happens in the short or medium term, what kind of leaders would emerge? Is there a Hugo Chávez among the armed forces' junior officers? Who might be more likely, a Leonel Fernández who governed the Dominican Republic well in the late 1990s and again since 2004 or an Arnoldo Alemán in Nicaragua who is under house arrest for corruption and engages in mafioso politics? Would Cuban society produce a Lula—a civilian who rises from the ranks of labor—or an urban-based Zapatista-like movement? Is there a Cuban of African ancestry who could stir his or her compatriots to claim their due share as Morales is doing in Bolivia? When the time comes, the answers to these questions would tell us whether a successor regime has consolidated or a transition is in progress and, if so, whether Cuba is on the road to democratic consolidation or, instead, has settled into a hybrid regime.

TWO

Cuba's Civil-Military Relations in Comparative Perspective

Looking Ahead to a Democratic Regime

JORGE I. DOMÍNGUEZ

- Cuba wins victory at war in Angola in 1975–76 against South Africa's invasion forces.
- Cuba wins victory at war in Ethiopia in 1977–78 against Somalia's invasion forces.
- Cuba wins victory at war in Angola in 1987–88 against South Africa's invasion forces.

Comparable sentences cannot be written about the armed forces of Argentina, Brazil, or Mexico on the eve of their respective moments of political regime change, nor about those of communist Poland, Czechoslovakia, or Bulgaria at a similar juncture. In the last third of the twentieth century, none of the Latin American and Central and Eastern European countries that transitioned from authoritarian to democratic regimes deployed its military to fight and win an overseas war. Argentina invaded the South Atlantic islands in 1982, but it was defeated by the United Kingdom soon after. The Soviet Union invaded Afghanistan in late 1979, suffered a decade-long war of attrition, and eventually withdrew in defeat.

Cubans think that their country is unique—a trait that they share with citizens of every country. But Cubans are correct in saying that their armed forces differ from those in former communist Europe or Latin America. In the 1970s and 1980s, the level of competence and professionalism achieved by Cuba's victorious armed forces and their long-standing success in projecting military power overseas ranked them among the world's most competent. Cuban soldiers proved effective in fulfilling their wartime missions.

THE LONGER-TERM SOCIAL LEGACIES OF CUBA'S REVOLUTIONARY ARMED FORCES

The success of Cuban arms overseas has significant effects on Cuban society. At least two of those effects are likely to linger: the claims that military veterans will make on the state and the residues of the social prestige of military institutions. These legacies may pose practical problems for a democratic regime, even if such prestige may be tarnished in the future if some officers are shown to have abused power or some managers of state enterprises linked to the military prove to have engaged in corrupt acts.

In Cuba today, with just over 11 million people, more than 300,000 soldiers have served overseas. These soldiers understandably believe that they served their country well as patriotic, dutiful citizens and that they deserve honor and respect for their service even if the government that sent them abroad may have been wrong to do so. No doubt they also believe that the Cuban state owes them pensions, disability payments for those who qualify, and health care treatment for the diseases and other disabilities acquired during their service. They probably believe that the spouses and offspring of comrades killed while in service abroad also deserve the state's protection. In a Cuba marked by open politics, war veterans are likely to form political movements to defend and advance their interests, lobby the government, and run for office.

In the early decades of the twentieth century, veterans of Cuba's wars of independence did so. Veterans of Cuba's most recent wars are likely to do so on their own, or as members of the Communist Party or other parties that back their concerns, perhaps adapting for this purpose the already existing Asociación de Combatientes de la Revolución Cubana.

The military has had social prestige as Cuba's most effective institution. The endurance of such prestige would make it harder to construct a democratic civil society. In early 1988, Cuba's military magazine, *Verde olivo,* published a mother's complaint about her seventeen-year-old son who "is giving me terrible headaches, left school, and is mixed up with a gang that cannot teach him anything good . . . I do not know what to do with him, and so I appeal to you to see whether you can help me: get the draft to take him. I know of other similar cases in the neighborhood and, to everyone's peace of mind, they changed when they became soldiers; now they are more serious and responsible."

Self-serving as this statement might appear, *Verde olivo*'s editors were uncomfortable with some of its implications. They agreed that military service fosters "habits of discipline, organization and good conduct" but they stressed that the military should not be seen as a "reform school for kids in trouble." The government, however, has long promoted the view that the armed forces are the school for the nation precisely for the reasons that motivated this mother to want to have her son drafted, even in the midst of the second Angolan war. She is but one example of many Cubans who have held the nation's soldiers in high regard.

The Cuban armed forces are a direct descendant of the French revolution's *levée en masse* (mass conscription). The nation-in-arms defends the nation, not a highly paid volunteer force. The rate of participation in Cuban military organizations—armed forces and military reserves—has been consistently many times higher than that of any Latin American country in the last forty years of the twentieth century (without counting service in the militia as it was reorganized at the start of the 1980s). Many Latin American countries have military conscription, but with many exemptions to avoid military service. Cuba's conscription laws have included deferment and associated provisions, but they are much closer to the standard of universal military service. It has been a people's army.

The Cuban army has not been used against its citizens. In 1989, units of the Chinese army followed orders and fired on an unarmed crowd of civilians in Tiananmen Square. Nothing like that has happened in Cuba. The closest analogy is a riot that took place near Havana's harbor in 1994, which broke out in response to a foiled attempt at hijacking a boat to emigrate. Interior Ministry special troops—not army units—put down this riot without shooting and with discipline and professionalism.

COMPARATIVE EXPERIENCES: FEW COUPS, RISING CIVILIAN SUPREMACY

Notwithstanding those possible social legacies, the comparative experience is encouraging in terms of the prospects for a peaceful regime transition in Cuba and for the consolidation of democratic civilian supremacy over the military.

Since 1976, the only successful military coups in Latin America have occurred in Peru in 1992 and Ecuador in 2000. *Successful* coups have become extremely rare in countries that transitioned from authoritarian to democratic regimes. Coups remain more common in Africa, where there are few democratic regimes and where institutions of control over the military—even within the military—are weak. Yet even on that continent, successful coups against democratically elected civilian presidents have become less frequent since 2000. Since 1976 in Latin America, Ecuador's Jamil Mahuad was the only constitutional president, elected in free and fair elections, overthrown by a military coup. Even in this case, domestic and international pressure quickly forced military plotters to turn over power to Ecuador's constitutionally elected vice president and Congress. In 1992 in Peru, President Alberto Fujimori led the coup against Congress, the courts, and the political parties. In the fall of 2000, Fujimori's presidency ended in disgrace, and civilian supremacy has made substantial strides in Peru since then. After 1982, moreover, no successful military coup led by the high command took place in Central or South America, even against dictators, except for the overthrow of long-ruling dictator Alfredo Stroessner in Paraguay in 1989.

Unsuccessful coup attempts have been more common. In the first decade following their regime transitions, Argentina, Ecuador, El Salvador, Guatemala, Panama, and Paraguay each suffered one or more coup attempts. Coup attempts reappeared in Venezuela starting in 1992, three-and-a-half decades after its democratic transition. The first decade of the new century has seen attempted coups just in Ecuador, Paraguay, and Venezuela. In Argentina, the armed forces remained in the barracks throughout the catastrophic economic implosion of 2001–2002.

The news from East Asia is also good. In the 1980s and 1990s, constitutional governments were established in Indonesia, the Philippines, South Korea, Taiwan, and Thailand. The military played a role in enacting the transitions in Indonesia, the Philippines, and Thailand. Except for a successful coup in Thailand in 2006, no other coup has succeeded in recent years—not even in 1997 in the wake of the East Asian financial crisis. A constitutional crisis was settled peacefully in the Philippines when Vice President Gloria Macapagal Arroyo replaced President Joseph Estrada. (Latin America has also witnessed congressional impeachments of presidents in Brazil, Ecuador, Guatemala, Paraguay, and Venezuela, and the resignation of presidents in the face of widespread protests in Argentina and Bolivia.)

News from former communist Central and Eastern Europe is just as impressive. The transition from communist regimes retained civilian supremacy over the armed forces in every country. The actual transfer of power was free of military intervention in politics, except in Romania, where the military played a key role in deposing and executing President Nicolae Ceausescu. No coup has overthrown a Central or Eastern European constitutional government. The armed forces learned to comply with civilian authority under communist regimes; those habits persisted in the new democratic regimes.

There is greater variation in the former Soviet Union, but still few coups have been attempted. Estonia, Latvia, and Lithuania follow the Central and Eastern European pattern: no coups, and civilian authority prevails over the military. In the Central Asian states and the Caucasus region, communist regimes have been replaced with highly personalistic, authoritarian, or semi-authoritarian regimes. In each case, a key politician has held power since the end of the communist regime or, as in Belarus, come to power later and then snuffed out democratic politics. In these regimes, the connections between the president and the top military command are close; it is a conceptual stretch to affirm that there is civilian supremacy over the armed forces. Yet it is no less remarkable that coups or military rule have been rare even in the states that emerged from the former Soviet Union. The most famous failed coup took place in August 1991—a dramatic scene in the final act of the collapse of the Soviet Union. Ethnically divided Moldova has been de facto ruled in part by the military, and war was decisive in ousting Serbia's Slobodan Milosevic. All in all, however, the absence of military rule is impressive. The successors of the Soviet armed forces learned the habits of compliance to civilian authority, and those habits endured past regime change.

Civilian supremacy prevails as well in the four remaining communist countries in East Asia. The armed forces have not prevented the substantial reorientation of economic policy in China or Vietnam, nor have they derailed repeated successions in the top political leadership in these countries or in Laos, or the dynastic succession in North Korea. Communist China has suffered only one (failed) coup attempt, led by Lin Biao in the late 1960s. Military behavior thus far conforms to the worldwide pattern of military compliance to civilian authority.

Central and Eastern European countries and the European successor states of the Soviet Union have also successfully broken the link between the military and the Communist Party. These post-communist states adopted constitutions and legislation to establish civilian supremacy over military and domestic security forces. Most have civilian defense ministers. There are few instances of military officers intruding into civilian politics, except at the behest of politicians in power. President Boris Yeltsin ordered the military to storm the Russian parliament in 1993. In Romania and Hungary, military forces have at times been deployed in connection with labor strikes or other forms of civil unrest; these circumstances remain highly exceptional.

In Latin America, too, the military's ability to enforce its claimed political prerogatives and immunity from prosecutions related to human rights violations has declined. In the late 1980s, the Brazilian military sought to restrict labor's freedom to strike by creating laws and deploying troops against strikes in strategic sectors. The military's share of the budget also increased during the first half of the 1980s. In the second half of the 1980s, however, Brazil's civilian politicians whittled away these military claims, liberalizing strike laws, eschewing the sustained use of troops as strikebreakers, and decreasing the military share of the budget. Despite years of military resistance, in 1999 Brazil established a ministry of defense to exercise civilian authority. The Chilean military's immunity from human rights prosecutions, and its claimed exemption even from providing key information regarding human rights violations, cracked in the late 1990s through a confluence of international legal action against Augusto Pinochet and bold new decisions from Chile's Supreme Court. In the mid-1980s, Chile's military expenditures accounted for 10 percent of gross domestic product (GDP); by the end of the 1990s, that proportion was below 4 percent. Military influence grew in Peru during the Fujimori presidency but was sharply curtailed during Valentín Paniagua's effective interim presidency and subsequently under President Alejandro Toledo.

Across Central America, military budgets and personnel have been cut deeply. Most pertinent is the case of Nicaragua, whose military establishment fell from approximately 85,000 to 15,000 troops during the 1990s. Nicaragua's defense expenditures, which had consumed more than one-sixth of its GDP in the mid-1980s, dropped to just above 1 percent at the end of the 1990s.

Why is there such good news? For the former communist countries —and for others, such as Taiwan and Mexico, with strong and enduring legacies of civilian supremacy—the answer is unexpected but clear. Intrinsic to the professionalism of their armed forces was due obedience to civilian authority. This pattern held across regime transitions. The military did not search for coups in their toolkit to solve the new problems they faced. The Soviet armed forces were once impressive; their top generals, however, did not know how to carry out a successful coup. The same held true elsewhere in the communist and single-party world. Many professional military officers, in fact, welcomed the greater autonomy that came with severing ties with a communist—or any other—ruling party.

Latin America, long the land of the coup and the home of the inept politician, had to learn, and its history of military rule contributed to the learning. After 1980, the frequency of military coup attempts in Latin America has seemed to be related to the level of military professionalization: the lower the level (Ecuador, Guatemala, Paraguay), the more likely the coup attempts. This is also consistent with observable patterns in Africa. Yet for Latin America this breaks the pattern that prevailed in the 1960s and 1970s, when the more professional the military, the greater the likelihood and success of coup attempts. What explains the inversion of this pattern? Their professionalism notwithstanding, for the most part Latin American militaries governed badly, often damaging the military institutions in the process. This also fits the South Korean experience in the 1980s and the closing years of General Suharto's presidency in Indonesia. As a result, most officers were less inclined to attempt coups.

The "supply" of coups dropped. The "demand" for coups fell as well.

Except for General Augusto Pinochet's Chile and, thanks to an oil boom, the Ecuadorian military government in the 1970s, no authoritarian regime that yielded power during the "democratizing moment" (1979–90) managed the economy well. Civilians thus stopped demanding military coups to solve economic problems. Moreover, all authoritarian regimes repressed public liberties; some committed appalling acts of cruelty. The demand for coups also fell thanks to the growing popularity of parties of the right, which meant that many business elites no longer had to rely on coups to advance their objectives. Center-right politicians won many elections after democratization in Brazil, Chile, El Salvador, Guatemala, Nicaragua, and Peru.

International factors also mattered. The end of the Cold War deprived would-be coup makers of anticommunist national security rationales and U.S. support for possible coups. The United States became more likely to support democratic regimes. The European Union took a strong interest in the consolidation of constitutional governments in Central and Eastern Europe. Argentina, Brazil, and the United States helped to stop coup attempts in Paraguay. The Organization of American States, with strong support from the United States and most members, helped to thwart various coup attempts.

On their own, southern South American countries undertook effective steps to greatly decrease the risk of militarized interstate conflict and thus the need to allocate substantial resources to the armed forces. Impressive improvements have occurred in the international security relations between Brazil and Argentina, Argentina and Chile, and Chile and Peru. Peru and Ecuador reached, at last, a peace agreement and border delimitation.

The European Union (including its predecessor entities since the 1957 Treaty of Rome founded the European Economic Community) has helped to sustain civilian supremacy after regime transitions in both southern and Central and Eastern Europe, providing the post-communist armed forces with positive incentives for compliance. Accession to the European Union was open only to democratic regimes, and European patterns of civil-military relations were one test of democracy. In Portugal, Spain, and Greece, democracy benefited substantially from the pull of Europe. Spain suffered only one unsuccessful coup attempt in the first decade after its transition, and none since. Portugal's armed forces were key actors during the transition from authoritarian rule, though it took a decade to reassert civilian authority over the military. And at the start of the twenty-first century, Turkey undertook reforms to subordinate the military to civilian authority in the hope of qualifying for EU membership.

Today, Eastern European states seeking membership in the North Atlantic Treaty Organization (NATO) or the European Union are less likely to inflame ethnic issues. In the 1990s, the only exceptions to this were Slovakia and Croatia; by the start of the new century, Poland, the Czech Republic, Hungary, Slovakia, Romania, Bulgaria, and the three Baltic states had accepted and were moving toward Western European standards regarding the treatment of minorities and political dissidents. The three Central and Eastern European NATO members (Poland, the Czech Republic, and Hungary) made the deepest cuts in paramilitary and internal security forces, greatly reducing the prospects of repressing their own citizens; their armed forces, now part of NATO's joint command structure, are for their own and the alliance's external defense— not to be used against their own people. The three next best prospects for

NATO membership—Bulgaria, Romania, and Slovakia—have also greatly cut their internal security troops, to the same democratic effect.

Civilian control over the military is weakest when two factors combine: a low international threat and a high domestic threat, as perceived by the military. Either or both could be exaggerated and still affect military behavior. This combination contributed to the military coup epidemic throughout Latin America in the 1960s and early- to mid-1970s. It also helps to explain why communist Poland and Bulgaria had more internal security forces than they had regular armed forces and why all the communist regimes had very large internal security forces. The threat to these regimes is often greater from within the society. This is why NATO and especially the European Union have developed two related policies. One addresses possible external threats to Central and Eastern European countries by making them part of the Atlantic alliance. The other requires Central and Eastern European countries to reduce their internal security troops and adopt democratic standards for dealing with the domestic opposition and dissidents.

Finally, the logic of democratic politics chips away at military prerogatives and immunities. Electoral competition unleashed by democratization reduces the formal prerogatives of the armed forces, the scope of issues in which they intervene, and the degree of influence they have on these matters. Civilian power may lag or zigzag, but it expands relentlessly. International factors provide incentives to nurture these domestic changes and to support them once they are under way.

COMPARATIVE EXPERIENCES: WEAK CIVILIAN EFFECTIVENESS IN POLICY SETTING AND OVERSIGHT

The comparative evidence is less encouraging regarding the capacity of democratic civilian institutions to set policy and oversee the armed forces. This problem, therefore, requires special attention as Cuba ponders its future.

In Central and Eastern Europe, the development of effective parliamentary oversight over the armed forces, of competent and independent civilian experts within the ministries of defense, and of an informed mass media lag substantially compared to other elements of democratic transition. The severity of these problems varies. The Hungarian parliament has been able to regulate military doctrine and missions, as well as the size and budget of the armed forces. In contrast, Romania's military and security institutions have been vulnerable to politicization because politicians have employed the army to cope with labor and other domestic actors; military promotions and the allocation of resources have also been politicized. In the 1990s in Bulgaria, the military remained more cohesive than in Romania and used that cohesion to resist reform regarding budgets, doctrine, training, and transparency. Central and Eastern Europeans often appoint civilians as defense ministers, but Russia has retained military officers in that post. Yet even in countries with civilian defense ministers, public debate, parliamentary oversight, and civilian executive branches capable of defining and overseeing defense policy are limited. Instead, professional officers carry out these tasks. Civilian supervision often means no more than respect for the authority of the president and prime minister, while the military and security services retain very substantial internal authority. Many "civilians" who work as experts in defense ministries are retired military officers.

The Latin American experience is similar. Throughout the region, and notably so in Central America, civilians lack the expertise and professional capacity to make defense policy, provide effective supervision over the military, or debate defense and security issues responsibly. Neither civilian executives nor parliaments are well equipped to address these fundamental elements of democratic governance.

Brazil lacked a defense ministry until the twenty-first century, hitherto relying on separate ministries for each military service. Even now, most tasks of policy setting, auditing, and supervision remain in the hands of military officers. Brazil's tradition of a strong and highly capable foreign ministry, however, ensures that there is effective civilian leadership for broad international strategy.

In Venezuela, Hugo Chávez, both as coup plotter and subsequently as president, politicized the Venezuelan armed forces. In April 2002, he was nearly deposed when military officers supportive of his political opposition acted to overthrow him. Venezuelan civil-military relations under President Chávez are a textbook example of what democratic regimes should avoid: a president who manipulates military promotions, budgets, and the deployment of forces for his political gain, and an opposition movement that hunts for coup makers within the disgruntled officer ranks.

In Latin America, Chile has developed the largest, though still small, set of civilian cadres in its Defense Ministry—which has been headed by a civilian since 1990—to set defense policy, govern the armed forces, allocate resources, and monitor the military. Yet Chile has yet to develop a good parliamentary capacity to complement these executive roles. In short, civilian weakness in military policy-setting and oversight is often the key problem for democratic consolidation in the arena of civil-military relations.

CHANGES IN CUBA SINCE 1990

Significant political and military changes, begun gradually in the late 1980s, could contribute to future democratic politics in Cuba:

1. Cuba no longer has international allies asking it to retain a large military.
2. Since the start of the 1990s, but especially since 2000, Cuba has agreed to militarily significant treaties. It signed the Non-proliferation of Nuclear Weapons treaty, the Prohibition of Nuclear Weapons in Latin America treaty, and treaties prohibiting the wartime use of chemical and biological weapons.
3. President Fidel Castro's government brought back the armed forces from overseas, incurring the political, financial, logistical, and personnel costs of repatriation. In the mid-1980s, tens of thousands of Cuban troops were routinely posted abroad, mainly in Africa. No international obligations require Cuba to retain troops abroad today.
4. Pressured by the loss of Soviet subsidies and the collapse of Cuba's economy, the Castro government cut back the military budget. In 2002, the nominal value (unadjusted for inflation) of Cuba's defense and internal order budget was still 14 percent below the 1985 level. As a percent of GDP, military expenditures dropped from 7.3 percent in

1985 to 4.1 percent in 2002 (the latter level, however, was still about twice that of Hungary and Poland and about a third higher than that of Brazil and Colombia).

5. Since 1990, Cuba stopped obtaining expensive military equipment and decided against the maintenance of much of its older equipment. As much as three-quarters of the equipment of the Revolutionary Armed Forces may be in storage. All of the Cuban navy's larger ships were mothballed. Cuban air force pilots are down to fifty flying hours per year, approximately half the number of flying hours of the Chilean air force and one-third of Venezuela's. The state of readiness of the armed forces as a whole has declined, making fuller demobilization easier.

6. Personnel cutbacks matched budget cutbacks. In 2001, the Cuban armed forces had 46,000 troops, approximately 28.5 percent of their number in 1985. In 2001, Cuba also had 39,000 army ready reserves. The Interior Ministry possessed 20,000 state security troops and 6,500 border guards. The 70,000-strong Army of the Working Youth worked on economic activities, and the one-million-member Territorial Militia provided support functions in emergencies.

7. Cuba's birth rate has remained below the population replacement level since 1978. In 1985, the ratio of soldiers to persons ages 20–24 was approximately 146 per 1,000. In 2001, that ratio dropped to 68 per 1,000. The reduction in the number of troops reflected, but also greatly exceeded, the decline of the 20–24-year-old cohort. Increasing demographic constraints would make it difficult for Cuba to rebuild its armed forces.

8. In the early 1990s, Cuba shortened conscription from three to two years.

9. Cuban officers complied with these cutbacks in military personnel and resources. The supremacy of the party leadership has remained uncontested. In 1989, Division General Arnaldo Ochoa, decorated Hero of the Republic of Cuba for leading Cuban forces in two wars in Africa, was arrested and shot, along with other officers, all accused of participation in drug trafficking, smuggling, and other crimes. Still other officers were imprisoned and dismissed for related reasons. Also in 1989, Interior Minister Division General José Abrantes was

dismissed and imprisoned for dereliction of duty. These events remain murky but seem unrelated to the budget and personnel cutbacks because these were enacted well after those events.

Not every change in Cuba since 1990 augurs well for an eventual democratic civilian governance, however. Cuba has faced a "high military threat" from the United States since 1960, while domestic opposition to the regime has been low since the mid-1960s. Consistent with the comparative pattern, that combination helps to explain the high military subordination to civilian authority in Cuba. In the 1990s, however, the regime's domestic political weakening enhanced the political role of the military. Before 1980, no military officers other than the armed forces and interior ministers belonged to the country's most important political entity, the Political Bureau of the Cuban Communist Party. At the 1980 Second Party Congress, three division generals were added as alternate Political Bureau members. At the 1991 Fourth Party Congress, the post of alternate member was eliminated and the size of the Political Bureau expanded to twenty-five, with three division generals as full members besides the armed forces and interior ministers (although the military's share in the party's Central Committee was cut in half between those two party congresses). At the 1997 Fifth Party Congress, the size of the Political Bureau fell to twenty-four but a fourth division general was added.

Cuba's vast overseas military deployment to Angola and Ethiopia explains the timing of the addition of division generals to the Political Bureau as alternates in 1980, and when the Fourth Party Congress met in 1991, those deployments ended. It is the country's domestic politics that explain the post-1991 additions. As support for the regime weakened, high-ranking active-duty officers played a more active role in the Political Bureau—participating in general political decisions—making it more difficult to disentangle "civilian" from "military" and harder to formulate policies to build democratic civilian supremacy.

In the 1990s, the armed forces also acquired a more significant, albeit indirect, role in the economy. Until the end of the 1980s, the military had exported cadres to run public agencies. The Army of the Working Youth performed various economic tasks, especially in agriculture. In response to the economic slowdown of the late 1980s and the crisis of the early 1990s, the armed forces increased their economic activities. Since then, military-run state enterprises have played a more prominent role in the production of goods and services for both the military and civilian sectors. Retired military officers have been authorized to establish quasi-private business enterprises that operate as if they were private business firms with the state as the sole shareholder. They matter especially in tourism, Cuba's most dynamic economic sector since 1990. The more successful firms already raise their own financing for expansion. They double as a supplementary pension system for retired officers. The prospects for democratic control over the military become poorer once officers possess substantial political power, guns, and wealth—the iron triangle of antidemocratic military power.

As Carmelo Mesa-Lago indicates in chapter 8, the military and internal security forces have their own pension schemes that are financed entirely by the state. After twenty-five years of service, regardless of age, officers collect a full pension that equals the last year of salary—a considerably better deal than civilian pensions.

The military and internal security budget nearly doubled in current prices between 1997 and 2002 (the cumulative 1997–2002 consumer price inflation rate was below 10 percent). Much of that increase is attributable to internal security concerns: combating higher crime rates in Havana, ensuring the safety of 2 million international tourists who visit every year, cowing the political opposition, and containing the vulnerability of police officers to corruption by raising their salaries. Nevertheless, this budget's real purchasing power is difficult to estimate because some of it is spent in pesos and some in dollars. At the parallel market dollar-peso exchange rate, Cuba's defense and internal security budget dropped from about $164 million in 1990 to $28 million in 1997, then rose to $49 million in 2002. In constant pesos, the 2002 military and internal security budget was probably still below 70 percent of its value in 1990.

SCENARIOS FOR THE FUTURE

It is not my purpose in this chapter to speculate about how Cuba might move past a "poof moment"—that historical instance when the old political regime either changes enough or is replaced so that policies characteristic of civilian democracy can be applied successfully. For the purpose of this analysis, assume that moment will happen.

Lessons from the comparative analysis of civil-military relations are pertinent past the poof moment. In the 1980s, democratic politicians, scholars, and ordinary citizens worried about the threat of military coups unless democrats exercised extreme caution. We now know that military coups have become rare. Politicians should not be reckless, but, based on the newer comparative evidence, they need not be timid. International factors helped to ensure this. The strong opposition to coups from governments throughout the Americas, southern Europe, Central and Eastern Europe, and East Asia, and the incentives that wealthy democracies can offer, have contributed to the decline of coups everywhere. The four scenarios that follow start from the premise that coups are unlikely in Cuba's future.

Military institutions everywhere are conservative institutions. They prefer to retain their procedures, organization, chain of command, and relations to the external environment. Military organizations in Central and Eastern Europe and Latin America since 1990 have often resisted reform and, in some Central and Eastern European countries, have become politicized. Yet the comparative evidence also shows that reform is possible. After transitions to democracy, most military institutions have sought political prerogatives and immunity from accountability for past misdeeds. The comparative evidence shows two points. First, it takes time—typically not less than a decade—to chip away at those prerogatives and immunities. Second, democratic politicians can succeed in such endeavors if they persevere.

The most difficult aspect of establishing democratic civilian control over the military has been empowering civilians to perform as decision makers. There are few civilian defense experts in executive branches. Parliamentary politicians often know even less. And the lack of expertise of the mass media in defense and security matters impedes thoughtful public debate. The scenarios that follow focus on this practical problem of civilian capacity to govern the armed forces.

Since 1990, Cuba has shown that it can cut its military budget and the number of its troops. Military compliance has been notable. Cuban officers know that there are no new overseas wars in their future, no vast untapped international or national resources for military rebuilding, and no fancy military weaponry or equipment to protect. They know that the trend is inexorably downward.

Scenario 1

Prior to the poof moment, the most likely, or baseline, scenario for Cuba's near future is a dynastic succession, not unlike North Korea's, from President Fidel Castro to First Vice President Raúl Castro. General of the Army Raúl Castro holds all the formal titles to be the successor. He has been a long-serving, distinguished armed forces minister and the architect of Cuba's most effective institution. He earned respect from professional officers for his management of massive military deployments overseas. Raúl Castro has long been active in the Communist Party's internal organization and has substantial support as a result. His most likely overarching model would resemble that of the People's Republic of China. Military officers would remain in the party's Political Bureau and Central Committee. The Communist Party would retain its political monopoly, but there would be a greater market-oriented economic opening. As in China, military enterprises, or business firms run by retired military officers in collaboration with the armed forces, would be significant. This regime reconfiguration would have little impact on the fundamental aspects of civil-military relations.

Scenario 2

Assume that the armed forces and the internal security forces are abolished, the Ministry of Revolutionary Armed Forces and the Interior Ministries are disbanded, and the mission of the new security forces is refocused on controlling crime. Those circumstances constitute the scenario that best solves the problem of democratic governance over the military.

The key premise behind this scenario is a fundamental rethinking of the threats to Cuban security. Only one state has ever posed a credible international threat to Cuba: the United States. The U.S. government contemplated the annexation of Cuba from the start of the nineteenth century, seized it in 1898, held it as a protectorate between 1902 and 1934, and sought to counter and overthrow its government after 1960. Cuba, an island archipelago, has only maritime boundaries, which have been defined through international agreements or can be so defined through diplomatic negotiation. The main unratified maritime boundary is that with the United States.

Mexico experienced a similar history. It lost the northern half of its territory to the United States in 1848 and was the object of repeated U.S. military intervention in the second decade of the twentieth century. The United States remains an overbearing, intrusive and interfering presence in Mexico even when bilateral relations are good. But in the early 1940s, Mexican leaders reached two conclusions. First, Mexico could not resist a U.S. military invasion, and it was not worth it to build the military establishment required to deter and confront it. Second, Mexico could devise political, economic, and cultural strategies to cope with the United States, mitigating the adverse side effects of the relationship while harnessing the dynamic and liberating growth potential of the U.S. economy and culture. Scenario 2 presumes that Cuban leaders would reach a comparable decision. If a democratic Cuba decides to work with the United States, then this otherwise credible threat to Cuban security disappears.

This scenario would work best if the United States could behave with restraint, repealing the 1996 Helms-Burton Act's call for a U.S. government "protectorate" over Cuba. It would help if the United States, Canada, and Mexico welcomed Cuba into the North American Free Trade Agreement, with a long transition period to enable the Cuban economy to adjust. It would be equally beneficial if the United States offered to renegotiate the treaty that governs its use of the naval base at Guantanamo and agreed to return the base and its surrounding territory to Cuba immediately or on a fixed schedule. (In the latter case, the United States would pay rent at contemporary prevailing rates for U.S. bases elsewhere and fly the flag of the Republic of Cuba over the base.) These suggestions do not require the U.S. Congress to vote for foreign aid to Cuba, though that, too, would help. The European Union, Canada, and the Latin American countries could encourage and constrain the United States as it learns, for the first time in its history, to behave appropriately with regard to Cuba. It is a tall order because it requires both Cuba and the United States to adjust to each other in ways they never have.

Abolition of the Cuban armed forces would build on existing trends. They have been on a demobilization path for nearly a decade and a half. The standing armed forces are no longer large; the ready reserves are easily demobilizable, which would free its members for productive activities. The costs to Cuba of refurbishing and maintaining its mothballed equipment would be high; Cuba would welcome help in disposing of these weapons and equipment. The abolition of the military would save more than 3 percent of gross domestic product (GDP) at levels prevailing in 2002. The abolition of conscription would free up thousands of young Cubans. Abolition of the armed forces, moreover, addresses the most serious problem that democratic civilians encounter upon the transition from authoritarian rule, namely, how to govern the military in a new democratic context. No military, no governance problem.

Over the centuries, however, Cuba has faced a second international threat, albeit with changing characteristics: pirates. The Caribbean's history of transnational nonstate violence reemerged in the last quarter of the twentieth century as international crime, especially but not limited to international drug trafficking. Cuba's geographic location astride the American Mediterranean makes it a prime target for transnational illegal traffic. Cuba will require police forces to address this threat in collaboration with international institutions and neighboring governments.

How should such forces be structured? The current Interior Ministry is the wrong model. It operates on a military model, headed by Army Corps General Abelardo Colomé; its officers have military rank and organization. Moreover, state security troops define the enemy within—a typical design for an authoritarian regime, not a democratic one. A new ministry of public safety would be headed by a civilian and staffed by civilians. It would create and run a national police force that would possess specialized units to confront well-armed organized gangs on Cuban territory.

One branch of Cuba's new police force would replace the current militarized border guards. Its navy and air force would be disbanded as part of the abolition of the armed forces; Cuba would not need submarines, destroyers, MiG bombers, or combat fighter aircraft. Maritime police would be equipped with fast boats and coast guard cutters, and aerial police with helicopters. The new police would discard dated navy and air force equipment, receive different training, and have new missions defined for them by their civilian superiors. Cuba would need help to obtain and transfer such equipment for its aerial and maritime police.

Scenario 2 requires dismantling the iron triangle of antidemocratic military power: political clout, guns, and wealth. All ties must be severed between the political parties and the personnel in the new security forces. Demobilized soldiers must turn in their weapons to the police. These two steps may be relatively unproblematic if there is a peaceful transition of political regime, as was the case across Central and Eastern Europe, but more dangerous if there are high levels of violence as part of a regime transition or threats of revenge against retired officers. As they did in Central America, the United Nations and the Organization of American States could help complete this military demobilization. State enterprises run by the Armed Forces Ministry should be privatized, but the full privatization of quasi-private business enterprises may present thornier problems. The risk of insider privatization, that is, the seizure of effective ownership of firms by those who have been managing them, is greatest for quasi-private business firms. This has been a key part of Russia's experience; international assistance would help to lower this risk.

Scenario 2 is more likely to become a reality, however, if evidence is uncovered regarding corruption in military-run state enterprises or in quasi-private business firms managed by retired military officers. Such evidence would lower the Revolutionary Armed Forces' legacy of public prestige. An example of such a corruption scandal broke out in late 2003 in the quasi-private firm Cubanacán, which is staffed by many retired officers. The greater the number of such scandals, the more likely Scenario 2 becomes.

Scenario 2 will work best if items already on the agenda of the Cuban transition are addressed. First, democratic Cuba must honor and respect the accomplishments of soldiers who fought on behalf of the Republic of Cuba far from home. Cuba's future iconography must so acknowledge it—a task made easier by the void in according such public honor created by the Castro government's emphasis on celebrating the rebellion of the 1950s and the international guerrilla service in the 1960s more than the sacrifices of Cuban troops in the 1970s and 1980s. Second, veterans of international military service must be guaranteed free lifetime health care, and disability and old-age pensions indexed to the domestic cost of living. The full privatization of quasi-private business firms also makes it imperative to provide reliable pensions to retired officers who might otherwise have expected to work for these firms. Special hospitals and clinics for military and internal security personnel would be incorporated within the national health system. The calculation of pension benefits would also be the same as for the civilian population, though the time to retirement with a full pension (twenty-five years) would remain unchanged. Third, a democratic Cuba must supply the quality of public education and the context of civic life that would lead the mothers of the future to look for nonmilitary ways to build character, a sense of responsibility, and good behavior.

Finally, this scenario expects democratic Cuba to retain, transform, retrain, and reposition—but employ—one of communist Cuba's key resources, namely, a first-rate professional foreign service. Cuban diplomats will need to protect the nation's interests, foremost in relations with the United States but also in international organizations and elsewhere. They will have to work to constrain and harness the United States to assist a democratic, peaceful Cuba committed to economic growth.

Scenario 3

Scenario 2, some may argue, is utopian. Cuba is unlikely to become an instant Costa Rica. Cuba's contentious history may give rise to organizations that employ violence against the new democratic regime. Unhappy demobilized officers and soldiers may become easy recruits for organized crime, as has happened in northern Central America. Cuba will need, therefore, an army capable of defending the democratic state against its expected enemies. The new mission of the security forces would be to maintain public order. The remainder of Scenario 2 would apply, but this diagnosis argues for the creation of an army under a ministry of defense or the location of a new army within the new ministry of public safety. In either case, these forces would be counted in the thousands,

not the tens of thousands. They would be well trained and highly professional; international assistance would be welcome.

This scenario calls attention to the possibility that a transition could
go astray. High levels of organized crime, armed protest (some criminal,
some political) from demobilized soldiers, and sustained social unrest
related to a process of economic adjustment could increase the need to
retain a military to preserve public order and defend democratic institutions. Under these political circumstances, moreover, the armed forces
may be subject to politicization; the capacity of democratic civilian institutions to govern the armed forces may be problematic.

Scenario 4

Scenarios 2 and 3, some may argue, incur needless direct and opportunity costs in forgoing Cuba's international experience, which includes
the participation of its highly professional and experienced armed forces
in combat and advisory missions abroad. Instead, Cuba may remain internationally active to improve its bargaining relationship with the United
States and other countries while fostering citizen pride in the country's
new global democratic role. In this fourth scenario, democratic Cuba
would become an active participant in United Nations peacekeeping
operations. Cuba would retain a small professional army, and possibly a
navy and air force, for international service. It would contribute to international peace and security and carve for itself an arena of influence to
leverage resources with international actors. These Cuban forces could
support the police, a mission foreseen to some extent in scenarios 2
and, especially, 3 when international or domestic criminal threats warrant their deployment. The new mission of the armed forces would be to
serve Cuba's international objectives.

The United Nations would pay for Cuba's international military
deployments and for the sustenance of Cuba's military capacity for such
purposes. Cuba's army would serve under a defense ministry. The standing army may be five thousand troops, with the remainder available
from fifteen thousand ready reserves for UN service abroad (Cuba relied
mainly on its ready reserves during its three African wars). This deploy-
able military force would be one-quarter of the size of its comparable

components as the twenty-first century opened. Such a military establishment would be large enough also to address the concerns noted under scenario 3.

Only three non-African countries have professional armies with the experience and capacity to deploy forces to African countries and perform ably and with discipline in both combat and more traditional peacekeeping functions: the United Kingdom, France, and Cuba. All three have experience in combat and noncombat military activities in Africa. Cuban forces in Angola and Ethiopia fought in combat in three wars but also acquired noncombat experience protecting the rear guard of Angolan and Ethiopian forces. All three countries also have "soft power" in Africa, that is, each has significant influence beyond its military power. In Cuba's case, tens of thousands of Africans from throughout the continent have studied in Cuba and earned their professional degrees on Cuban scholarships. Many Cubans and Africans enjoy aspects of each other's culture, and many have intermarried.

Cuban forces have four advantages in Africa over the British and the French. First, Cuba was not a colonial power, and its presence would carry none of that history. Second, Cuban officers have experience across Africa's linguistic and cultural landscape, having served in English-, French-, Spanish-, Italian-, and especially Portuguese-speaking countries. Third, a large fraction of the Cuban military is composed of Afro-Cubans. And fourth, Cuba has had the largest internationalist civilian advisory presence in Africa, including its health care personnel.

Would Cuban soldiers voluntarily participate in combat and non-combat roles under United Nations auspices? Many Cubans volunteered for internationalist service during the 1970s and 1980s for reasons ranging from patriotism and belief in socialist solidarity, to better prospects of career advancement and material benefits for family, to the search for adventure. The comparative evidence on peacekeeping experiences of personnel from other countries suggests five common cross-national motivations not unlike those of Cubans in the past: adventure, economic gain, humanitarian goals, personal development, and career objectives. Economic gains are often higher for military reservists, which argues for a composition of a future Cuban force reliant on reservists. One concern, corroborated by soldiers of various countries, is that military personnel serving in peacekeeping missions support the mission more at its start than at its end. This was probably true of the Cuban military's experience in Angola and Ethiopia. On balance, however, service under UN auspices serves well both the international community and the sending country and its soldiers.

Argentina's experience may be particularly relevant for Cuba. The Argentine armed forces drastically demobilized after its transition to democracy in the 1980s. A smaller military, starved for funds, was a source of discontent and repeated mutinies. In the 1990s, the decision to participate in UN peacekeeping operations gave the Argentine armed forces a new honorable role, provided new career opportunities, and brought in funds for the military's needs at home. It also upgraded the professional standing and skills of Argentine officers through the development of interoperability with Western European forces deployed in Croatia and Cyprus. This experience contributed to international peace and domestic democratic consolidation.

Scenario 4 requires that Cuban civilians head and staff the Defense Ministry, set defense policy according to instructions from the chief executive and the Foreign Ministry, provide for multifaceted training for international peacekeeping operations, and foster parliamentary and public participation in debates over Cuba's prospective international obligations, budget commitments, recruitment, and training. This has not been easy in most Central and Eastern European and Latin American countries (a major scandal regarding illegal international weapons transfers plagues the Argentine experience) and it may be a principal reason for a democratic Cuba to forgo Scenario 4. In a democratic Cuba, moreover, there may be no political demand or support for such international military roles.

CONCLUSIONS

Cuba's transition to democracy is likely to be slow, marked by phases with varying degrees and speeds of political opening, and constrained by a persistently strong Communist Party and popular suspicion of U.S. policies. Its attitude toward the United States will determine whether it can abolish or greatly downsize its armed forces. Military demobilization has been under way since the early 1990s, but its continuation may be more difficult for a government not headed by either Fidel or Raúl Castro, who have enjoyed the respect and loyalty of the military high command.

Nevertheless, the comparative experience and Cuba's own since the late 1980s give reasons for hope. Military coups have become very rare. Military resistance to reform can be overcome in due course. The international milieu now favors these outcomes. Cuba has already accomplished significant military demobilization, including deep cuts in budget and personnel, with full military compliance. A future democratic Cuba can build on these experiences to adopt one of the three scenarios that advance civilian democratic rule.

THREE

The Cuban Constitution and the Future Democratic Transition

Lessons from Central and Eastern Europe

GUSTAVO ARNAVAT

Almost two decacdes after the implosion of the Soviet Bloc and the commencement of the democratic transitions of Central and Eastern Europe, when or how Cuba will follow a similar path remains uncertain. While Cuba did make an effort to respond to a new world order through notable—if carefully targeted and managed—structural economic reforms in the 1990s, these developments were not accompanied by any significant liberalization on the political front. If Cuba is to transition successfully and legitimately to a multiparty democracy—as did Poland and Hungary, among other former socialist republics—fundamental legal reform is essential. The ultimate goal of such reform should be the development of a democratic and constitutionally-based rule-of-law culture that serves the interests of both the state and its citizens.

One of the first tasks undertaken by transition movements in Central and Eastern Europe was to review the Constitution and other fundamental laws in light of the new political and economic realities. The purpose of these normative modifications was two-fold: first, and of most immediate concern, to establish the ground rules under which the transition would occur, and second, to lay down the framework that would permit the transition to take root and flourish in the long-run. Although conditions in Cuba differ from those of Central and Eastern Europe, the shared experience of communism and Cuba's deeply rooted legal system suggest that constitutional reform is also likely to be an effective point of departure for a democratic transition.

Effectively restructuring a state's legal system is a formidable task that, in many instances, can take one or more generations to implement. The process of reform includes repealing or modifying existing laws and regulations and adopting new ones to meet the demands and expectations of a recently empowered and democratized population. It also involves the more difficult task of restructuring existing institutions or establishing new ones whose aim is to implement and enforce the nation's new normative regime. The process of reform in Cuba will undoubtedly be affected by both domestic and international pressures, but the experiences of Central and Eastern European nations demonstrate that these forces can be addressed in a manner that facilitates the establishment of a liberal democracy and a market economy.

LESSONS LEARNED FROM THE CONSTITUTIONAL REFORMS OF SOME EMERGING DEMOCRACIES

The Case of Poland

Constitutional Revisions

Poland's Round Table Agreement of 1989 produced a number of amendments that significantly altered its 1952 Constitution. Among the most notable structural changes were the establishment of a bicameral legislature and the Office of the President, which assumed many of the executive responsibilities previously held by the Council of State. The Constitution was also amended to extricate Marxist terminology from its text and to end the Polish United Workers' Party's monopolistic hold on state power and its dogmatic role as the guiding force in society. The Constitution was further modified to reflect guaranteed civil and property rights commensurate with the establishment of an open society and market-oriented economy.

The architects of Poland's transition had originally envisioned the ratification and enactment of a new Constitution. In December 1989, the Sejm, Poland's lower legislative chamber, appointed a special constitutional commission to undertake such a project. But because the Round Table Agreement limited Solidarity's participation in the Sejm to no more than 35 percent of its seats despite Solidarity's significant popularity among Poles, the legitimacy of the commission's work was repeatedly called into question during the drafting process. Other internal political disputes, including some within the ranks of Solidarity, led to delays in drafting a new constitutive law. This disappointed many who had hoped that a new Polish Constitution would go into effect on May 3, 1991, the bicentennial of Poland's Constitution of 1791, Europe's first freely-adopted written Constitution.

These obstacles, however, did not obstruct the passage of the necessary legal reforms for Poland to progress in the restructuring of its economy as well as in the promotion of a more open, liberal democracy. Between 1989 and 1992, the 1952 Constitution was amended nine times. Realizing that a comprehensive constitutional draft was impossible during those early transformative years, the Polish government enacted what is often referred to as the Small Constitution. Although limited in scope, it nevertheless achieved the critical task of defining the relationship between the executive and legislative branches of the government.

Finally, in 1997 Poland adopted a comprehensive constitutive law to supersede the 1952 Constitution and the Small Constitution. Chapter II of the new document contains an extensive list of individual rights (e.g., freedom of movement, including the right to leave the national territory), economic rights (e.g., property rights and the right to choose one's occupation and place of work), and political rights (e.g., the right to petition any government body and the right to assembly and association) that form the basis of a liberal democracy. In addition, Chapter II contains a number of important social and cultural rights that attempt to provide a safety net, such as the right to social security—either as a result of unemployment, disability, or retirement—and equal access to publicly financed health care services and education.

Many participants in Poland's constitutional drafting process believed that the new Constitution contained too many compromises because it had been produced by the National Assembly, which at the time was simultaneously engaged in legislative and political battles. In other words, one can argue that the completed document is a reflection of Poland's political reality at the time of its enactment rather than a collection of independently drafted and high-minded provisions intended to withstand the test of time. Such criticism, however, may be unwarranted, since a democratic state's Constitution cannot avoid or ignore the contemporary political context in which it was given life.

Constitutional Tribunal

Every Polish citizen has the right, subject to the exhaustion of other legal or administrative remedies, to bring a case before the Constitutional Tribunal if his or her "constitutional freedoms and rights have been infringed." The tribunal is an independent state organ charged with determining the constitutionality of Polish laws. It consists of fifteen judges who are not affiliated with any political party. They are selected exclusively by the Sejm and appointed for nine-year terms. Since its inception, the majority of judges sitting on the Constitutional Tribunal have been professors of law.

Paradoxically, the seeds of the Constitutional Tribunal were planted in the early 1980s after the imposition of martial law. The concept of judicial review of legislative acts was revolutionary for any socialist state because of the well-established socialist doctrine of legislative—albeit party-controlled—supremacy in the affairs of the state. Although the 1952 Constitution was amended in 1982 to permit the establishment of such a tribunal, enabling legislation did not go into effect until 1985, with the court commencing operations in 1986.

Until the adoption of the 1997 Constitution, the Constitutional Tribunal could only issue advisory (i.e., nonbinding) opinions concerning the constitutionality of statutes passed by the Sejm and, since 1989, the National Assembly. If a statute was considered unconstitutional, it had to be submitted to the Sejm, which then had six months to override the ruling by a two-thirds majority vote.

Between 1986 and 1988, the tribunal considered the constitutionality of only three statutes, and struck down one, in 1988. In 1989, as the political climate began to change in Poland, so did the tribunal's resolve to uphold the Constitution. In that year, it considered eight statutes and struck down seven. With the arrival of six Solidarity-appointed judges in December 1989 (half of the number of judges permitted on the court at that time), the Constitutional Tribunal greatly increased its prerogative in addressing constitutional deficiencies in statutes. For example, from January 1, 1990, to June 30, 1994, the tribunal considered the constitutionality of fifty-two statutes and invalidated (in whole or in part) forty of them.

Poland's Constitutional Tribunal proved to be a fairly moderating and independent force during the early years of the transition, even when positions held by key transition figures are considered. For example, in 1995, President Lech Walesa, who often sparred with the Sejm over issues of political power, tried to have the Sejm dissolved—under the authority granted to him at the time—because the state budget had failed to pass within the allotted three-month period required by law. Walesa wanted to include the one-month period that he had held the budget for review in the calculation of the three-month period. Although the Constitution's language was vague on the methodology for measuring time, the Constitutional Tribunal exercised its independent judgment and rejected Walesa's argument.

Furthermore, the Constitutional Tribunal was generally steadfast in applying those portions of the 1952 Constitution that called for social justice, particularly in response to the so-called shock-therapy techniques whose aim was to quickly restructure the country's economy. In one example, the Constitutional Tribunal struck down a provision to the 1991 Employment and Unemployment Act that severely limited the time period to pay out benefits to unemployed workers who were the sole providers of their household income. The tribunal concluded that the provision violated basic human needs and was inconsistent with the constitutional principle of social justice. In another example, the Constitutional Tribunal struck down, as vague and overly broad, statutes that were generally aimed at punishing former members of the Communist Party or employees of the notorious Ministry of Internal Affairs by withholding their pensions or other state benefits.

The Case of Hungary

Constitutional Revisions

Although Hungary has a strong legal tradition, it never had a written Constitution until the socialist Constitution of 1949, which, like that of Poland's in 1952, was modeled after the Soviet Constitution of 1936.

The negotiations between the Opposition Round Table and the then-ruling communist government (led by the Hungarian Socialist Workers Party) resulted in six amendments to the 1949 Constitution between 1989 and 1990, effectively rewriting 95 percent of its clauses. During this period, Hungary also adopted legislation to foster the development of a market economy.

The preamble to the amended 1949 Constitution clearly indicates that the drafters only intended for this document to be in effect "until the country's new Constitution is adopted." More than fifteen years after the last major revision, however, the 1949 Constitution, albeit with significant modifications, continues in effect. It explicitly states that the "economy of Hungary is a market economy" and that the state "recognizes and supports the right to enterprise and the freedom of competition in the economy." Chapter XII of the document delineates the fundamental rights and freedoms available to Hungarian citizens, including the right to privacy and freedom of expression, religion, and the press. In addition, the amended 1949 Constitution contains important social rights, such as the right to social security in case of illness, disability, or retirement, as well as guaranteed education and the right to "the highest possible level of physical and mental health."

Constitutional Court

The Constitutional Court is charged with the responsibility of protecting the 1949 Constitution through the review of the constitutionality of statutes as well as through the more expansive protection of constitutional order and fundamental rights. The court was established by an amendment to the 1949 Constitution, as well as the Constitutional Court Act, which was passed in November 1989.

Interestingly, during the early months of Hungary's transition, the weakened communists favored the establishment of the Constitutional Court—perhaps more than the opposition—because they saw it as a possible guarantor of their rights in an uncertain future. There was also a genuine concern that the absence of a tribunal to adjudicate the actions of the various political actors engaged in negotiations could have a paralyzing effect on a peaceful transition and possibly result in the violent overthrow of the established order.

The negotiations called for each side to choose two judges, with a fifth independent judge acceptable to both sides. It was agreed that the newly and freely elected parliament in 1990 would select the next five justices (for a total of ten), with an additional five justices to be selected following the second parliamentary elections in 1994. Prior to the election, however, the maximum number of justices on the court was reduced to eleven. Judges are elected by parliament for nine-year, once-renewable terms and may not be members of any political party. They enjoy immunity similar to that of members of parliament and may only be removed by other members of the Constitutional Court sitting in plenary session.

One of the most notable features of the court's jurisdiction concerns its ability to declare as unconstitutional not only legislative acts that are inconsistent with the Constitution but also the *omission* or failure by the legislature to pass enabling laws called for by either the 1949 Constitution or other legislation. The court, typically, sets a date by which such enabling laws must be ratified, although it has no effective way to enforce these types of rulings, and some have been ignored. Another notable characteristic of the Constitutional Court is the granting of standing to anyone who feels aggrieved under the Constitution. Unlike its Polish counterpart, however, the court allows any person to bring forth a claim without first having filed it in the lower courts, exhausting administrative remedies, or proving direct interest in the outcome of the case. This procedure was established because of the prevailing belief that the lower courts or government agencies would fail to act quickly or impartially enough to address injustices requiring immediate attention.

The Constitutional Court has become known for its judicial activism, often filling in gaps and reconciling contradictions in the Constitution. One of the first examples of this assertiveness involved the invalidation of the death penalty. Article 54 of the 1949 Constitution provides that "everyone has the inherent right to life and to human dignity," and another states that the imposition of the death penalty shall not be "arbitrary." Supporters of capital punishment argued that the latter provision in the 1949 Constitution implicitly permitted its imposition. Within the court's first year, the League against Capital Punishment brought a case before the court that was resolved against the state on the grounds that the right to life was deemed to be the most important fundamental right within the text of the Constitution. The court argued, furthermore, that Article 8 provides that the observance and protection of the rights enumerated in the Constitution (instead of the implicit rights of the state) were to be the primary duty of the state. Despite contemporaneous opinion polls suggesting that a majority of Hungarians favored the death penalty, the parliament did not amend the Constitution in order to reconcile the ambiguity found by the Constitutional Court. Although the court's analysis is certainly open to debate, this decision and similar ones challenging the enactment of various laws (or the failure to enact required laws) firmly established the court's independence within Hungarian society.

As in Poland, the Constitutional Court had a moderating effect on the treatment of former Communist Party members, including those who may have been involved in suppressing the 1956 uprising. In 1991, the parliament voted to lift the statute of limitations on treason, murder, and fatal injury committed between December 21, 1944, and May 2, 1990, "provided that the state's failure to prosecute for said offenses was based on political reasons." The Constitutional Court struck down the law because it contained many ambiguities and increased the possibility of arbitrary application, citing, instead, the need to provide "legal certainty," which is implied by the 1949 Constitution's grounding in the rule of law.

During its first six years of operation, the Constitutional Court struck down approximately two hundred statutes. Public opinion polls in 1993 and 1995 suggested that the court was more highly regarded than the legislative and executive branches.

General Lessons

Several lessons can be gleaned from the cases of Poland and Hungary.

- The first and most important step for legal reform is to amend the existing constitutional structure to permit the establishment of a multiparty system, free and open elections, the enhancement and protection of individual liberties, and the promotion of economic growth through private economic activity and the infusion of foreign capital.
- Although it would be ideal, for the sake of legitimacy, that a new Constitution or amendments to the existing one be made following free and open elections, events unfold in accordance with the particular political, social, and economic pressures existing at the time of the transition. Thus, while Hungary has been relatively successful in developing its postsocialist legal system, the amendments to its 1949 Constitution were made before free elections were held for its parliament. The amendments were never ratified directly by the population at large nor has Hungary promulgated a new Constitution to replace the socialist one. In contrast, Poland initially amended its 1952 Constitution several times prior to free and open elections for the Sejm, but passed its Small Constitution in 1992 and, finally, its permanent Constitution in 1997—in each case following free and open elections.
- The constitutional courts of Poland and Hungary have played critical roles in establishing and protecting the rule of law, particularly as it relates to reviewing the constitutionality of legislative acts. To assure the effectiveness of these tribunals, its judges have been ac-

corded the highest degree of independence. Typically, these judges are appointed for a relatively long period of time and are not permitted to be members of any political party or to engage in political activities. One of the reasons why constitutional tribunals have been effective is because they are seen as protectors of the constitutional rights of both reformers and former members of the socialist order. Indeed, these courts have played a moderating role in connection with laws aimed at punishing former regime supporters, thus promoting the establishment of the rule of law and, indirectly, the acceptance of previously inconceivable political change by the old order. This is not to suggest that especially egregious instances of abuse of power, particularly when combined with loss of life, should escape justice, but any legal procedures and their attendant sanctions should be consistent with the spirit and letter of a transitional Constitution.

- The greatest advancements in the promotion of the rule of law in Central and Eastern Europe have occurred in those nations where civil society had established the deepest roots. Because representatives of civil society enjoyed widespread support, they consequently had the most power to negotiate and effect change within the existing constitutional order.

- External inducements, such as the prospect of joining the Council of Europe, the North Atlantic Treaty Organization, and, eventually, the European Union, have proven to be important in persuading these new democracies to undertake necessary transformations in their legal system. For example, each country had to negotiate a judicial chapter and to implement legislation to conform to the European Convention on Human Rights if it hoped to gain entry into the Council of Europe.

- Emerging democracies benefited from the technical assistance provided by legal scholars and law-related nongovernmental organizations, such as the American Bar Association's Central European and Eurasian Legal Institute (CEELI). CEELI was established in 1990 and provided transition governments with assistance on constitutional and other legal drafting, as well as the training of judges.

CUBA'S LEGAL SYSTEM FOLLOWING THE COLLAPSE
OF THE SOCIALIST BLOC

Before describing changes to Cuba's legal system since the early 1990s, it is important to briefly examine Cuba's existing Constitution of 1976 and how it came into being. Although one of the most widely professed goals of the 26th of July Movement was the restoration of Cuba's liberal 1940 Constitution, Fidel Castro made clear his intentions concerning the Revolution's future legal foundations during his May Day speech of 1961. He declared that "the Constitution of 1940 is already too antiquated and too old for us; we have advanced too far for that 'outgrown suit' . . . which was good for its time [but] which was never carried out; and that constitution has been left behind by this revolution, which . . . is a socialist revolution. . . . We must talk of a new constitution . . . and this constitution will . . . be a socialist constitution."

The search for such a Constitution began in earnest in 1974, when a group of approximately twenty Communist Party and government officials began work on what would ultimately become the Constitution of 1976. In order to avoid criticism that the new Constitution would lack legitimacy because it was not drafted by a popularly elected constitutional assembly (as had been the case with the Constitution of 1940), the government invited the public to attend discussion groups and comment on the preliminary text during a five-month period of examination. The text was then put before the electorate in a national referendum and, according to government sources, was approved by 97.7 percent of the voters.

The socialist Constitution essentially codified the government's unity-of-power model of governance that was typical of other socialist countries at the time. This model runs contrary to the separation-of-powers structure associated with liberal, representative democracies. Its central purpose is the protection of the socialist state created by the Revolution. The Communist Party is declared the "superior leading force of the society and the State, organizing and guiding the common efforts aimed at the highest goals of the construction of socialism and advancement toward the communist society."

The new Constitution expanded social rights such as access to public education, housing, and health care, as well as women's rights. With respect to individual rights, the socialist Constitution built on many of the rights enumerated in the Constitution of 1940 but at the same time limited them when they came into conflict with the social or collective goals of the Revolution, as determined by the government. For example, it declares, "citizens have freedom of speech and of the press *in keeping with the objectives of socialist society*" (emphasis added). Another provision, in particular, eviscerates many of the rights explicitly recognized by declaring, "none of the freedoms which are recognized for citizens can be exercised . . . contrary to the existence and objectives of the socialist State, or contrary to the decision of the Cuban people to build socialism and communism."

Concerning the judiciary, the socialist Constitution contains language that, on its face, appears to promote the concept of judicial independence, declaring, "judges, in their function of imparting justice, are independent, and owe obedience solely to the law." This provision, however, is belied by the fact that the National Assembly has the power to appoint as well as recall national-level judges—a power that appears to be, at least textually, unfettered. Further limiting the independence of judges is an overarching provision stating that "all organs of the State," including courts, " . . . operate within the limits of their respective authority, and are obliged to strictly observe socialist legality, and to ensure respect for it in the life of the entire society." In other words, the ultimate role of judges is to serve the Revolution's objective of promoting and protecting a socialist state, even at the expense of individual liberties. To further ensure that no law will be misinterpreted or misapplied by a court, the socialist Constitution empowers the Council of State to "give existing laws a general and obligatory interpretation whenever necessary" and to "issue general instructions to the courts through the Council of Government of the People's Supreme Court." As a result, Cuban courts do not exercise true judicial review concerning the legality or constitutionality of any act by either the executive or legislative functions of government.

The demise of the Soviet Bloc in the late 1980s aggravated the recession that the Cuban economy already suffered. In 1990, the government proclaimed the euphemistically named "Special Period." This new phase provided an opportunity to amend Cuban law under the socialist

Constitution as well as Cuba's foreign investment and corporate management regimes.

In 1992, the National Assembly amended, for the first time, the Constitution of 1976. Approximately 60 percent of the articles to the socialist Constitution were altered and a portion, though certainly not the majority, of the dogmatic Marxist-Leninist terminology was eliminated. On the political front, the direct election of National Assembly deputies and provincial assembly delegates was established (municipal delegates have been elected directly since 1976). In regard to personal freedoms, there was a subtle expansion of religious freedom with the state no longer declaring itself officially atheist.

On the economic front, efforts to attract foreign capital through the development of the tourism sector led to important changes concerning the recognition of property rights by "mixed enterprises," essentially joint ventures between state-controlled companies and foreign partners. To facilitate this, Article 14 was amended to limit the state monopoly to the "fundamental means of production" instead of the previous "means of production," which was more expansive.

These constitutional changes led to initiatives that legalized the widespread use of the U.S. dollar by Cuban citizens (although changes in 2005 partially reversed this policy) and authorized self-employment for some 150 occupations, enabling an estimated 200,000 Cubans to seek limited private enterprises such as operating small restaurants in their homes or selling used books. These private-sector activities, however, are highly regulated, and changes in 2004 indicated that the government was beginning to scale them back. In addition, the government enacted legislation to attract foreign investment through the establishment of duty-free zones, banks, and other types of financial institutions. The most noteworthy legislation is the Foreign Investment Law of 1995, otherwise known as Law No. 77. It opened all sectors of the Cuban economy—except the education, health care, and noncommercial military sectors—to foreign participation.

To be sure, Cuba opened its economy to foreign investment in 1982 with the passage of Law No. 50, but it had little success in attracting foreign investment. Thus, Law No. 77, together with a number of changes to the socialist Constitution discussed above, was enacted to be more effective in sparking interest among potential investors. Unlike Law No. 50, which only permitted minority investments of up to 49 percent of a joint-venture company, the new law authorized three types of investments by foreign parties: joint ventures involving both Cuban and non-Cuban corporate entities; international economic association agreements, which do not require the establishment of a separate legal entity (as with the case of a joint venture company); and companies whose shares are owned wholly by a non-Cuban investor. Law No. 77 also authorized entities created by foreign investors to own property, including real estate, and provided guarantees against uncompensated expropriations—an assurance the old law had failed to provide.

Law No. 187, the Enterprise Optimization Law, was enacted in 1998 to address the inefficiencies created by Cuba's centrally planned economy. The law's objective is to increase the efficiency and productivity of state-owned enterprises by promoting decentralization in their management. Qualifying companies are now allowed to conduct their affairs with far less state intrusion than in the past as long as standards and procedures imposed by the state are met and detailed business plans approved. Some observers believe that Law No. 187 may even serve as a prelude to the privatization of these enterprises, although there is no indication that the Cuban government is considering such a transformative change in economic policy.

The legal changes to encourage foreign investment and the subsequent investment increase have produced four results that should facilitate Cuba's transition to a free market economy. First, foreign investors provide not only capital but technological and managerial skills, including the administrative and financial skills necessary to run an enterprise in a competitive global economy. Even where no local partner is participating in an enterprise, local employees are undoubtedly being exposed to business norms that would have otherwise been absent in a purely socialist society. Among the business norms being transplanted to Cuba by foreign entrepreneurs is the expectation of a rational and predictable legal system that is protective of sound corporate interests.

Second, the government also recognizes that the private sector, while adept at taking business or financial risks, has a strong aversion to political risk. By committing to protect foreign investors, the government is promoting the rule of law not as the naked instrument of the Revolution but as a set of rules that can be relied upon to pursue predictable results. Predictability creates and reinforces the concept of the rule of law, which is essential in any future transition in Cuba.

Third, the participation of foreign businesses and individuals in the Cuban economy is causing a paradigm shift in Cuban society, which, prior to the start of the Special Period, had received a very different and critical message concerning the role of private enterprise, particularly as pursued by Western interests. To be sure, the socialist Constitution recognizes personal property rights and the right of individual farmers to own their land, but the Constitution reserves the right to engage in large-scale economic projects to the state (through controlled corporate bodies) and to foreign investors. One can only assume that this contradiction, favoring the treatment of non-Cuban entities, has frustrated many Cubans and piqued their desire to participate in a more meaningful way in the fomenting of economic activity.

Finally, the role of lawyers—deliberately downgraded by the government during the initial years of the Revolution because of their perceived roles as counterrevolutionary enablers of the bourgeoisie class—has been rehabilitated in order to meet the demands of investors who seek advice on the Cuban legal system. It is essential to note, however, that this rehabilitation actually began in the 1970s and 1980s as part of the institutionalization process and the establishment of the National Union of Cuban Jurists, which is a state-sponsored bar association. At present, the vast majority of practicing lawyers work either as judges or prosecutors for the state, directly with foreign-owned businesses, or as part of one of several collective law firms that represent private individuals in a vast array of legal matters. Cuba's legal profession, however, has a long way to go before it can be at the full service of a transition. The current low number of lawyers on the island and the absence of standards fully supportive of a free-enterprise system need to be addressed.

Notwithstanding the relatively positive, if small, steps toward religious freedom and a more open economic environment resulting from the 1992 amendments to the socialist Constitution, recent moves by the government have signaled a reverse in reform politics. In June 2002, the socialist Constitution was amended in an attempt to impede any future modifications in favor of a politically pluralistic and market-oriented society. Specifically, the Constitution's relevant amendment provision, Article 137, now reads: "this Constitution may be amended only by the National Assembly by resolution adopted by a roll call vote of no less than a two-thirds vote of the total number of members, except to the extent to which it refers to the political, economic and social system, the irrevocable nature of which is established by Article 3, Chapter I, and the prohibition against negotiating agreements as a result of aggression, threat or coercion on the part of a foreign power." Article 3 was also amended to read: "socialism and the revolutionary political and social system established in this Constitution . . . is irrevocable, and Cuba will never return to capitalism."

The 2002 amendments, combined with the arrest and imprisonment in the spring of 2003 of seventy-five people representing Cuba's embryonic civil society—following a period of carefully managed tolerance—suggests that the rights and freedoms currently available to the nearly 200 million citizens of the former socialist republics in Central and Eastern Europe (other than Russia) remain elusive to the 11 million inhabitants of Cuba.

POSSIBLE SCENARIOS CONCERNING CUBA'S LEGAL TRANSITION

How or when a transition to a liberal democracy in Cuba will occur is unknown. No one can confidently predict whether the departure of Fidel or Raúl Castro from the nucleus of governance will inevitably lead to the immediate and sweeping liberalization of the political and economic spheres in the same way that the fall of communist leaders throughout Central and Eastern Europe led to radical change. Although there is speculation that Raúl Castro may pursue a Chinese- or Vietnamese-style restructuring of the economy, such changes, while fundamental and welcome (if they occur under his watch), would be unlikely to be accompanied by any opening on the political front. Will a transition and attendant changes in society result from a process of negotiation between the more moderate elements of the Cuban Communist Party and members of an as-yet-to-be-defined opposition group, as occurred in

Poland or Hungary? Or will political change come more dramatically, although relatively peacefully, due to the sudden collapse of the regime, as occurred in the former Czechoslovakia? Perhaps change will come rapidly but violently, as occurred in Romania. Or will it come as a result of a transformation closely and primarily controlled by the people already in power, as occurred in Russia or Bulgaria? All we know for certain is that the answer will be provided in due course by the people of Cuba and the country's leadership.

There is also the possibility that a true transition will be preceded by a period during which a succession government consisting of the Communist Party's current leadership is able to survive without making any critical structural changes. Given the entrenched nature of state institutions, the effectiveness of the internal security apparatus, the relatively small—if growing—civil society on the island, and the uncertain resolve of the international community to try to persuade a new government to pursue an alternative to the Revolution's failed socialist experiment, this scenario should not be easily dismissed. Indeed, Fidel Castro's transfer of power in July 2006 to his brother Raúl Castro and other government officials suggests such a succession plan is underway.

What is certain is that any transition to a liberal democracy with an economy based largely on market principles cannot proceed without the deliberate and comprehensive transformation of its core legal system. The architects of Cuba's transition will need to concentrate much of their attention on reviewing and revising many existing laws—a task that will be time consuming and challenging. But they are likely to find that, for the most part, their task will be one of assertive reform and revision more than the immediate, outright abrogation and replacement of laws. One of the terms used to describe the initial changes in the legal systems of Central and Eastern Europe is likely to be apt in describing what will take place in Cuba: "refolution," a cross between corrective reformation and revolutionary changes.

There are two reasons for this observation. First, Cuba has a legal system with deep roots established by the Spanish in the fifteenth and sixteenth centuries. A large portion of Cuba's civil code and code of civil procedure, for example, reflects to those of present-day Spain. Its penal code and code of penal procedure, also based on Spain's, are fairly sophisticated. But certain provisions of the penal code will need immediate attention, specifically those that give too much discretion to state authorities to apply vaguely worded prohibitions relating to threats to order or state security. Furthermore, the vast majority of matters handled by Cuban courts have little or nothing to do with political matters, nor are they related in any way to the socialist nature of the Cuban government. Naturally, existing laws will be improved over time with the participation of new voices in Cuban politics, as is the case in every liberal democracy. In short, Cuba today is not a "lawless" society from a normative point of view, and much of its legal system can be incorporated in some fashion into the legal system of a transition state.

Second, it is unlikely that in the short run the people of Cuba, if they are the ones directing their transition (as one must assume), will opt for radical change and the attendant economic and social dislocation that it could produce. Indeed, such dislocation could precipitate a strong political backlash that might compromise the transition itself, as occurred, if temporarily, in various Central and Eastern European states, including Poland. Only in East Germany was the legal system radically and immediately transformed, through the adoption of West Germany's, and this occurred only because of the extremely generous economic incentives offered by the absorbing state. An examination of the new or revised constitutions of the former Central and Eastern European states shows a desire to maintain a constitutionally mandated social security safety net in order to ease the volatility that accompanies most transitions.

A transition implies the resurrection of a multiparty political system and the establishment of a full-fledged private-property regime, which cannot occur without constitutional change. Thus, one of the first tasks of a transition government will be to commence a process of either amending Cuba's socialist Constitution or adopting a new one. Both options involve two related concepts: the substantive changes to be made in order to attain the objectives of the transition government, and the process by which those changes are made and ratified in order to maximize the legitimacy of the completed project.

Concerning the first point, the drafters of the constitutional text are most likely to be guided by two sources: the Constitution of 1976 and the Constitution of 1940. To be sure, they may eventually decide to draft a totally new Constitution that bears little resemblance to either, but this is unlikely in light of Cuba's long constitutional history. This history includes three pre-independence texts (the Constitutions of Guáimaro [1869], Jimaguayú [1895], and La Yaya [1897]), the 1902 Constitution (enacted by Cuba's first republican government and written subject to the approval of the United States during its occupation of the island), the Constitutions of 1933 and 1935, the Constitution of 1940 and the Constitution of 1976. Indeed, given their historical contexts, there are striking similarities among these documents. The constitutional model to be chosen, however, must ultimately be decided by the people of Cuba.

Some legal scholars in the Cuban diaspora believe that the Constitution of 1940 should be restored. This Constitution stands out for a number of key reasons. First, it resulted from the efforts of a popularly selected constituent assembly that represented a diverse group of opinion leaders, including members of Cuba's prerevolutionary Communist Party. As mentioned above, the restoration of the 1940 Constitution was a key rallying call for Fidel Castro and his revolutionary fighters. It also reflects a governing structure that is more reminiscent of a liberal democracy, with an established system of checks and balances as well as a constitutional court (a tribunal for constitutional and social guarantees) akin to the ones described above under the present constitutions of Poland and Hungary.

Beyond its claim to enhanced legitimacy and independence from foreign meddling, the Constitution of 1940 is notable for the surprisingly large number and progressive nature of the political, social, economic, and cultural rights contained within its text. Article 20, for example, declared, "any discrimination by reason of gender, race, color, or class, and any other kind of discrimination destructive of human dignity, is declared illegal and punishable." This antidiscrimination provision applied to all members of Cuban society, not just the government. Article 25 prohibited the imposition of the death penalty, except for treason or espionage during times of war and other very limited circumstances. Articles 43 through 59 established state obligations to the institutions of marriage and the family, as well as the right to a free education through the high-school level. Article 60 declared, "labor is an inalienable right of the individual," and further mandated the state to "employ all the resources within its power to provide employment for everyone who lacks it" and to "ensure for every worker, be he a laborer or a professional, the economic conditions necessary for a dignified existence." Article 66 granted every worker one month of vacation per year and declared that the working day "shall not exceed eight hours." Article 67 prohibited the termination of employment of any expecting mother within three months of the expected due date and required an employer to provide her with six weeks paid leave both prior to her due date and following delivery.

The primary disadvantage of the Constitution of 1940 is that it reflects a Cuban society that existed more than sixty-five years ago. Also, because of its suspension in 1952, that Constitution is not well-known to Cubans on the island who, after all, are the ones who will be most affected by Cuba's legal transition. In addition, depending on the perceived role (in the eyes of Cubans on the island) to be played by the Cuban diaspora during the transition, the 1940 Constitution's close association with members of the diaspora may render it an unattractive choice.

The Constitution of 1976 is the other sensible model for a transition government to consider, in much the same way that the Polish and Hungarian leaders began their legal transitions: by amending their existing socialist constitutions. In each of those cases, however, the amended texts were intended to be transitory, although only the Poles actually succeeded in adopting a new permanent Constitution. Its greatest advantage is that it reflects contemporary Cuba and is well known to the vast majority of Cubans. It could be easily modified by stripping all Marxist doctrinal language from the existing text; codifying the free establishment of political parties and a free-enterprise system, including enhanced rights concerning the ownership, maintenance, and disposition of private property interests; reducing the role of the Communist Party and related organizations and the state, including the military, in economic and social matters; and permitting greater individual freedoms that are guaranteed by a truly independent judiciary, in particular, a constitutional court with judicial review of the acts of the legislature and the executive. Restructuring the roles of the legislative and executive functions of government would also require special consideration, but either a presidential or parliamentary system can be fashioned from the existing text.

The practical effect of the 2002 amendments to Cuba's socialist Constitution is that any substantial change to the socialist Constitution must be approved by a majority of eligible Cuban citizens, even if the resulting Constitution is intended to be of a temporary nature. Although the new language contained in Article 137 (the Constitution's amendment provision) gives the impression that such amendments would be impossible, this problem could, theoretically, be addressed through a two-step vote sequence reflected on the same ballot. The first vote would be in favor of an amendment to Article 137 itself, with the aim of eliminating the "irrevocability" proviso (required because it affects the power of the National Assembly). The second vote, conditioned upon passage of the amendment, would refer to the numerous amendments required in order to begin to build a liberal democratic state, including excising the 2002 revisions to Article 3, which refers to the irrevocability of the communist system.

The transitional government's adoption of a new constitutional text broaches the critical question of process because it addresses the issue of its legitimacy. Adhering to the steps discussed above in order to deal with the problems presented by the 2002 amendments will give instant legitimacy to the transition movement. One should not, however, underestimate the difficult nature of this type of amendment procedure. A more practical approach, especially if the situation calls for immediate action to restore public order and trust, is for all sides working in good faith toward a transition to accept the inevitable but temporary adoption of alternative methods to amend the existing Constitution if it is determined to be the best model to override the rigid and antidemocratic provisions found in Articles 137 and 3 of the socialist Constitution. Ironically, this approach would not be unprecedented in Cuban history because it is the same method, in effect, used by the 26th of July Movement to justify the adoption of the Fundamental Law of 1959 instead of restoring the Constitution of 1940. Prudence would dictate, however, that any amendments be ratified directly or indirectly by the Cuban people as soon as practicable.

Accordingly, most critical is that a new and permanent Constitution be seen as legitimate; in other words, that it be seen as reflecting the will of the people. This can result either from the nature of the body that drafts the Constitution (the more representative the body, the more legitimate the Constitution will be deemed) or how it is ultimately ratified (the more direct the popular vote, such as through a plebiscite, the more legitimate the Constitution will be deemed). Ideally, both sources of legitimacy would be present.

One example from outside of the former Central and Eastern European bloc may be helpful. Spain began a transition to a liberal democracy shortly after the death of Francisco Franco. The transition was led by a moderate prime minister, Adolfo Suárez, who had been an active supporter of Franco. Although Suárez had been a fierce opponent of Spain's political left, he was a pragmatist who also understood that continuing Franco's policies of brutally repressing dissidents was becoming ever-more intolerable in the eyes of the international community, a situation that would have held Spain back as his government tried to modernize the country's economy and integrate it with the rest of Western Europe. Suárez also recognized that, for a transition to be viewed as legitimate, changes to the Constitution needed to be made by a legislative body fully representative of the Spanish people. Thus, he began to work with moderate leaders of dissident groups, including the communists and, within eighteen months after being sworn in as prime minister, national legislative elections were held. A new Constitution was drafted by a special committee of that legislature, and it was ratified in a special national plebiscite.

Because of Cuba's rich constitutional history, as well as its recent experience in connection with amending the socialist Constitution, the people of Cuba should be familiar with the concept of constitutionalism and the mechanisms by which constitutions are adopted or amended.

Regardless of the model that proves to be the most influential, it is imperative that a revised or new Constitution firmly grant a judicial body, such as a constitutional court, the power of judicial review over the acts of the legislature and the executive. Furthermore, measures must be established, either in the Constitution or in enabling legislation, to ensure the independence of that judicial body. This court would represent a radical departure from Cuba's existing judicial review process, but if it is effective in guaranteeing individual rights, then it should prove popular among most political actors involved in the transition, as well as the Cuban people.

As noted previously, one of the major lessons from the experience of the emerging democracies in Central and Eastern Europe is the powerful incentive provided by external organizations. Membership in the Council of Europe and, ultimately, the European Union had an enormous influence on the desire of these countries to continue to make necessary changes to their legal systems. Clearly, Cuba would not qualify for such membership. On the other hand, there will no doubt be financial and other incentives provided to a transition government that is focused on bringing true reforms to Cuba, including its legal system. Among others, it is not difficult to imagine that the World Bank, the International Monetary Fund, the International Finance Corporation, and the Inter-American Development Bank would be interested in providing financial and technical assistance. Bilateral assistance can also play an important role. Cuba is no stranger to such help, having benefited economically from its special relationship with the Soviet Union during the Cold War and, most recently, Venezuela.

In addition, a large number of Cubans in the diaspora, including lawyers, are likely to be interested in assisting Cuba to achieve its transition goals. Many of them have developed professional capabilities that are likely to be of enormous help as Cuba restructures itself and its legal system. For these legal experts to be welcomed and effective, however, they will need to become familiar with—and appreciate—Cuba's rich legal history and its existing civil law system. They must also understand that changes to Cuba's legal system are unlikely to take effect overnight and, most importantly, that the process of change must be driven primarily by those who inhabit the island since they have the most at stake in the future transformation of Cuba.

One of the early tests of the establishment of a new legal order in Cuba is likely to involve the resolution of the many claims that have been filed against the Cuban government for property that was expropriated through nationalization or confiscated by the revolutionary government, particularly in the early years of the Revolution. This is a highly complex and emotional issue given the number of claims by non-Cuban corporations and individuals as well as former residents of Cuba and the many more that, in theory, may be filed by Cubans living on the island.

An effective resolution will undoubtedly require a combination of both legal and political finesse. Resolving the issue in a just way that takes into account the many equities involved, including the interests of current residential property holders in Cuba, will also go a long way in re-establishing the respect for private property that is a hallmark of a market economy—not to mention an essential element in the restoration of individual freedoms in Cuba. Until property claims are resolved, it will be difficult to set the stage for the privatization of state-owned enterprises and to secure significant investments involving properties whose titles may be under adverse claim.

Since both investment and privatization are sure to be the focus of transition and post-transition governments in their attempt to revive the private sector and raise needed funds, the need to address property claims becomes ever more apparent. Cuba's transition will have to deal with many of the obstacles encountered by postcommunist states in Central and Eastern Europe. But despite any similarities with these nations, Cuba must forge a path to transition that builds from its own experience and history. The interaction between the key players in the transition is particularly important, as is the involvement of the Cuban people in creating or amending their Constitution. The Constitution should serve as a building block for the transition by providing a legitimate framework for establishing the rule of law. The success of Cuba's transition rests very much on two elements: constitutionality and cooperation. It is with these key elements that a peaceful transition in Cuba can occur.

FOUR

The Good, the Bad, and the Ugly

*The Normalization of Cuba's Civil Society
in Post-Transition*

DAMIÁN J. FERNÁNDEZ

The story of civil society in transitions to democracy is the story of the good, the bad, and the ugly. Cuba will likely be no exception. Cuban civil society will face similar challenges and opportunities as its counterparts have confronted elsewhere, albeit with its own national peculiarities.

Civil society is understood as the social sphere where multiple formal and informal autonomous organizations articulate diverse interests and identities and mediate between the citizens and the state. It is a requisite of democratic governance. The standard interpretation of the emergence of proto–civil society in communist regimes tends to be a benign one, and rightly so. In Cuba, a type of proto–civil society is already in place, as the not-so-latent social pluralism suggests. Once the state opens the door (or fails to keep it shut), autonomous organizations will proliferate.

In Central and Eastern Europe, the former Soviet Union, Latin America, and China, wherever one-party states asphyxiated the independent public sphere, the emergence of nongovernmental organizations (NGOs) has been nothing short of revolutionary. The quest for autonomous space—social, economic, and political, both personal and public—was one of the factors that ushered transitions to democracy and has been its driving force since. In turn, democracy has nurtured civil society by creating opportunities for organizations to act in a relatively unconstrained fashion. That is the good part of the story.

But the bad and the ugly were quick to surface in post-transition societies as well. Popular organizations lost support. Apathy overtook engaged optimism. The "NGO frenzy" of the initial years ushered in dangerous social fragmentation rather than beneficial pluralism. A host of actors placed demands that new governments, which were confronting monumental economic and political tasks, were hard pressed to meet. In the process, expectations were raised and deflated, which in turn fed pessimism and contributed to the population's disengagement from the civic sphere.

The transitional time after communism generated incivility. Personal security has become one of the top concerns of citizens throughout Eastern Europe and the Commonwealth of Independent States (CIS). Criminality and corruption have spread like wildfire. Too often, governments and states, if not accomplices of organized crime, have barely kept it at bay. Political legitimacy and efficacy have been compromised as a result. In sum, transitions to democracy have resulted in the spread of both civil and uncivil society. A similar pattern is likely to unfold in Cuba. The degrees of goodness, badness, and ugliness will depend on the specifics of the Cuban case, including the timing of the transition, the modality it takes, its political economy, and its leadership.

What assets and liabilities does Cuban society possess that will influence the emergence of a new civil society? In what ways will the emergence of civil society both foster and undermine a democratic transition? To what extent will a transition tend to produce not only civil society but its opposite as well? Will the least favorable aspects of civil society be dependent on specific macro and micro factors? What scenarios of transition are better suited to produce robust independent associations? By focusing on three pillars of contemporary Cuban society—the human rights movement, the Catholic Church, and young adults—one can detect patterns of civil and uncivil society on the island that are likely to continue.

TEN LESSONS OF CIVIL AND UNCIVIL SOCIETY IN POST-COMMUNISM AND POST-AUTHORITARIANISM: The Experience of Central and Eastern Europe, the Commonwealth of Independent States, China, and Latin America

The experience of civic life after transitions in the Soviet Union, Central and Eastern Europe, Latin America, and China has been variegated. Even within the former communist bloc countries the degree of divergence is striking. The initial enthusiasm of the early 1990s has been replaced by a nuanced tension between potentiality and achievement. Early expectations for civil society were so lofty that it should not come as a surprise that some remain unfulfilled. Civil society was expected to

- protect against state interference in private affairs;
- control state power and hold it accountable;
- socialize individuals in democratic practice;
- aggregate and represent interests outside political parties;
- forge bridges between class, gender, racial, and political divides in society by bringing people together in ways that reduce social conflict; and
- fill needs that the state is unable or unwilling to address.

This is no small task.

Differences notwithstanding, the spectrum of cross-regional experiences can be summarized in ten key lessons.

1. Pre-transition civic life is a good indicator of the future robustness of civic associations. Societies in which formal (i.e., institutional) levels of pluralism were high before democratization have fared much better than those with fewer autonomous organizations. In Poland, the transition was pushed from below by civil-society actors such as Solidarity, the Catholic Church, and intellectuals. Catholicism and nationalism played catalytic roles in mobilizing organized and informal social sectors. In the later years of the communist regime, the Polish state found it increasingly difficult to control a pluralist society.

In Hungary, civil society did not develop as strongly due to its absorption by the second economy and the informal sphere of private networks. Moreover, the decision of Hungarian communist elites to orchestrate reforms from above provided only a modicum of space for citizen participation within official structures, reducing the need for alternative organizations, and, in effect, preempting civil society and delaying the growth of pro-democratic forces. Where the Catholic Church became an icon of opposition, as in Poland and Chile, proto–civil society gained power by way of the state, facilitating the transition and a healthy nonstate sector. Where the landscape of autonomous organizations was barren, as in the former Soviet Union, civil society has generally failed to become an effective force, resulting in states that are far from democratic.

2. Different stages of transition have been accompanied by different phases of civil society activism.   Civil society tends to exhibit cycles of engagement and disengagement. During the mobilization phase against the *ancien régime* and in the early phases of transition—usually coinciding with reformist policies or elite contention inside the state—proto–civil society has tended to grow vigorously. With the institutionalization of democracy, a decline in the robustness of civil society is common. Once political parties are formed, constitutions ratified, and elections held, the energy of civil society tends to wane. Accompanying the cycle of disengagement has been a sense of disappointment with democratic institutions (but not with democracy broadly speaking) as economic crisis and weak performance erodes pro-engagement attitudes.

3. In a few key cases, civil society leadership has nurtured political society.   Civic leaders have assumed leadership roles in political parties. The case of Solidarity is the most notable one, but the experience was similar in Hungary, Chile, and Czechoslovakia. In those countries, the dissidents of yesterday became the elected officials of today. But they are the exception rather than the rule. A vigorous civil society, though, contributes to the quality of politics by making governments more responsive and accountable to the population.

4. Widespread popular engagement and a deep-seated civic culture remain elusive in many post-transition societies. Even in countries with a robust NGO sector, only small percentages of the population belong to civic organizations, and the development of civic values has been daunting. Throughout the former Soviet bloc and in Latin America, one can speak of the rise of an uncivil society characterized by political apathy, lack of personal security, mafias, criminality, and a host of other uncivil behaviors. In countries with high levels of education and urbanization, civil society and civic participation tend to be stronger than in more rural settings with less educated populations.

5. External actors, particularly multilateral institutions, can foster civil society organizations in important, if limited, ways. The political magnetism of the European Union has pulled societies in Central and Eastern Europe toward democracy; the closer to Western Europe, the greater the pull. Western Europe's role in helping to diffuse norms and values (in tandem with material support) undergirds democratization as it contributes to the development of an international society of NGOs that operates transnationally. External actors can also exert a less than positive influence, such as the case of Russia over Belarus.

6. Civil society is conducive to democracy even in the least favorable settings such as Belarus, Moldova, and Uzbekistan, where the transitions are far from consolidated. Even in nondemocratic contexts, civil society acts as a democratic conscience and plays a liberalizing role by demanding liberties, transparency, and accountability. In Ukraine, an organized and mobilized civil society was effective in overturning fraudulent election results in 2004.

7. Civil society alone cannot be responsible for democratic governance. Civil society cannot run and win elections or reform the state or end a culture of informality and corruption. A more realistic perspective on what civil society can do is in order. Civil society can safeguard a space for personal and group freedom, serve some group interests, address specific needs, and stand against governmental practices that corrode democracy—though not always successfully.

8. *Since democracy is not everyone's natural or uncontested choice, it must work to the advantage of most citizens.*   If it does not, pessimism and antidemocratic feelings take hold, which in turn tend to reduce engagement in the public sphere. In countries such as Russia, where the economic transition was most painful and accompanied by few long-term rewards, the appeal of civil society has diminished. What is not totally clear is whether poor economic performance causes the decline in the social capital or whether weak social capital leads to lackluster economies and skewed distribution. Surprisingly though, despite anemic economic performance, rising inequality, eroding standards of living, and unfulfilled expectations in many post-transition societies, few sectors of the population have advocated a return to the politics of the past.

9. *Public support for democracy rests largely on the acceptance of democratic rules rather than on participation in or the vitality of civil society per se.*   That is, although an active NGO sector is supportive of democracy, widespread civic engagement might be desirable but not required for a liberal democratic order with electoral competition.

10. *The timing of economic reforms in communist systems affects the development of civil society.*   In countries where socialist states embark on a process of opening markets, the ruling party can act as an economic and political gatekeeper without ushering in a process of political transition. This is a lesson one can draw from China and Vietnam. It requires a correlate: although the Chinese model provides the state with additional resources, it also unleashes dynamics at the social level that, in the long run, challenge the one-party system and contribute to the formation of civil society.

CUBA IN COMPARATIVE PERSPECTIVE

Cuban society has changed dramatically since the mid-1990s. Today it is more diverse, with grey zones of autonomy from the state. As such, it has both assets and liabilities for civil-society formation in specific and for civility in general. The landscape of what can be called a proto–civil society on the island covers a range of types of organizations, from opposition groups to state-governed agencies that, with more or less success, try to push the borderline of what is permissible. Between those two points, religious institutions, self-help organizations, cultural groups, and other independent associations operate, although under intense government restrictions if not outright repression. At the same time the traditional socialist civil society—the group of organizations controlled by the Communist Party and the state—has atrophied.

Cuba's proto–civil society falls somewhere between the extremes of the pluralism of Poland and the barren landscape of the former Soviet Union before transition. An infrastructure of resources exists on which future actors can build civil society, including a highly educated urban population. But liabilities are also present.

In two important ways Cuba resembles Hungary. The Catholic Church is not a strong mobilizing force, and nationalism as a compelling ideology has been appropriated and co-opted by the government rather than by the opposition. In Cuba, potential sources of civil-society initiatives have been channeled into informal practices, networks, and the black market. But Cuba is not Hungary, at least not yet. The Cuban elite has not shown the will to make concessions through a reform process orchestrated from above. In terms of social pluralism, Cuba is somewhere between Poland and Hungary, but neither model fits perfectly. The economic reforms of the 1990s resemble more the Chinese experience than that of other reforming socialist or authoritarian states.

While Cuba is not as formally pluralistic as Poland was before transition, the dissident and opposition community is much more substantial than the Czechoslovakian and Hungarian counterparts were in the late 1980s, despite the wave of repression in 2003. Today, there is a formal opposition on the island, and the world knows its leaders and what they stand for. But Cuba is not within the political gravity of an international institution such as the European Union. The Western Hemisphere's democracy rules are not as formalized or operational as those of the European Union. Cuba's political field—the United States, Latin America, and the Organization of American States—has a mixed history of support for democracy.

THE CUBAN CASE

Social Dynamics and the Emergence of a Proto–Civil Society

Today, there are more than 350 independent organizations. Most of them are small, but they have significant potential for changing Cuban politics in the future. There is also widespread informal resistance, and social actors with new identities and interests (dissidents, business managers, and owners of private restaurants, among others) are shaping a proto–civil society in Cuba. The state is less able to make citizens act in prescribed ways: many Cubans have disengaged from formal politics as opportunities for autonomous and efficacious political participation have been foreclosed. Fear has corroded social trust, making collective action almost impossible, but that too is changing. Networks of family and friends act as conduits of resistance and accommodation at the informal level, and an opposition-led initiative, the Varela Project, obtained more than 25,000 signatures on a petition demanding a series of political and economic reforms. The number of Cubans in dissident organizations has mushroomed. The Catholic Church has assumed a self-assured posture in relation to the government as it has expanded the ranks of the laity. Young adults and other social sectors, such as artists and intellectuals, have challenged state control in economic and social matters (e.g., freedom of expression and religiosity). Even within the formal structures of the state and the Communist Party, latent discontent, quiet divergence of interests, and submerged pluralism exist.

The emergent proto–civil society is composed of human rights, opposition, single-issue, and religious associations. Several factors, however, conspire against the expansion of civil society. Tired of politics and mobilization, Cubans are seeking to satisfy their interests and find meaning in the personal realm. The demands that the economy of survival places on individuals result in a necessary self-centeredness. Combined with a heavy dosage of fear, these tendencies and attitudes are a poor conduit for civic participation in independent organizations, particularly given the risks associated with such activities. Most Cubans are not ready or willing to join alternative organizations. Many have divided loyalties and seem disoriented regarding the future. The confrontation with the United States, always a factor in Cuban politics, reduces the space for civil society by polarizing the debate on the future of the nation.

The Human Rights Community and the Opposition

The genesis of the Cuban human rights movement dates to the 1960s, when exiled activists and the Organization of American States tried, against the odds, to put the issue at the forefront of international public awareness. In 1976, the first human rights group was formed on the island. Since then, the movement has expanded and become more diverse, confrontational (through civil resistance), and visible. A new generation of leaders, more representative of the population—black and white, men and women, from all walks of life and from all regions of the country—assumed the reins of the movement. They have found a reluctant ally in the Catholic Church and increasingly supportive friends in the international community. The movement has not only survived but thrived. Today Cuba has a well-established human rights community.

Since 2004, there has also been an institutionalized opposition on the island, one that has survived despite waves of repression. The fact that the Varela Project, led by Oswaldo Payá Sardiñas of the Christian Liberation Movement, persuaded more than 25,000 Cubans between the late 1990s and 2004 to sign a petition demanding a referendum (the Constitution requires 10,000 signatures for a referendum) represents a watershed in the history of Cuban socialist politics. The Project calls for a modest five-point set of political and economic proposals, namely freedom of speech and assembly, amnesty for political prisoners, permission for Cubans to establish enterprises, a new electoral law, and elections within nine months.

The Project's logic is to use the socialist Constitution to change the regime from within. By succeeding in meeting and surpassing the signature requirement for a referendum, the organizers demonstrated the reduction in state capacity to control society and the pent-up demand for change. Furthermore, the Project is pursuing reforms through civic engagement and legal, peaceful means—good harbingers of civil society in the future. The moral and political capital thus accumulated in past years will serve these groups well under different conditions.

Although membership in civil-society organizations on the island reaches well into the thousands, most of the individual groups have remained quite small and fragmented. They have not been able to forge a common front since 1996, when the government disbanded the Cuban Council, which served as an umbrella for the most prominent dissident and opposition associations. Ideological and institutional diversity, however, can be interpreted as a virtue rather than a sin. The multiplicity of leaders and organizations is both a condition for democracy and a strategy for survival, making it harder for the government to eliminate the movement in one sweep.

What unites members of the human rights and opposition community is their autonomy relative to the state and their call to establish the rule of law according to international legal standards. They demand the right to exist legally. They oppose the one-party state and the limitations on individual rights. Though differing on the degree of state intervention they would accept in the economy, all agree on political and economic liberalization. By rejecting violence and supporting a peaceful transition, their discourse and practice are weaving a democratic pattern into Cuban political culture.

Human rights and opposition activists are forced to spread their message by word of mouth. Not surprisingly, independent political associations have not been able to mobilize the population because they lack the resources and the opportunity and because the costs associated with dissidence—which can involve harassment, imprisonment, and exile—are still high. Members of opposition groups are continuously under surveillance and threat of imprisonment. The secret police infiltrate their organizations, undermine their unity, discredit them, and unravel their plans. Pervasive fear keeps ordinary Cubans from joining their ranks.

Another dilemma confronting the movement is its relationship to the outside world, particularly the United States. While the human rights and opposition movements need U.S. assistance, the Cuban government focuses on that dependence to discredit their authenticity and nationalism. To make matters worse, U.S. policy under the George W. Bush administration has unwittingly played into the hands of the Cuban government by bilateralizing an issue that is national, international, and transnational. Furthermore, the Bush administration's decision to tighten the travel restrictions has made it more difficult to get resources to the activists. As in other moments in Cuban history, the U.S. factor tends to fracture and polarize Cubans. In this case, the dissident community is divided along pro- and anti-embargo camps, which complicates further an already complex situation.

The Catholic Church: The Only National Independent Institution

The Catholic Church is the only autonomous institution with national reach on the island, which places it in a privileged position with significant, if not always welcomed, responsibilities. After a period of dormancy from the early 1960s to the early 1980s, the Cuban church experienced a reawakening. The newfound activism was due in part to the initiative of the Cuban National Ecclesial Encounter, the 1986 national gathering of church leaders and members that promoted a course of action to attract believers to the flock. It convened at a time of deepening crisis in Cuban society that was eventually compounded in the 1990s by the economic effects of the dissolution of the Soviet Union. With the collapse of the moral and material universe of Cuban socialism, people were in need of new sources of hope, meaning, and identity. Many Cubans turned to religion; researchers on the island today estimate that 82 percent of Cubans have religious beliefs. Since the collapse of socialism in Europe, attendance at services and vocations has increased sharply. Approximately 5 percent of Cubans regularly practice Catholicism, compared to 2 percent in the 1980s. The numbers of baptisms, confirmations, and communions are on the rise as well. In 1988, 14,400 baptisms were held; in 1994, the number reached 70,081. By the early 2000s, the church had expanded its social presence and power of convocation, and religious celebrations now often attract hundreds if not thousands of participants.

The reasons for institutional strengthening of the church are numerous: the internal decisions of the leadership, demands from the grassroots for a more active church, the economic crisis, and the lessons learned regarding the church's role in transitions from communism and dictatorship elsewhere. Changes in government policy contributed to the church's newfound stature as well. The Communist Party eased the restrictions on religious practice and reduced its social cost. The Fourth Party Congress lifted the ban on believers joining the Cuban Communist Party. In 1992, the new constitution declared Cuba a secular rather than an atheist state. Cuban authorities legalized the celebration of Christmas in 1997 and have allowed several public masses since then. Processions have been granted legal permits. At the same time, the church has become a center for distribution of material resources, especially medicines and other forms of assistance to a needy population.

Pope John Paul II's visit to the island in January 1998 identified new opportunities for the church and showed a society responsive to it. His masses brought together tens of thousands in the largest congregations of Cubans outside state-directed mobilizations since 1959. Yet the church faces serious constraints—internal, governmental, and social—as it tries to find its place, course, and voice in an unpredictable environment.

The defining feature of the Catholic Church—and religion in general—in contemporary Cuba is encapsulated in a paradox: growing strength amid continuing weakness. The Cuban Catholic Church and its Protestant sisters are minority institutions and well aware of their limitations. As of the late 1990s, the Catholic Church had 269 priests (1 per 35,000 inhabitants). About 4.5 million Cubans are nominally Catholic (that is, they were baptized), representing about 41 percent of the population—half the number of people who profess some kind of religious belief. Even the most popular religious festivity—that of Saint Lazarus—attracts fewer than 100,000 people. At most, 500,000 Cubans participate in religious services (both Catholic and Protestant) on any given Sunday.

The priority for religious organizations in the next decade is to extend and deepen their roots in Cuban society. It will not be an easy task because most Cubans are distanced from formal religious practice. In addition, government regulations continue to limit the space for religion in society and severely restrict its expansion, despite relaxation of the parameters in the early 1990s. The growth of Afro-Cuban religions and *espiritismo* (spiritism) poses an additional challenge of no small consequence, as does the general cultural tendency toward informal practices and away from institutions. Moreover, the church's ambivalence toward involvement in political matters might become a liability in the future.

The caution exhibited by the Catholic Church regarding human rights groups and the opposition movement poses another layer of difficulties for the institution. The hierarchy has defined a pastoral mission of evangelization and reconciliation. It is unlikely that the church will serve as an umbrella for the opposition to the regime or for civil society in general. But by opting for relative detachment from politics, the church runs the risk of alienating many inside and outside the country and undermining its potential constituency.

The Catholic Church does count on a measure of moral capital. It offers a compelling spiritual and moral message, independent of the government. The three major challenges it will face in the medium to long term are how to connect with the population, how to manage church-government relations, and how to contain the rise of other competing religious practices and institutions.

In the short to medium term, the church has an agenda with objectives that range from the minimalist to the maximalist, from continuing its evangelical mission to attracting a greater number of believers and increasing the number of priests and nuns allowed into the country. It also hopes to repair churches and expand the purview of Catholic charities throughout the island. In the longer term, the church desires access to media and eventually permission to establish its own radio station and Catholic schools. During a time of transition, the church would like to be a power broker and a leading force for reconciliation.

The church has contributed to the emergence of a proto–civil society on the island by its sheer existence and that of its adherents, by forming a cadre of lay Catholic activists, and by supporting norms that are conducive to civil society development (e.g., support for economic reforms and citizen rights). Also, by holding processions in public spaces, for example, it has helped to "de-privatize" religion, which might have a demonstration effect on the rest of the population in terms of legitimizing public pluralism. To a lesser but still important extent, the church has protected human rights activists and dissidents behind the scenes.

Young Adults

Life is frustrating for the young adults in Cuba. Their frustration is a symptom of the dissonance between their expectations and reality as well as of the failure of official political socialization. Frustration is also the result of the state's inability to make good on promises made, and it is a harbinger of social transformation. In the early twenty-first century, the desire of young Cubans for change is manifest. One can hear it in their music and slang. One can see it in their membership in alternative organizations, in their multiple manifestations of informal resistance, and in their exit—both symbolic and literal—from official politics. Like young adults elsewhere, they want the opportunities and lives that their educational levels should make available to them but do not.

Current issues of contention among young Cubans may play out in the future around three axes: the political, including their participation or nonparticipation in the political process; the social, including corruption, criminality, and pervasive informality; and the economic, having to do with their sense of equal access to opportunity, of unmet material needs and expectations, and access to the labor market. As these intersect with overarching issues of transition, they will influence the development of democracy and the construction of an active civil society.

In this process, the biggest challenge will not come from "good communist youth" who internalized revolutionary nationalist dogmas expounded in schools and state organizations. On the contrary, the greatest source of political and social disruption will tend to be the dissocialized, the marginal, the school dropouts, and the unemployed. That is, the failure—not the success—of communist institutions will cause the thorniest social, political, and economic problems in a post-Castro Cuba. For it is precisely the disassociated population—which has become adept at skirting the system and surviving by engaging in illegal behavior—that will fray the fabric of civil and political life. To make matters more complex, any post-transition government will have to redefine the social contract, reformulate a national imaginary, and address the pent-up economic demands of the population in the context of a dismal economy if it is to gain legitimacy and support. The tasks are monumental; the outlook is not bright.

The politics of young adults have played a defining role and will continue to play one in the future, not only politically but, more important, socially. What is at stake is not only the replication of the regime but the future quality of civil and political society. Cubans between the ages of 18 and 35 could constitute the single most explosive social group for the regime and its successors. The issues concerning young Cubans are shaped by structural limitations, institutional legitimacy, efficacy, and political culture; they have to do with class, race, and ideology. As such, the politics of the young serves as a prism through which one can better detect the tensions and fissures in state–society relations at present and how these can contribute to the development of civil and uncivil society in the future.

A significant, although undetermined, segment of the young uphold new standards of political judgment based on performance rather than promise, on legal rationality rather than charismatic authority. Interviews with young adults on the island make clear that they compare the theory of Cuban socialism with its practice; and the resulting distance has undermined their support for the political system, generating disenchantment and disappointment. This is expressed in a variety of behaviors, including political apathy, that are marked by either refusal to participate or ritualistic participation; by the *doble moral*, a dual set of behaviors, attitudes, and opinions, one set for the public sphere and one for the private; by migration or self-imposed alienation; and self-generated (usually illegal) mechanisms for satisfying material and non-material needs.

Another important reason for the political distinctiveness of the younger generations is the emergence of a youth identity since the 1980s that is marked by values such as individualism, autonomy, and consumerism. Such values have been expressed in attempts to create independent organizations—particularly cultural ones—in the latest wave of migration, and in participation in self-employment, formal and informal.

In fact, the insertion of young adults into the labor market has not met expectations, and one of the reasons for their confrontation with political authority is their reduced socioeconomic possibilities. In addition, the political discourse of the top leaders (and of state institutions) is out of sync with the interests of the young, and it has alienated many.

The young have seen their possibilities for mobility and consumption fade. High expectations fueled by education, urbanization, and the socialist discourse have come to naught, leaving the young (and many of their elders) at odds with the political and economic system and without formal spaces in which to voice contending perspectives. The economic crisis has had a negative effect on the educational and labor profile of young adults. In the early 1990s, Cubans younger than thirty-five years of age made up 50 percent of the employed labor force while representing 40 percent of working-age Cubans. They exhibited notable educational achievement: by the 1980s, 60 percent had some level of professional training. Since the crisis of the early 1990s though, young Cubans account for 74 percent of the unemployed; many shifted to self-employment, particularly within the tourism sector, and the ranks of the underemployed swelled.

The young accommodate to and resist governmental demands. Cuban publications regularly comment on how the young evade agricultural work, voluntary service, and meetings of the neighborhood committees. They skip school, drop out, dodge the draft. Criminality has increased among their generation. In some poor neighborhoods the situation is critical.

Resistance to official ideology and its codes is evident in a variety of ways: in music and fashions, tattoos, relations with tourists, and graffiti. In the early 1990s, crimes perpetrated by young Cubans increased. The majority of victims of homicides were between the ages of twenty-six and thirty-five. Drug use escalated as well. The situation is so serious that the government and the Communist Youth have conducted prevention campaigns against crime and antisocial conduct. Criminality is not only national but international, revolving around tourist centers and at times associated with drug networks. The emergence of such criminal associations foreshadows what may come after Castro: mafia-style transnational operations. On a different scale, youth organizations and teacher associations have long tried to combat academic misconduct and fraud to no avail. Fraud has a corrosive effect not only on academic institutions but on social life in general.

This crisis of values is the major challenge confronting the government today and one likely to continue in the future. Exhaustion with the heavy-handedness of state socialization has resulted in a generalized rejection of politics. Young adults, as well as their elders, want to be free from politics. Throughout the globe, political apathy is widespread. With few exceptions (e.g., the antiglobalization movement), youth participation in civil and political society is waning. In the case of Cuba, however, decades of coerced participation in a hyperpoliticized environment where institutions are not representative or efficacious accentuate the trend.

As mentioned earlier, a serious challenge for a post-Castro Cuba will not be the youth socialized under the guidelines of Marxism-Leninism or Martianismo (the ideology based on José Martí's thought with a heavy dosage of Fidelismo). The most problematic will be the disassociated youth, who have discarded ideology, are used to breaking the law on a daily basis, and have little to lose. They will be less able to compete in the labor market because they lack the skills to succeed in a formal economy. Criminal entrepreneurship and participation in mafia-style groups will be more likely avenues. If national and transnational networks develop and spread corruption throughout Cuban society, the young, who are rich in informal network capital, will be active agents in them.

Changing the sociopolitical attitudes and values of younger Cubans will be a Sisyphean task. The problem of desocialization seems insoluble in the short term and even post-transition. Changing the structure of opportunities to provide incentives for political, social, and economic participation will mitigate but not eradicate the negative tendencies that the regime today bemoans. Civic education has proven only marginally successful the world over; will young Cubans be any less impervious to official campaigns aimed at instilling civic values?

The rejection of politics also entails the repudiation of traditional national symbols. What symbols and myths would a new government employ to garner the population's imagination and good will? What new social contract could it develop to muster support among generations that are willing neither to listen nor to believe? How should the government address such issues when the available methods are precisely the ones that have been rejected? How can political society reconstitute itself in a democratic manner if participation is perceived as meaningless? What type of civil society can emerge in a context that lacks the social capital appropriate for cooperation? Although expectations might have been reduced after years of economic crisis, there is still unsatisfied demand for consumer goods, employment, private enterprise, and social mobility. Young Cubans want to be fully modern, economic citizens whose material opportunities match their educational profile. Meeting these expectations with an empty treasury will be impossible. How could a new government muster and sustain popular good will if it is unable to deliver materially?

Any transition government will be confronted by a host of immediate and long-term problems regarding young Cubans: political apathy, migration, brain drain, pent-up demands for economic goods, rising inequality, potential class conflict, racial tension, prostitution, drop-out rates, and criminality. Just as pressing will be the creation of a new foundational myth that, if widely accepted, would legitimize the new government. Given young Cubans' exhaustion with propaganda, such an effort may fall on deaf ears. Without economic deliverables, political citizenship and civil harmony will be difficult to sustain, particularly in a democratic context.

SCENARIOS OF TRANSITION AND THEIR EFFECT ON CIVIL SOCIETY

The development of civil society will depend on the timing and speed of transition, the degree of political openness, and the government's economic policies.

Scenario 1: The Succession Scenario

In this scenario political change would be minimal in the short term and the likely economic reforms would tend to be modest. Political control and social stability would be paramount for the new leaders. The regime's

principal institutions would remain in place and unaltered; elite cohesion would be sustained. The pace of necessary reforms—to secure
legitimacy and economic gains at a basic level—would be slow and measured. The space for the development of civil society would be similar to
that under the present regime.

But the physical disappearance of Fidel Castro would tend to em-
bolden the organized opposition, the church, and informal resistance at
the grassroots level, generating fissures in the top leadership sooner rather
than later. Even modest economic reforms would support the emergence of a civil society. Overall, in this scenario the pressures from below
are likely to increase and challenge the regime. The successors would find
it difficult to maintain the status quo in the medium or short term.

The church and the opposition organizations would assert themselves and find a renewed cause for marshalling their power and articu-
lating their message at the domestic and international levels. Based on its
long-held position on national reconciliation, the church would support
a national dialogue and would find its position to be strengthened. It
would likely display an uncharacteristically assertive role and call for social peace and reforms at the same time. The Varela Project would gain
greater immediacy, and Payá's call for a national dialogue would resonate with the church's message. The new government would have to
continue resorting to repression to quiet these voices.

The biggest wild card in this scenario is how the citizenry would
react. Are riots and social disturbance likely? Or would they give the successors the benefit of a honeymoon period? The answers to these questions depend on a number of variables: the conditions at the time when
the succession occurs, how the succession itself is managed immediately
after Castro's passing, and the economic reforms introduced shortly thereafter. If the economic situation at the moment of succession is akin to
the direst levels of 1993–94, the government will have to act quickly and
intelligently to contain the population. If material benefits are not forthcoming relatively early, the citizenry, especially the young, will likely become increasingly difficult to control. Criminality and informality will
increase. Corruption will continue to fray the fabric of Cuban social life.
Apathy and disengagement from politics will be pervasive and at some
point social violence is to be expected. Pressures to emigrate will escalate.

If the new government is able to deliver economic gains, its legitimacy and ability to govern will be strengthened without the need for concessions to the advocates of civil society or for altering the space for autonomous organizations. Nevertheless, the government will have to address the atrophy of mass organizations, pervasive social informality, the lack of representativeness, and pent-up demands.

Scenario 2: The Transition Scenario

The transition scenario implies abrupt and meaningful change in the politics and economics of Cuba. Whether led from the top down or the bottom up, this sort of transition would lead to the establishment of a democratic regime. New (or redefined) leaders and institutions would pave the road toward an open, competitive political system that would respect civil rights and protect private property. Opportunities for groups to organize and participate would be radically expanded. But this process is fraught with uncertainty and obstacles, not the least of which is deciding who would govern and how to manage an economic transition while sustaining social peace and providing a modicum of welfare as democracy is allowed to flourish.

The church would be able to extend its reach into society as it gains greater access to the media and establishes religious schools, among other activities. It would also be well situated to act as a mediator, or even as a leader, in a national reconciliation effort. Not everything, however, would be ideal for the Catholic Church. Other post-transition experiences indicate that attendance at services declines after a transition takes place. It is unlikely that the Cuban church would face as dramatic a drop as those in Poland or Chile, where the Catholic Church had a considerably stronger presence. But the church might have to deal with criticism that it did too little too late, or even that it was an accomplice to the regime, if it continues its present policies.

Opposition and human rights groups might be big winners in this scenario. The rule of law would recognize their rights of association and their freedom of expression. Some leaders, such as Oswaldo Payá, Marta Beatriz Roque (president of the Assembly to Promote Civil Society in Cuba), and Elizardo Sánchez Santa Cruz (president of the Cuban

Commission for Human Rights and National Reconciliation), might be able to parlay their credentials as bona fide political candidates and reconstitute their organizations into political parties. Others will not have the personal or institutional resources to do so. International support (including from Miami) would play an important role in the process of transforming members of the opposition into electoral contenders and developing civil society on the island. Independent associations might grow out of the old state institutions. Labor unions would put pressure on the new government to pursue issues like unemployment and wages. Some actors who originated in communist institutions might well advocate a hard line.

Social tensions and imperiled governability would likely emerge in a full transition scenario. The rough road of economic recovery and the likelihood of increasing social inequality would tend to exacerbate already existing patterns of apathy, disengagement, informality, and polarization. Winners would be empowered and losers disempowered. Nonetheless, a democratic transition and a market economy constitute the scenario that provides the greatest hope for addressing political and economic challenges. How those challenges are met will depend on the quality of leadership and institutions as well as on the behavior of civil society and society in general.

Scenario 3: The China Scenario

While imposing strict limits on human rights, civil liberties, and autonomous organizations, the Chinese government expanded the parameters for individual and group behavior that are not overtly political under market socialism. Chinese society has experienced profound changes in terms of class, culture, and lifestyle without political transformation.

The Cuban Communist Party could oversee a liberalization of the economy under one-party rule. In this Chinese scenario, development of civil society would be slow, conflictual, partial, and constrained. The broadened sphere of economic activity and cultural diversity would usher a movement away from totalitarianism and toward authoritarianism, providing much-needed breathing room for individuals and groups but not political openness. The church and other religious associations could find greater space and fewer restrictions to pursue their evangelical mission, but human rights activists and dissidents would not fare as well. Young Cubans would find their principal economic concerns addressed and, thus, those pressures eased. Economic reforms per se, however, would not erase the political dissatisfaction resulting from issues of inefficacy and lack of representation and autonomy.

The China scenario cuts both ways, providing answers to some of the challenges facing Cuban socialism while raising others. Economic changes would begin to satisfy citizens' expectations, and social actors would test the limits of what is permissible. A major confrontation similar to the protests in China's Tiananmen Square in 1989 might occur in Havana or in the eastern provinces, where social tension has been highest.

The political economy of market socialism would strengthen party leaders at the provincial and local levels, which in turn would attract a new crop of cadres and would reinforce the party overall. If the party becomes a venue for social mobility and economic security, conformity will be cemented. The impetus to go outside the official channels will be reduced and civil society thwarted. Party politics will not be without tension and cleavages. Factions will likely emerge and tend to coalesce around the winners and losers in the new economy. While the China model would bring some economic hope and social space, it would also raise the prospect of elite division and accentuated contradictions that could, in the end, encourage the formation of civil society.

THE SPECTER OF THE BAD AND THE UGLY IN THE MIDST OF THE GOOD

In a political transition, the most daunting task involves fostering a generalized attitude supportive of democratic citizenship. The hardware of pluralism—that is, the institutional formation of NGOs—is easily attainable. Once the legal framework is in place, independent organizations multiply, especially in the context of economic liberalization. The key will be to avoid hyperfragmentation in civil society, which can erode the common good and horizontal linkages.

The legacy of decades of government insufficiency and the failure of official socialization, however, could be a fertile breeding ground for incivility and uncivil society. Some of these negative prospects can be altered by providing incentives for work, making room for private enterprise and creating opportunities for efficacious political engagement. Moreover, the transition to a market economy and the concomitant reliance on individualistic values will work against collective pursuits. This is the reality under which civil society actors and real democracies must operate.

The Cuban people have values, resources, and some autonomous organizations that might be conducive to a vibrant civil society. Considering its relatively high level of education, high degree of urbanization, and social diversity, Cuban society has a partial foundation on which to build independent organizations and represent social pluralism. The stronger the civil society is that emerges, the more likely it is that a democratic transition—albeit imperfect—will be forthcoming.

FIVE

Gender Equality
in Transition Policies

Comparative Perspectives on Cuba

MALA HTUN

Revolutionary Cuba upholds some of the world's most progressive policies for gender equality. Women and men enjoy equal rights; abortion is free, legal, and safe; divorce is easy to obtain; the family code requires that men and women share in childrearing and other domestic tasks; maternity leave is generous; and the state sponsors a network of affordable day care facilities for working mothers. The island's efforts in this regard resemble those of other communist countries. Believing women's economic emancipation to be a key part of forging a socialist order, states from China and Vietnam to members of the former Soviet Union and the Central and Eastern European bloc eliminated obstacles to their equal participation, including customary family laws and belief systems about female incapacity. Cuba's approach to gender equality also contains elements of continuity with its liberal pre-revolutionary traditions. The country legalized no-fault divorce in 1918, decades before other Latin American states did. During the 1930s, a national maternity insurance program, a progressive maternity code, and equal work laws were introduced. The 1940 Constitution granted men and women equal rights.

Have these policies changed patriarchal customs? If Cuba begins a transition away from socialism and a one-party state, what will happen to its progressive approach? Do the experiences of other new democracies offer any lessons relevant to the island's future? As forecasts, these experiences invite broader reflections on the role of the state in forging gender equality and, more specifically, on the type of regime best suited to advance women's rights. Is gender equality more likely to be achieved under a socialist government like Cuba's than in a liberal democracy? Can equality be preserved amid political liberalization and market reforms? What are the advantages and disadvantages of different political regimes for progress toward gender justice?

Official socialism in Cuba, like its counterparts elsewhere, has tended to stress positive freedoms, that is, the material conditions enabling people to exercise certain rights. The regime enacted social policies to educate, feed, house, and provide health care. It succeeded in bringing women into the workplace, integrating educational institutions, and building social services to support working mothers. Yet the Cuban Communist Party's curtailment of civil liberties and its monopoly over civic organizations has precluded the articulation of alternative visions of gender emancipation and the development of a society able to critique and influence state policy. Important sources of inequality—such as domestic and sexual violence—have mostly remained unaddressed.

Liberal regimes, by contrast, prioritize negative freedoms. They build hedges defending individual autonomy of thought, decision, and action from state intrusion. These rights protect people from the capricious decisions of those in power. Historically, however, liberalism has been compatible with domestic patriarchy and the oppression of women. Though Western liberal regimes in the developed world have made important advances toward gender equality, the emergence of new democracies coincided with the resurgence of patriarchal and nationalist movements hostile to women's rights. What is more, the freeing of politics in many nations produced a deadlock on gender policy issues such as abortion. Liberal democracy opens space for the organization of civil society but offers no assurance of a particular set of policy outcomes.

GENDER EQUALITY AFTER DEMOCRATIC TRANSITIONS

The track record of Western liberal democracies suggests that democracies promote women's rights. Most of these societies—particularly in Northern Europe and Canada—have made considerable progress toward equality between women and men. Yet it would be a mistake to attribute these results to democratic politics alone. In Latin America, Asia, Africa, and the Middle East, nondemocratic regimes have often presided over the liberalization of laws related to gender issues as well as over marked improvements in women's status. Authoritarian governments committed to modernization have ruptured patriarchal structures in the home. Anticlerical dictatorships have undermined the power of religious institutions over marriage and family affairs. And military regimes seeking greater economic growth have drawn women into the workforce and institutions of higher education.

In fact, the record of new democracies is mixed when it comes to gender equality. Transitions in Central and Eastern Europe and Latin America produced some contradictory results. In the former, some countries rolled back liberal laws on abortion and reproduction and abandoned policies to support working mothers. Women's representation in political office plummeted. Democratization also coincided with the resurgence of patriarchal and nationalist discourses that crowded out feminist movements. In Latin America, democratization created an opportunity for debate and change that had been repressed under military governments. But the transition also opened space for the mobilization of conservative movements and generated political stalemate on at least one important policy issue: abortion. These experiences highlight some of the advantages and disadvantages of democratic politics as a means to achieve gender equality. An inherently open-ended process, democracy makes no guarantees about outcomes. It can provide only opportunities for continued contestation.

Central and Eastern Europe

Central and Eastern Europe offer one model for what to expect in Cuba. Socialist regimes there also supported legal equality and enacted social policies to help working women. Abortion was legal and divorce easy to obtain. How did the transition affect these issues? In the first place, abortion became hotly contested, one of the first items on the policy agenda of new democracies. Under communist rule, abortion had been free, legal, safe, and widely used as a method of birth control. Liberal abortion policies were upheld, however, not out of respect for women's right to reproductive freedom but to keep women in the workforce and families small. Unlike in the United States and Western Europe, feminist movements in Central and Eastern Europe had not mobilized in defense of elective abortion as a matter of personal liberty, privacy, or a woman's right to control her body. In new democracies, the situation changed. In many countries, including the former East Germany, Hungary, Poland, Serbia, Slovenia, and Croatia, conservative and religious groups launched attacks on liberal abortion policies and introduced bills to restrict access to abortion, if not ban the procedure completely.

These efforts were most successful in Poland, where the conservative assault on abortion dovetailed with the growing strength of the Roman Catholic Church. The bishops had served as power brokers in the political transition: they contributed to the emergence of the Solidarity movement and helped protect other dissident groups from official repression. In the 1990s, the bishops enjoyed legitimacy and political clout, and they used this capital to demand change on abortion. The practice was positioned as an immoral relic of the communist past, and politicians jumped on the anti-abortion bandwagon to affirm their commitment to democracy. In 1993, the Polish parliament approved a law criminalizing abortion under almost all circumstances. A more liberal law was introduced in 1996 but overturned by the Constitutional Court in 1997.

In Germany, conflict over abortion almost derailed reunification. The East allowed free abortion on demand in the first twelve weeks of pregnancy. In the West, permission was granted only if the pregnancy resulted from an illegal act or if it imposed serious hardship on the woman.

Two doctors were required to approve the process, which was often lengthy. As a result, most women went to neighboring countries for abortions. Amid emotional battles between the defenders of elective abortion and conservative Christians from the West, a compromise was forged to allow each side to retain its laws for two years. Though then-chancellor Helmut Kohl had wanted to prosecute Western women who went to the East to abort, the Social Democrats threatened to withhold support for the agreement unless he relented, which he did at the last minute. In 1995, Parliament passed a law permitting women throughout Germany to abort in the first trimester of pregnancy, but only after undergoing counseling intended to reverse the decision. What is more, abortion is rarely covered under the national health care system.

Elsewhere, attacks on abortion were less successful, and some countries even broadened reproductive freedom. In Romania, where abortion had been severely punished under the Nicolae Ceausescu regime, the second act of the provisional government that assumed power after his fall was to liberalize abortion. In Slovenia, parliamentary resistance and protests by feminists against conservative proposals led to the inclusion, in the new Constitution, of an article granting citizens the right to make decisions about the birth of their children.

Abortion rates remained high. In Bulgaria, for example, where liberal policies were unaffected by the transition, contraceptive use increased but did not lead to a drop in abortions. In the 1970s and early 1980s, pregnancies ending in abortion hovered around 50 percent; in the 1990s, however, it increased to around 58 percent. Birth rates dropped: the total number of births per year halved between 1970 and 1995. This was a common trend in the region regardless of abortion statutes: fertility rates declined to below replacement levels. In Poland in 1980, the number of children per woman decreased from 2.3 in 1980 to 1.3 in 2000; in the Czech Republic, from 2.1 to 1.2 in the same years; in Romania, from 2.4 to 1.3; and in Hungary, from 1.9 to 1.3.

Equitable family laws from the past were largely preserved (though divorce became more difficult to obtain in Poland). But official and popular discourse throughout the region began to idealize the patriarchal family and its male-breadwinner and woman-housewife model for family relations. Being or having a wife who stayed at home was elevated into a status symbol. The rising prestige of the church and its values also coincided with an emphasis on traditional motherhood.

Though relatively weak, feminist movements have tried to deploy alternative discourses. Attempts by Western feminists and international organizations to stimulate a bigger movement have encountered obstacles posed by different gender structures. For example, unlike their counterparts in the West, women in Central and Eastern Europe did not view careers as their path to autonomy and self-realization. Wage work was a duty imposed by the state, not a path to freedom. What is more, whereas feminists in the West have often sought state intervention to equalize family relations, punish domestic abusers, and protect the rights of vulnerable people, women in the East viewed the state more suspiciously. Rather than a target of intervention, the family was the only site safe from the intrusions of the state.

Post-socialist transitions produced widespread suffering: the first few years were characterized by a decline in real wages and a sharp rise in unemployment. Poverty also increased: data from the late 1990s show that the share of the population classified as poor reached 18 percent in Hungary, 19 percent in Bulgaria, and 24 percent in Poland. Subsequently, there was a recovery in employment and growth indicators, though wages remained below their pre-reform levels in several countries. Economic restructuring, however, produced cutbacks in social provisions like day care as well as price increases for domestic goods and services, exacerbating the burdens assumed by women.

Women remained a significant share of the workforce: in Hungary, women were 43 percent of the labor force in 1980 and 45 percent in 2000; in Poland, 45 percent in 1980 and 46 percent in 2000; in the Czech Republic, 47 percent in both years; in Bulgaria, 45 percent and 48 percent. Many are employed by small businesses and new industries that have arisen with the free market. Yet occupational segregation continues, with the result that women's wages are lower than men's.

Under communist rule, women's representation in decision making was relatively high because the party attempted to balance the presence of different sectors and official organizations in leadership. Yet in the first elections following the transition, women's presence in power dropped.

In Poland, women made up around 23 percent of delegates to the pre-1989 unicameral Parliament; after the first free elections held in 1991, their participation declined to 9 percent of the lower house (Sejm) and 8 percent of the Senate. In the communist Parliament of Czechoslovakia, women's representation hit a maximum of 23 percent but fell to 11 percent in the first free elections, held in June of 1990. In Hungary's last elections held under communist rule (in 1985), women won 27 percent of parliamentary seats; they assumed only 7 percent of positions in the free elections of 1990. Women occupied 21 percent of seats in Bulgaria's last communist Parliament, but only 9 percent of those in the country's first democratic assembly.

Subsequently, however, women's presence began to rise. In 2004, they made up 20 percent of Poland's Sejm, 17 percent of the Czech lower house, and 26 percent of Bulgaria's Parliament. Their numbers stayed low in Hungary, at 10 percent. Electoral rules in most countries of the former Yugoslavia (Bosnia and Herzegovina, Kosovo, Macedonia and Serbia) now include gender quota rules (minimum levels for women's participation as candidates in general elections), and in Slovenia, parties use quotas voluntarily. Agencies that assisted in postwar reconstruction—the United Nations, the Organization for Security and Cooperation in Europe, and the Stability Pact for South-Central Europe—helped apply international norms regarding women's empowerment to the design of new electoral institutions. Results, however, are mixed: women make up 18 percent of the Parliament in Macedonia and 17 percent in Bosnia but only 8 percent in Serbia and 12 percent in Slovenia. In Croatia, women are 18 percent of Parliament, without quotas. As in the advanced democracies of the West, there is considerable variation in women's presence in public office, something attributable to differences in electoral institutions, the details of quota laws, and their enforcement and variation in party ideology.

In summary, with the exception of the attacks on elective abortion (which were only partially successful), progressive policy frameworks basically survived the transition intact. What changed the most were the social policies communist regimes had installed to translate the letter of the law into practice. Maternity leave, day care, free education, health care, job security, and so on had made it easier for women to work outside the home and rendered them less dependent on men (though more dependent on the state). Economic reform undermined aspects of this old support structure, leaving women and families to fend for themselves. It is important, however, not to exaggerate the contrasts. Communist social policies never fully alleviated women's domestic burdens, and the sexual division of labor persisted. In this respect, there is considerable similarity between the different regimes. Yet major changes occurred in social and political discourse. Officials who had stressed sex equality and atheism under communism turned to alternative models: more often than not, these were supplied by Roman Catholic doctrine and conservative nationalist movements. The dominance of such discourses makes it harder to adopt policies designed from a feminist perspective in post-socialist democracies.

Latin American Lessons

Latin American democratic transitions may be equally instructive for Cuba because they share a common cultural heritage, and similar external actors—the United States, the Organization of American States, the Vatican—are likely to influence the process. Cuba's past and present regional allies—not just Hugo Chávez in Venezuela but also leftist and socialist parties in other countries—may also play a role. As in Central and Eastern Europe, the Western Hemisphere's experiences have also been mixed. Political openings generated new social movements and uncapped old debates, but the mobilization of conservative groups, party competition, and crowded policy agendas stalled some progressive changes.

For example, no Latin American democracy has liberalized restrictive laws on abortion, and at least two (Chile and El Salvador) ban the practice under all circumstances, including when the pregnancy poses a threat to the woman's life. Chile delayed the long-sought legalization of divorce until March 2004, fourteen years after the end of General Augusto Pinochet's rule, and women still do not enjoy equal property rights in marriage. Several countries maintain archaic laws on rape, declaring, for example, that it constitutes a crime against custom and not against a person and, therefore, it is not actionable by the state.

Though feminist movements mobilized around political transitions and succeeded in persuading parties to incorporate some of their demands, other forces—churches and conservative movements—have taken advantage of democratic politics to mobilize and defend their views. For example, the renewed legitimacy of Roman Catholic bishops helps explain official conservatism in Chile. Bishops played an important role during Chile's transition, bringing together opposing forces to negotiate as well as sheltering dissidents and human rights activists from the worst abuses of military rule. Such admirable actions indebted democratic politicians to the ecclesiastical hierarchy. Upon assuming state power in the 1990s, they were reluctant to challenge the church and its allies in parties of the right on controversial issues such as abortion and divorce. The result was a policy deadlock in spite of growing rates of marital breakup and extremely high rates of illegal abortion.

This suggests that if Cuban politicians desire to seek the church's good graces or if they feel indebted to it for past charitable behavior, they may feel compelled to join anti-abortion coalitions. On the other hand, if the government clashes with the bishops over other issues (economic reform, secular education, human rights), it will have little incentive to conform to Catholic principles on abortion. The state may seek even to discredit the church by endorsing policies it opposes.

In Latin American history, some of the most propitious moments for liberalizing reform on controversial issues have come about during religious conflict. Thus, one of the first acts of the anticlerical Mexican revolutionary government in 1917 was to legalize divorce. In Colombia, nineteenth-century Liberal governments had the same agenda for divorce, as did Juan Perón in 1954 in Argentina.

Such political maneuvering is not always related to the religiosity of the population. Even though few Latin Americans attend church on a regular basis, they still hold the institution in high esteem. Latinobarómetro surveys show that more people have more confidence in the church than in any other national institution, including the judiciary, armed forces, mass media, police, political parties, the president, and Congress. Such confidence increases the church's political leverage.

In the absence of conservative churches or movements, legislative and bureaucratic procedures can still stall policy changes. Bills and proposals with broad support can languish for years and even decades when legislators have little incentive to make them priorities. In Brazil, it took the national Congress twenty-six years to approve a new civil code, the provisions of which—including equal rights for married women and mothers—were hardly controversial. Originally submitted by the government of General Ernesto Geisel in 1975, it was finally sanctioned in 2001. The code was considered a low priority and kept getting shoved aside by other matters. Unlike budgetary amendments such as those allocating funds to municipalities, it was an issue from which few legislators could extract tangible advantage. Nor was a new civil code a matter on which political parties had staked their fortunes. Indeed, some of the greatest challenges to feminist advocates involve not *overcoming opposition* but compelling politicians and state officials to focus their attention on gender issues. Negligence is as salient an obstacle to gender equality policy as principled dissent.

In Latin America, the mere existence of electoral democracy has not led inexorably to feminist policies, but political freedoms created space to debate equality in multiple arenas. As former Argentine Supreme Court Justice Gustavo Bossert said to me in an interview, "Everything changed with democracy. When the authoritarian government left the scene, censorship and self-censorship ended." Civic organizations have not just lobbied the state but also sought to raise public awareness and promote cultural changes, the sine qua non of real progress.

International organizations have played important roles. Many gender-related issues were thrust onto the policy agenda of Latin America's new democracies when governments signed on to global agreements or when transnational networks helped to publicize them. Such networks —composed of individuals working in international agencies, domestic civic organizations, national governments, and so on—unite people with shared interests in promoting change in human rights, domestic violence, the environment, reproductive health, political empowerment, and other policy issues. They strengthen domestic advocacy groups by transferring skills and resources. They also help legitimize new concepts: the idea of women's rights as human rights, for example, trickled into national politics from the global level; so did definitions of reproductive rights endorsed by the 1994 Cairo Conference for Population and Development.

Regional and international networks were the driving force behind the adoption of gender quotas in twelve Latin American countries in the 1990s. Eleven introduced laws establishing minimum percentage quotas for women's participation as candidates in national elections and a twelfth, Colombia, created them for senior appointments in the executive branch. After Argentina pioneered a quota law in 1991, female politicians from different countries met to debate the successes of the Southern Cone and to develop strategies for lobbying for quotas at home. Then, the Fourth World Conference on Women, held in Beijing in 1995, approved gender-based affirmative action in politics. Other United Nations documents and European Union agreements established a global benchmark that women constitute 30 percent of power holders. In this way, international accords helped spread the idea that promoting female leadership is something that modern, democratic countries do. Leaders wanting to join such a community took note. Women's scarcity in the statehouse became a sign of backwardness.

GENDER EQUALITY UNDER SOCIALIST REVOLUTION

Cuba has made progress toward equality between the sexes, particularly in the area of law and official discourse. At its first congress in 1975, the Cuban Communist Party approved a document called "Thesis: On the Full Exercise of Women's Equality," which declared that "it is the task of the party and its members—at the same time that they foster the objective conditions for the growing integration of women into economic, social and political life—to carry forward in all spheres of national life an ideological effort designed to eliminate the holdovers of the old society, seeing to it that all the people take part in this struggle." At least in theory, religious, patriarchal, and nationalist doctrines relegating women to the home and granting men exclusive power had no place in this new society. The nation's Constitution proclaims that "women and men enjoy equal rights in economic, political, cultural, social, and family life" and that "the state guarantees women the same opportunities and possibilities as men to insure their full participation in the development of the country."

The Family Code, sanctioned in 1975, goes a step further by offering detailed descriptions of the equal duties of the two sexes in marriage and parenting. It states that "both partners must care for the family they have created and must cooperate with each other in the education, upbringing and guidance of the children according to the principles of socialist morality. They must participate, to the extent of their capacity or possibilities, in the running of the home." Even spouses who work outside the home to support the family through wage work are not spared from domestic responsibilities, and the code urges them to practice their profession in a way compatible with their obligations at home. Children are considered equal regardless of the civil status of their parents; mother and father jointly exercise *patria potestad* (parental rights); and spouses are equal executors of marital property. The code avoids gendered language, making reference to spouses, parents, guardians, and providers.

The nation permits individuals to exercise considerable discretion over their intimate decisions. Abortion, for example, is freely permitted. The 1979 criminal code prohibits only those abortions performed for profit, outside of official institutions, or by someone who is not a physician. As legal scholar Olga Mesa Castillo points out, "fetal or embryonic life is no longer the juridically protected good and what remains as a legal object is only the life or health of the pregnant woman." Divorce is also easy to obtain. Cuba was one of the first countries in Latin America to legalize the practice (in 1918) and permit it without proving fault. The revolutionary Family Code followed this tradition of no-fault divorce, issued on the basis of the mutual consent of the spouses or when a court establishes objectively that the marriage has broken down (a process that can be initiated at the unilateral request of either partner). A 1994 decree law then established "notarial divorce," something unprecedented in the world. The law permits notary publics to preside over a divorce when there is mutual consent; people are not required to have the suit processed through the courts.

The Family Code upholds marriage as the centerpiece of the family (a declaration somewhat at odds with the ease of actually dissolving one). Its broad and inclusive definition of marriage includes stable unions (but *not* same-sex unions) and permits couples to have their partnership legally recognized with retroactive effects to its origin (as long as the parties meet the normal criteria for a marriage, such as being of minimum age and not wed to anyone else). Already, the Cuban Constitution of 1940 had been progressive in this respect. Ahead of its time, that document declared stable unions to have the same effects as marriage (though the two bonds remained theoretically distinct). Other countries have gradually changed their laws to grant stable unions many of the same effects as marriage, but Cuba goes further: when recognized or legalized, a stable union *becomes* a civil marriage.

The regime also succeeded in integrating women into the public sphere. Women's share of the civilian labor force is around 43 percent, a figure that has stayed constant since the mid-1980s. In the late 1990s, women made up over 60 percent of university students. To alleviate women's domestic responsibilities and promote their equal participation in political life, the state has endeavored to provide a network of day care centers, maternity leave, school lunches, free education at all levels, and high-quality public health, including attention to women's health and family planning.

Finally, women have made gains in formal decision making. The Federation of Cuban Women has long been lobbying senior leaders to promote women, and the country's own revolutionary discourse supports their equal political representation. The Federation's research wing, led by Mayda Álvarez, has published numerous studies on the obstacles to women's leadership. In 1986, the central committee of the Communist Party endorsed affirmative action for women and blacks. Though the resolutions became only general guidelines rather than enforceable rules, a desire for diversity has influenced nomination decisions within the party.

Women's representation in elected office is higher at the national than at the local level. Cuban women make up 36 percent of National Assembly deputies compared to 23 percent of municipal delegates. In the rest of the world, women tend to be more numerous in local than in national leadership. In the United States, for example, women make up 22 percent of state legislatures (in six states, women occupy more than 30 percent of the state house), but only 14 percent of the House of Representatives. How can we explain the discrepancy in women's representation across levels of government in Cuba?

One hypothesis attributes the local-national gap to the fact that local jobs are more demanding. The National Assembly of People's Power usually meets twice a year, and most of the time it simply ratifies decisions made by others in the government, voting unanimously to approve bills introduced by the executive. Municipal assemblies, on the other hand, run restaurants, build housing, provide social services, and cooperate with state enterprises. Like national deputies, municipal councilors are unpaid, so most have other jobs and must perform their official duties at night and on weekends. Numerous studies have found that both the electorate and potential candidates believe that women's domestic burden constitutes a major obstacle to their ability to effectively fulfill these responsibilities.

A better argument focuses on differences in electoral regimes. The rules governing candidate selection at the national level permit party leaders to exercise more discretion promoting women. Candidates are proposed by nominating committees comprised of representatives of the mass organizations—for example the Central Organization of Cuban Trade Unions, the Federation of Cuban Women, and the Committees for the Defense of the Revolution—and the decision among them reflects concern for gender, racial, and sectoral balancing. Since the final number of candidates equals the number of posts to be filled, everyone selected by the nominating committee will gain a seat. Voters have only a choice not to endorse the entire slate; they may not pick some candidates over others.

In municipal elections, by contrast, voters actually exercise some choice. At least two candidates contest each post after their selection by committees of neighbors. This system permits party leaders to exercise less control over gender and racial balancing. These elections are more democratic, but they lead to a less diverse municipal assembly.

Though Cuba's laws appear well crafted, social practice has not always lived up to their spirit. Disturbing trends persist in the shadow of laws with good intentions. What is more, political repression precludes civic organizations from mobilizing to contest these discrepancies and compel adjustments in state policy. In spite of the exhortations of the Family Code, for example, studies show that women perform the overwhelming share of domestic duties. A 1996 survey by the National Office of Statistics found that while women dedicated an average of thirty-four hours per week to household chores, men spent only twelve. This unequal distribution appears to vary little according to the women's labor market participation, level of education, or type of family. The same study showed that both partners seem to accept domestic asymmetries as fixed, normal, and not a reason for intrafamily conflict.

Abortion is easily available in Cuba, and significant unmet demand for other methods of birth control keeps rates high. Though seen as less desirable than other family planning methods (one study revealed that 68 percent of the women surveyed are ambivalent about abortion), the procedure is simple and safe. In 1970, the abortion rate was 36 per 1,000 women; in 1980, 42 per 1,000; in 1985, 55 per 1,000; and in 1990, 46 per 1,000. After that, the abortion rate seemed to decline (hitting 24 per 1,000 in 1999), though these figures are deceptive. Many abortions occur through what are called "menstrual regulations," a vacuum suction of the uterus performed up to two weeks after a missed period. Such procedures are not officially counted as abortion. One survey of some two thousand women in a municipality in greater Havana revealed that 10 percent had undergone abortions in the previous year, one-third of which were performed as menstrual regulations. Thus, the actual number of abortions is likely to be higher than those reported by the government.

The availability of abortions helps keep fertility low: its rate has been below replacement levels since 1978. By 1998, it had dropped to 1.64 children per woman. Besides abortion, the most common method of fertility control is the intrauterine device, or IUD, which is rarely used in the advanced democracies because of its risks. Revealing ignorance about contraception among Cuban women, some surveys attest to major flaws in the country's sex education system. For example, when the Havana study asked women whether they would recommend, or not, certain contraceptive methods, fully 50 percent declared that they would not advise using the birth control pill on the grounds of it being ineffective, damaging to health, and a cause of sterility. Yet in fact, the pill is at least 95 (and, when used properly, over 99) percent effective in preventing pregnancy.

Cuban lawyers criticize notarial divorce for being too easy and providing insufficient protection for children. In fact, the National Union of

Cuban Jurists is quietly campaigning to have the law revoked. They claim that if divorce were more difficult to obtain, judges might be able to encourage reconciliation among spouses and impose more guarantees that children's interests would be protected. They also want to create a system of family courts and a code of family law procedure, transferring such matters from the competency of regular civil courts. Their argument is that the atmosphere and methods of civil courts are too blunt to deal with the intricacies and the emotions of family cases.

Meanwhile, in spite of the law's attempts to valorize marriage, fewer people are getting, and staying, married. Between 1985 and 1999, the number of divorces per 100 marriages almost doubled, from 36 to 69. The marriage rate (number of marriages per 1,000 people) was 8 in 1985, grew to 18 in 1992, and then dropped to 5 in 1999. Most couples opt for stable unions, not (initially) legally constituted civil marriages. One indirect measure of the practice comes from birth records. When women give birth at hospitals, they are asked about their civil status. Among women aged 20 to 24, 66 percent reported they were "accompanied" and only 29 percent "married"; figures for the 25 to 29 age group were 60 percent accompanied and 36 percent married.

Finally, though the presence of women in power has been growing, it is still low in those places that matter most. Though 36 percent of deputies in the National Assembly of People's Power are women, this is a largely symbolic body that meets briefly only twice a year (and it is hardly a forum of democratic decision making). More important are the Council of State and especially the Communist Party's Political Bureau, where women are only 16 and 8 percent of members, respectively. Women make up 13 percent of the party's central committee. These numbers have changed little even as women advanced in other spheres, including the economy. The upper ranks of the party have therefore become less representative of the gender composition of the workforce than at the time of its founding in 1965. At lower levels of party leadership, women are more numerous, but their representation is still disproportionate to overall participation: 1998 data show that women make up around 23 percent of party leadership in provinces and municipalities.

Cuba's experiences highlight several disadvantages with the socialist approach. First, progress toward equality depends on the will of the state and party. The fundamental concern of most socialist regimes is not to advance opportunities for individual women but to promote the interests of the state in securing full employment, economic growth, and societal transformation. As a result, without an electorate constituted by an engaged society to hold them accountable, senior officials may promote gender equality one day and undermine it the next depending on other priorities. In 1976, for example, the Ministry of Labor issued a resolution excluding women from approximately three hundred occupations, in direct contradiction to previously articulated goals of workplace equality. The formal rationale was a desire to protect them from on-the-job hazards; the real reason was to increase male employment. By the mid-1980s, protests by the Federation of Cuban Women succeeded in reducing the number of off-limits jobs to twenty-five, but not in revoking the general policy. Gender equality is not an absolute principle: it is easily subordinated to other goals.

A second disadvantage is that socialism's theory of gender emancipation—that it occurs through wage work and other public-sphere participation—is wrong. The theory focuses on only one dimension of inequality, and not even the most important one. Gender hierarchies are sustained through the division of labor in the home and through norms of sexuality, violence, militarism, and cultural stereotypes. In fact, the public participation of women may be burdensome if domestic inequalities and contradictions are not resolved. And on issues of private patriarchy, violence, and sexual orientation, to name a few, Cuba's track record is not good.

But an erroneous official philosophy of gender equality is not necessarily an insurmountable problem. Liberalism's idea that human emancipation occurs through an expansion of individual freedoms is arguably wrong. But although the core thesis of liberalism may be faulty, liberal societies tolerate vigorous debate about their own flaws. In Cuba, an incorrect theory is particularly damaging given the third disadvantage of socialist politics: repression of political pluralism. Progress toward equality on the island suffers for the absence of a civil society to challenge, revise, improve, and even help enforce state policy. Though the Federation of Cuban Women has long served as an advocate of equality, its influence and critical capacity are inhibited by its close ties to the state and the Communist Party. What is more, the mere existence of the federation preempts the growth of independent organizations that could help the state get it right.

CONCLUSION

Socialism and democracy are opposite models. The socialist commitment to gender equality derives from a doctrine upheld by political leaders and their actions to apply it. When this doctrine falters, there is no corrective mechanism except the gradual self-enlightenment of state officials. Electoral democracy provides no such overarching framework. Policy decisions reflect the competing interests and ideas of politicians and social forces. Their bargains, however, are temporary: civic organizations mobilize to alter the course of most policy choices.

Since 1990, Cuba has steered a third course. The government has abandoned many of its socialist principles and introduced economic reforms without freeing its politics. Combined with the hardships endured during the Special Period, the result has been a worst-case scenario for gender equality. Though everyone suffered, women (as well as blacks) may have suffered disproportionately. Retreating from socialist policies without ceding space for civic organization may jeopardize the revolution's progress toward gender equality.

Women, for example, have largely stayed in the labor force, but the economic crisis forced reductions in state services for working mothers. School meals were cut, and the state introduced a fee for day care centers. Meanwhile, the struggle for family survival has become more acute and women's roles, in turn, more demanding. Fuel shortages, for example, impose transportation delays and cause problems for cooking meals. Scarcity of foreign currency renders impossible the importation of new labor-saving appliances or the parts to repair old ones. A decline in industrial production makes it difficult to obtain canned and other easy-to-prepare foods, not to mention soap, toothpaste, laundry detergent, and other items for personal hygiene and household maintenance.

The equal participation of women has appeared to be in danger as employers favored men in their search for scarce jobs. In spite of good intentions, a decision in 2002 to extend maternity leave to one year is likely to have made employers additionally reluctant to hire potential mothers. What is more, by opening the door to joint ventures, dollarization, foreign tourism, and the growth of prostitution, the government created the conditions for new hierarchies to replace socialist egalitarianism. As the struggle for survival has grown more acute, latent social differences have been manipulated into justifications for unequal opportunities.

Cuban women are more numerous in less lucrative jobs and scarcer in better remunerated, cutting-edge occupations (such as those in the tourism, joint ventures, or the nonstate sector generally). In 1999, women made up 43 percent of workers in the state civilian sector as a whole, but only 24 percent of appointments in the highly coveted tourism industry. Of the twenty tourist agencies run by the state, only one, Formatur, had a woman director. Women are underrepresented in nonstate jobs, in rural cooperatives, and among the self-employed (27 percent in 1999). These figures suggest that women tend to be slightly more dependent on the old state economy than men, and increasingly marginalized from more dynamic sectors that have opened since the mid-1990s.

In a democracy, a free press, feminist groups, human rights movements, and opposition political parties act as watchdogs to expose and help negotiate the consequences of economic restructuring. The desire to court voters in competitive elections helps drive policy toward articulated public interests. Without the possibility of civic organization and political contestation, redressing inequities depends on the will of the state. Will the Cuban government use its scarce funds to create alternative economic opportunities for prostitutes? to subsidize day care centers? to provide abortions free of charge? State priorities are one question; state capacity may be even more important. A continuing economic crisis may not only threaten the ability of the state to compensate for the inequities of the market but also its ability to enforce those equality laws that remain on the books. Achieving gender justice thus requires greater economic growth and deeper political reforms.

SIX

Race, Culture, and Politics

ALEJANDRO DE LA FUENTE

"Five of us were fired from our jobs. The manager of the company did not hide to declare that he did not want black people there," a fifty-five-year-old black woman from Havana explained when she took her case to the district attorney of her municipality in 1997. She had been working in one of Havana's shopping centers that operate in dollars, but she suddenly lost her job, she asserted, because she was black. Her case is unfortunately not unique. According to *Carta de Cuba,* in 2001 the only black person working at Hotel Tortuga in the beach resort of Varadero was also fired. The manager of the hotel claimed that he did so "to avoid complaints from the tourists," but a member of the local union gave a different explanation: "They were after him for being black; he was the only black in the hotel."

Instances of blatant racial discrimination such as these have become painfully familiar in Cuba since the early 1990s, as numerous examples and testimonies can easily demonstrate. Just a few years earlier, however, they were much more difficult to find. The elimination of racism and racial inequality had been one of the main goals of the revolutionary government, and Cuban authorities had proudly declared racism eradicated on the island since the early 1960s. Although this was not the case, it is nonetheless true that the massive structural transformations implemented by the revolutionary government during its early years in power resulted in a dramatic decline of various forms of social inequality, including those associated with race.

Free and massive access to education, nutrition, and social services, coupled with an aggressive redistribution of national income, resulted in a social leveling unprecedented in Cuban history. By the early 1980s, several important indicators suggested that the Cuban experiment had been remarkably successful in reducing, if not eliminating, racial inequality, particularly in those areas that had received systematic attention and generous funding from the government. The life expectancy of people identified as "negros" or "mestizos" in the 1981 census was only one year below that of whites—a minuscule gap in comparison to other multiracial societies in the Americas such as Brazil and the United States. Rates of schooling were similar, even at the university level. Illiteracy, which was higher among blacks than whites in pre-revolutionary Cuba, had basically disappeared. Employment distribution remained somehow unequal but low compared to Brazil and the United States. Cuba was not the racial paradise that its authorities had frequently stated it was, but they could justifiably claim that the country's relative success in combating racism was one of the great achievements of the socialist society.

But the Cuban approach had serious shortcomings. To begin with, racial inequality greatly diminished in areas that were given priority by the government, such as education and public health. In areas where government programs were less successful, important differences associated with race remained. For instance, the government was never able to tackle the chronic housing shortage successfully. As a result, the regional distribution of the population continued to have strong racial undertones, with blacks concentrated in the poorest sectors of Havana and other cities. Although the government decreed the elimination of racism and created an ideal by which racist attitudes were not compatible with the Revolution, some of its own policies contributed, in fact, to the re-affirmation of the social importance of race and to the reproduction of ingrained racist stereotypes. For example, the rates of incarceration were much higher for blacks than for whites, reflecting (as well as feeding) the widespread belief that blacks were naturally predisposed to committing crimes. If anything, the disproportionate representation of blacks among inmates could be used to highlight their inability to benefit from the op-portunities that socialism had allegedly given them. The government also opposed Afro-Cuban religious manifestations and persecuted its practi-tioners at various points, thus reproducing and sanctioning the tradi-tional racist notion that identifies these cultural practices with savagery and barbarism.

One of the most important shortcomings of the government's ap-proach was its inability to deal with the cultural and ideological roots of racism. As some government officials have acknowledged, they expected racism to wither away once its perceived structural bases were dismantled. It did not. There were two main problems with the government's ap-proach. First, not all the "structural bases" of racism were dismantled, as the housing example demonstrates. Second, racism is not simply a question of unequal distribution of resources; it is a cultural and ideo-logical complex that needs to be actively and systematically dismantled. The official declaration of racism as a solved problem produced the opposite effect. It precluded any effective public discussion of race in Cuban society and identified this important theme with enemy attempts to create "divisions" within the revolution. Race and racism were turned into taboos, untouchable political themes in public discourse. This does not mean, of course, that they disappeared from Cuban life or ceased to affect social relations. Quite the contrary. The official mantle of silence probably facilitated the unchecked creation and reproduction of racial images that continued to affect interpersonal relations in families, com-munities, schools, and workplaces. As with other difficult subjects, these ideas were frequently packaged in allegedly harmless jokes and discussed mostly in private spaces. Their social influence was limited, however, because the government retained significant control over the distribu-tion of employment and other resources and remained committed to the vision of a racially egalitarian nation. This is precisely what changed dramatically in the 1990s: the government's centralized control over resources was significantly eroded and its egalitarian dreams sacrificed in part to the harsh imperatives of economic recovery.

THE EFFECTS OF THE SPECIAL PERIOD

There is consensus that since the early 1990s race relations—social interactions and exchanges between individuals believed to belong to different racial groups—deteriorated dramatically on the island. Visitors and observers are shocked by the frequency and virulence of racist remarks, indeed by the undisguised contempt with which many white Cubans refer to blacks and mulattos. They are equally startled by the low proportion of blacks and mulattos in positions of power, by their lack of representation in the media, by their low presence in the most desirable jobs, particularly in those dealing with tourists, and by their prominent participation in informal economic activities. Several surveys conducted in the 1990s show that blackness continues to be equated with the most degrading physical and ethical attributes—ugliness, laziness, incompetence, vanity, and ignorance—and is also identified with the most despicable behaviors, from robbery and peddling to prostitution and rape.

Some of the inequities that became evident in the 1990s were the result of historic factors, such as past discrimination (which accounted for unequal access to good housing, for instance) or the demographic and racial composition of the overwhelmingly white Cuban American community, which provides significant resources to family members on the island through dollar remittances. Cuban scholars have estimated that while 30 to 40 percent of people identified as white receive dollar remittances, only 5 to 10 percent of blacks do.

Other differences, however, are much harder to explain without acknowledging the active role that racial discrimination plays in shaping social realities. Among these is the dismally low participation of blacks and mulattos in the tourist industry, the fastest growing sector of Cuba's economy. Although tourism typically creates low-paying service jobs, these positions are coveted in Cuba because they provide personal access to tourists and their dollars. The low representation of blacks in this sector cannot be explained in terms of past discrimination or lack of proper qualifications. In fact, until the 1980s, when these jobs were not particularly attractive, blacks and mulattos were *over-represented* in what government documents defined as gastronomy and similar services. Their low representation in the tourist industry in the 1990s reflects a deliberate effort to minimize their presence in these attractive jobs.

It was at this juncture that the racist ideology mentioned above came to play a more active role in the allocation of scarce resources. In order to minimize the black and mulatto presence in tourism, white managers began to demand from prospective employees what they defined as a *buena presencia* (pleasant appearance), an aesthetic attribute that only people deemed to be white could fulfill. The same criteria has been applied to positions in so-called joint ventures—companies financed and partly owned by foreign investors in which Cuban employees typically receive a portion of their salary in dollars. By creating supposedly objective indicators of desirability and competence that can be used to exclude Afro-Cuban job seekers from the best positions, this ideology has helped to whiten the most coveted sectors of the labor market and to rationalize the process of exclusion. According to research done by the Center for Cuban Anthropology, blacks barely represent 5 percent of the labor force employed in tourism and other dollar-related activities.

Excluded from these jobs and with limited access to dollar remittances, many blacks and mulattos have sought since the 1990s to participate in the new economy via the informal sector. Many of these activities (hustling, peddling, and prostitution) are criminalized, thus reinforcing the embedded notion that blacks and mulattos are naturally inclined to an easy life of crime and corruption and averse to hard and honest work. When, in the mid-1990s, the residents of Havana experienced a swell of robberies and other crimes, whites quickly attributed this wave of criminality to blacks and to their incapacity to handle the economic crisis through other means. There was little or no evidence to sustain these perceptions, but a racial explanation for the problem was advanced nonetheless. And perceptions count. As many black and mulatto individuals can attest, it is not unusual for a black or mulatto person walking with a package to be stopped by the police and asked to furnish identity papers. This is the case even in areas where nonwhites are the majority of the population: "Here in Santiago [de Cuba], only blacks are asked to provide identity papers. That is racism," a white resident in the city told *Carta de Cuba*. An African American who visited the island in 2003 was baffled when guards kept stopping him at the entrance of his hotel. People kept explaining to him that he "looked Cuban" and, as he eventually learned, "the unwritten rule in Cuba is that if you are Cuban, you do not go to the good hotels, especially if you are black." Numerous testimonies confirm that whites are rarely stopped. And although hard data on police records is very difficult to obtain, people characterized as black or mulatto are grossly over-represented among inmates, with many observers estimating proportions as high as 80 or even 90 percent.

The growing racial gap that has characterized Cuban society since the early 1990s and the growing assertiveness of openly racial discourses in public life have contributed significantly to the perception that race is an important element in the crisis. Paradoxically, this perception is fed as well by the widespread belief that Afro-Cubans represent an important reservoir of political support for the current government, or that they may even be responsible for the longevity of the regime. As a Western diplomat based in Havana expressed in 1993, a political change will not take place until the blacks "start throwing rocks." They are supposed to be "Fidel's secret weapon"—what one of my white informants characterized, using appallingly derogatory terms, as "the bomb of *negrones* (loosely, "black savages")." Behind these expressions there is the belief that, if need be, the government can mobilize large contingents— "hordes" or "gangs"—of black and mulatto males to repress any popular demonstration against the current regime. In support of this assertion, people from Havana frequently point to a police force in which they claim blacks and mulattos—many of them immigrants from the eastern provinces of the island—are over-represented. Others note that there are relatively few blacks and mulattos among the rafters, supposedly an indicator that Afro-Cubans continue to support the Revolution.

Some observers have concluded, based on all these elements, that race may be the source of considerable trouble, perhaps even violence, in a post-Castro Cuba. An important additional ingredient in this vision is the Cuban American community, which defines itself as overwhelmingly white. The official media in Cuba have consistently depicted the

Cuban American community as a group of racists and conservatives who dream of restoring their old economic and social privileges. They would seek to recover not only their properties and material goods but also their privileged social and racial status. To put it bluntly, the return of the exiles would add a new layer of racism and tension to an already racially explosive situation.

Many of these perceptions about the alleged social deficiencies of Afro-Cubans or about their political sympathies are based on very shallow evidence or flawed assumptions. But along with the processes of growing racial inequality and tension described above, they rightly point to the salience of race in Cuban society. Although the economic crisis that began in the early 1990s affected all Cubans, blacks and whites experienced the crisis differently. Afro-Cubans will thus enter a post-Castro Cuba with specific grievances and needs that they will likely translate into concrete economic, social, and political demands. In this sense, race will indeed play an important role in Cuba's transition.

RACE AND POLITICS: TRANSITION PARADIGMS

How can we best understand the ways ideas of race will shape the political options of Cubans of different racial groups during this process? Will blacks and mulattos join multiracial social and political movements to channel their grievances and demands, as they frequently did in pre-revolutionary Cuba? Or will they resort to separate, autonomous forms of mobilization, as they also did in the past? Will the future Cuban state be responsive to these demands? Which policies could be implemented to address the race problem?

In order to answer these questions and to discuss possible transition scenarios, it is better to place them in the context of similar transitions. But the example of other communist countries is of limited value in this case. Although one may find tempting parallels with some of the Central and Eastern European transitions, given the salience of ethnic politics and ethnic strife in many of them, I believe that these similarities are of little relevance to the Cuban case. Unlike the ethnic communities of Europe, the Afro-Cuban population does not represent a group with a separate culture, territory, or language. Many cultural forms in Cuba are identified with their African roots (from Santería to countless musical expressions), but they are practiced and embraced by ample sectors of the population, regardless of race. These cultural expressions have been *nationalized,* and most Cubans consider them to be part of their own heritage. There exists some association between race and the geographic distribution of the population, but not in terms strong enough to identify separate black or white territories. Throughout the national territory, blacks and whites live in neighborhoods that are largely integrated, go to racially mixed schools and workplaces, and share integrated hospitals and other social services. The European ethnic paradigm is not the answer.

Closer to home, it is possible to situate the Cuban transition scenarios in at least two contexts. First, the Cuban transition should be discussed in reference to Cuba's own history. This is not an academic exercise: there is much to learn from Cuba's past. After all, this is not the first time Cubans have experienced a political transition in their modern history. Earlier transitions have held significant promises concerning more democratic and effective forms of political participation, and they offer important insights for the study of the current crisis. These transitions took place in 1902, when the U.S. military government of occupation was replaced by a constitutionally elected Cuban administration; in 1933, when the dictatorial regime of President Gerardo Machado was overthrown by popular forces; and of course in 1959, when another popular coalition forced dictator Fulgencio Batista out of power. Race was central to the social and political conflicts surrounding these periods of change—as central as it now appears to many contemporary Cubans.

The other useful context in which Cuba's democratic transition may be examined is that of Brazil. Despite their obvious differences, both countries share a similar history of slavery, racism, and racial mobilization. More to the point, in both countries, ideas of nationhood are intimately linked to the so-called myths of racial democracy, ideologies positing that all individuals, regardless of race, are members of the nation and as such have equal rights and standing in society. By idealizing race relations in both Cuba and Brazil as harmonious and fraternal, these nationalist ideologies of racial democracy have minimized racial conflicts and obstructed, if not de-legitimized altogether, racially defined forms of political mobilization. Last, but certainly not least, the relevance of the Brazilian case is based on its recent political history, which has some parallels with that of Cuba. Between 1964 and 1985, the country was ruled by military governments that suppressed most formal political activities, censored the media, and exercised tight control over labor unions and other organizations. As in Cuba, Brazilian authorities were quite unsympathetic to any public debate about the country's racial democracy. Unlike Cuba, however, the military regimes in Brazil were not committed to the elimination of social inequalities or to improving the lot of the poorest sectors of society.

The Brazilian transition gives us the opportunity to evaluate the viability and strength of racially defined political organizations in a democratizing environment within the constraints imposed by a nationalist ideology of racial democracy. It also shows the ability of a sympathetic state to implement fairly radical policies of reparation and affirmative action and the influence that transnational actors and events can have on domestic racial policies.

Political Transitions in Twentieth-Century Cuba

The prominence of race as a social cleavage in the current crisis is not new; each of these transitions has been characterized by high levels of racial conflict. These conflicts can be grouped into three categories. First, periods of transition have been characterized by intense debates over the meanings of *Cubanidad* (Cubanness) and its relationship with the racial groups that form the nation. Created in the long process of the wars for independence between 1868 and 1898, Cuba's dominant nationalist ideology posits that all Cubans, regardless of race, are equal citizens of the nation. This egalitarian ideology of inclusion, greatly advanced by Cuban patriot and intellectual José Martí (1853–95), was summarized in his famous dictum "Cuban is more than mulatto, black, or white." Martí invented a racially inclusive Cubanidad precisely because the island was inhabited by whites, blacks, and mulattos with different histories, aspirations, and visions for the future. He emphasized unity because it did not exist. Racial fraternity was a political creation, a platform from which to launch the project of an independent and viable nation. As a result, the concrete meanings and contours of this inclusive Cubanidad were hotly contested throughout the entire republican period.

Second, the salience of race in these periods of transition has never been confined to abstract debates about the meanings of what it is to be Cuban. Rather, these debates reflect contradictory social interests that invariably translate into various forms of organization and mobilization. Political transitions represent moments of uncertainty and change in which the nation is being refashioned, not just figuratively but in terms of power relations as well. In periods such as these, social and political groups, while claiming to represent "national" interests, seek in fact to advance their own programs and their own visions of *la patria* (the homeland). In these transitions, there have been groups interested in minimizing Afro-Cuban participation in the emergent political order. But each transition has also witnessed the rise of social movements that seek to transform society by enlarging the share of economic and political power of Afro-Cubans and other popular groups. Confrontations between these groups have led to high levels of racial tension, even violence.

Third, one of the strategies used most consistently in these transitions to legitimize the exclusion of Afro-Cubans from the new political order has been to blame them for the survival of the previous regime, or to single them out as its beneficiaries. The logic behind this strategy is clear: if blacks benefited the most from the fallen political order, it is legitimate to minimize their role in the creation of the new order. This is not Fidel Castro's privilege: blacks have allegedly been the "secret weapon" of every Cuban dictator, from Machado to Batista. The question was debated even during the establishment of the Cuban republic in 1902, when some questioned whether Afro-Cubans had truly represented the bulk of the soldiers in the Liberation Army. "When the war ended, the talk started about whether the blacks had fought or not," black veteran Esteban Montejo recounted.

Arguments over black participation in the war were part of larger discussions about the place of blacks within the Cuban republic. Mainstream politicians and intellectuals frequently claimed that there were no racial differences in the republic, as the Constitution of 1901 flamboyantly proclaimed. Racial fraternity had been achieved during the struggles for independence, and thus additional social action was neither required nor welcome. Afro-Cuban intellectuals, activists, and writers frequently used the same discourse of brotherhood to underline the persistent social subordination of blacks and mulattos in Cuban society. They treated Martí's vision as a program for future social and political action rather than an accomplishment. Efforts by black leaders to create their own organizations were frequently labeled as un-Cuban, on the grounds that they threatened the unity of the Cuban family. When in the first decade of the twentieth century a group of black veterans organized the Independent Party of Color (PIC), a racially defined political party intended to combat racism and increase Afro-Cuban representation in the government, it was banned. The veterans revolted in protest, leading to a white backlash and to the brutal repression of the movement. The revolt and repression against the PIC in 1912 can be interpreted as the ultimate expressions of the racial conflicts surrounding the establishment of the republic.

Racist violence was also widespread during the social conflicts that led to the establishment of the second republic in the 1930s. Some of the groups opposing the dictatorial regime of Machado (1925–33), espoused a vision of the nation in which Afro-Cubans would be relegated to a subordinate role. Some members of the opposition were connected to the Ku Klux Klan Kubano (KKKK), which presented itself as a "great army of racial defense" and was likely responsible for the bombing of several black clubs and associations in 1933 and 1934. In addition to these instances of violence, white racists sought to minimize the role of Afro-Cubans in the new Cuba by claiming that blacks had been the main supporters of the Machado regime. As white conservative politician Enrique José Varona stated, "The black race has been indifferent to the hardships suffered by our unfortunate republic during the struggle against the Machado tyranny." This charge rested on very weak and problematic evidence but amply diffused nonetheless, to the point that it became commonly accepted by many Cubans. Afro-Cubans reacted to these challenges through different strategies, including participation in cross-racial organizations such as the labor unions, the Communist Party, or the populist Partido Revolucionario Cubano Auténtico, or through the creation of autonomous organizations such as the Federación de Sociedades de la Raza de Color or the short-lived Partido Asteria. The very existence of these organizations, in turn, was used by white racists to proclaim that Afro-Cubans were taking advantage of the situation to overturn traditional racial hierarchies. "The black, with unbelievable insolence . . . has been extending its influence as a malignant plague," warned the KKKK. Racial tensions thus characterized the long process of transition between the fall of Machado and the reestablishment of constitutional democracy in 1940.

Similar tensions characterized the political conflicts surrounding the demise of Batista's dictatorship in 1958. Batista himself was widely considered to be a mulatto, which eventually allowed some white opposition leaders to find a racial explanation for his ability to remain in power. As in the early 1930s, white racists charged that Batista enjoyed the unconditional support of Afro-Cubans, who they claimed had benefited greatly during his administration. Evidence to support these claims was again scant, but the charge was repeated frequently enough as to be accepted by many Cubans, who even today assert that it was whites who had to do the fighting against Batista. This way the struggle could be framed as a fight between white young idealists and a corrupt and brutish army led by a "black" dictator. Contributing to portraying the conflict in racial terms were some of Batista's followers, who noted that the programmatic documents of the 26th of July Movement contained no provisions on racial discrimination and that blacks should expect nothing from what they described as the white opposition.

Attempts to keep blacks on the margins of the political order that began to emerge in January 1959 were largely fruitless, however, as black activists used the revolutionary momentum to press for racial equality and for greater Afro-Cuban participation in the structures of power. As in earlier moments of political transition and change, Afro-Cuban activists not linked to the previous regime raised their voices to make sure that questions of race would not go unaddressed and demanded an equal place in society. As in the past, these efforts met with some resistance, although on this occasion the support that the revolutionary government gave to the struggle for racial integration and equality from the start served to limit the political space for racist responses to emerge. Members of the upper classes complained that blacks did not respect social conventions of deference the way they used to, but similar complaints had been voiced whenever blacks had tried to assert a central place in

Cuban society and politics. A few conservative journalists attempted to deflate Afro-Cuban demands for greater equality by calling for a very long-term process of education and change, but that was pretty much the extent of the racist backlash. The groups that could have voiced such alternative views of the nation were in clear retreat after 1959. Besides, since most revolutionary programs were launched in the name of the "humble" and the "have-nots," opposition to them was frequently couched in the language of class rather than race.

The current crisis resembles those of the past in several ways. First of all, there are obviously individuals in Cuba who have begun to exclude blacks and mulattos from the most attractive jobs and occupations in some systematic ways. Second, passionate discussions about the uneasy intersections between race and Cubanidad have been taking place, although mostly in noninstitutional venues, as several recent compilations of testimonials show. That this time the debate has not spilled into the press, as in the past, is largely a function of the government's control of the media. Third, the belief that blacks are the main beneficiaries and supporters of the current regime mirrors previous racist attempts to minimize Afro-Cuban claims to equal participation in a post-transition political order. The evidence to support this view is frankly precarious, but this has been the case in previous instances as well. In fact, blacks and mulattos represent a significant proportion of the leadership of the opposition movement on the island.

Yet Cuba's future transition is peculiar in at least one important way. The current government has managed to eliminate formal competitive politics and prevent the creation of an organized opposition much more effectively than any other administration in the past. In previous transitions, Afro-Cuban political activism always benefited from institutional bases that do not exist now. Among these were the black social clubs and societies as well as the autonomous black press, not to mention the power mustered by some black and mulatto politicians within the mainstream political parties.

It is in this sense that the Brazilian case is of interest to this discussion. As in Cuba, the military governments in Brazil officially denied the existence of a racial problem in the country and endorsed the dominant ideology of racial democracy as an accurate reflection of social realities.

As in Cuba, the military regimes basically prohibited all forms of opposition politics: parties were abolished or allowed to operate under strict control, independent unions were disbanded and purged, strict censorship was established. As in Brazil, black politics in a formally democratic Cuba will likely take different forms, from autonomous and racially defined forms of mobilization to participation in cross-racial organizations defined around other social identities such as class. As in Brazil, racially defined mobilization will face important challenges. In addition to the lack of organizational resources, an emergent black movement will have to face the formidable challenge of a nationalist ideology that equates Cuba with racial fraternity and openly proclaims that all Cubans are equal, regardless of race.

The Brazilian Example

The Brazilian case offers several important insights about the ways in which racial politics are likely to be organized in Cuba, provided that a democratic transition takes place on the island. Black political activism reemerged in Brazil in the late 1970s, in the context of a timid political opening implemented by the military regime. Envisioned by the military as a tightly controlled process of democratization and change, this opening was seized upon by opposition forces to speed up and push forward the return to democracy.

Afro-Brazilian activists were among those taking advantage of these new political spaces. Initial organizational efforts revolved around cultural issues and agendas, sponsored by organizations such as the Center for Black Culture and Art in São Paulo, or by similar institutions in Rio de Janeiro, such as the Society for Brazil-Africa Exchange and the Institute for the Study of Black Cultures. These and other organizations began to analyze the situation of Afro-Brazilians and to study the development of black struggles elsewhere, particularly in Africa and in the United States. They published their own newspapers and journals, contributing to the formation of a politically conscious youth that would go on to play a leading role in the Brazilian black movement. Indeed, some members of these organizations participated in the creation of the Unified Black Movement against Racial Discrimination in São Paulo (popularly known as Movimento Negro Unificado, or MNU), which quickly became the most important racially defined voice in Brazilian politics. In its first national assembly in September 1978, the MNU gathered delegates from Rio de Janeiro, Minas Gerais, Bahia, Espritu Santo, and São Paulo.

Along with other local organizations, the MNU began a campaign to denounce the persistence of racial discrimination in the country. Taking advantage of the gradual opening and eventual return of democratic politics to the country in the mid 1980s, the black movement pressed political parties to incorporate antidiscriminatory statements in their platforms and supported the election of black candidates. In order to raise the consciousness of, and therefore rally, the Afro-Brazilian population, some groups within the movement advocated elements of cultural nationalism and negritude.

This movement made significant achievements. The very incorporation of the issue of racial discrimination in the political platform of most mainstream political parties represented an unprecedented public recognition that racism continued to be a problem in the Brazilian racial democracy. For the first time in Brazilian history, the newly elected democratic authorities created institutions charged with collecting information on racial inequities, disseminating such studies, and ultimately combating racism. In the state of Rio de Janeiro, the Democratic Labor Party appointed Afro-Brazilians to head several state secretariats, and the state assembly passed an antidiscrimination law in 1985.

The centennial of the abolition of slavery in 1988 provided the black movement with an opportunity to make significant gains. To begin with, a nationwide press campaign reassessed the persistence of racism in Brazilian society. The 1988 Constitution criminalized racial discrimination for the first time and asserted the territorial rights of occupants of lands of former *quilombos* (communities of runaway slaves). A new federal agency, the Palmares Cultural Foundation—named after the largest and most famous community of runaway slaves in Brazilian history—was created to promote blacks within the government and to channel state resources to Afro-Brazilians.

Nongovernmental organizations (NGOs) proliferated in this context as well. The Black Women's Institute (Geledés Instituto da Mulher Negra) is a good example. Created in São Paulo in 1988, its main objectives are to combat gender and racial discrimination: "the valorization and promotion of black women in particular and of the black community in general." Its programs cover a wide spectrum: reproductive health workshops, legal advice to victims of racial discrimination, the publication of a journal, and support for young Brazilian rappers with the production and dissemination of their music. Like many other NGOs, the Black Women's Institute also became part of a growing international network of organizations devoted to the elimination of racial discrimination. A document released on the occasion of the institute's tenth anniversary explained: "Our strategy was to give visibility to the racial problem in Brazil, attending all the world conferences organized by the United Nations in the 1990s, creating sensitivity in governments and civil society to discuss the growing problem of the exclusion of the poor and discriminated sectors of the world."

These international links, in turn, have had a significant effect on Brazilian racial politics. International agencies and foundations have funded Brazilian organizations and NGOs seeking to influence state policies in the area of race. They have also facilitated contacts with activists in other countries, similar organizations elsewhere, and international human rights organizations. Indeed, it was in preparation for the United Nations World Conference on Racism, Xenophobia and Related Forms of Intolerance (2001) that a government committee recommended the adoption of affirmative action policies, including the creation of racial quotas in universities and public institutions, an idea that President Fernando Henrique Cardoso had supported before. A noted sociologist, Cardoso devoted his early intellectual work to the question of racial inequality in Brazil.

Despite these significant successes, the black movement has failed the most important test of all in a competitive political system: mobilizing substantial numbers of voters during election time. Most black candidates running for office have not been elected. The proportion of Afro-Brazilians in the federal Congress remains a dismal 2 to 3 percent. Scholars and activists generally agree on two principal reasons for the movement's failure to mobilize and capture the sympathy of the masses of Afro-Brazilian workers. The first refers to social stratification within the black population. The organizations that compose the black movement, and their leaders, frequently represent the interests and aspirations of the black middle class, and these are only partially compatible with the interests and aspirations of the masses of Afro-Brazilian workers. The second factor concerns the continuing strength of the ideology of racial democracy. Although the mainstream media, public officials, and state agencies have all publicly admitted and even promoted the notion that racial inequality afflicts Brazilian society, the nationalist ideology of racial harmony and fraternity continues to enjoy significant ascendancy among ordinary Brazilians—and for good reasons. Although racism and discrimination affect blacks at all social levels, these issues are particularly overt and vicious when it comes to upwardly mobile Afro-Brazilians, especially those trying to enter the more exclusive social and occupational spaces of the middle classes. At the bottom of society, where most Brazilians regardless of color face the gripping realities of poverty and hunger, race appears as only one in a multitude of formidable social barriers. Afro-Brazilian workers have therefore been giving their support to cross-racial political forces that they feel better represent the interests of the poor and the working class. According to various surveys conducted in the 1990s, most Afro-Brazilian workers could not support the black movement because they had not even heard of it. It is no surprise, then, that by the 1990s the membership of the most important national political organization of the black movement, the MNU, had declined to only a few thousand.

RACIAL POLITICS IN CUBA'S TRANSITION

We can now discuss, based on Cuba's historical experience and on the example of Brazil, some of the ways in which race and politics are likely to interact in a transition. Will Afro-Cubans organize a racially defined political movement? What are the odds for such a movement to succeed? Would this lead to racial violence?

The growing racial polarization that has characterized Cuban society since the early 1990s has already led to various expressions of Afro-Cuban discontent and to some efforts at organization. As in Brazil, these initial expressions of protest have taken place in the relatively safer context of culture (as opposed to politics), where questions about the social meanings of blackness and denunciations about the subordinate place of Afro-Cubans in society can be voiced with less fear of political retribution. Signs of an emerging black cultural movement are apparent in various areas: music, visual arts, theater, and religion. All of these expressions seek to carve out a social and cultural space from which Afro-Cubans would be able to reassert the centrality of blackness to Cubanidad and protest racial discrimination.

The paintings presented in a 1999 art exhibition at the Center for the Development of Visual Arts in Havana exemplify this quite clearly. Organized by artists who self-identified with various racial labels, the exhibition was devoted to the theme of race. Its very title, "Queloides," represented a thinly veiled denunciation against racism, as it refers to the scars that appear in black skin after it is wounded. In case authorities and viewers missed the not-so-subtle allusion to racism in the exhibition's name, they were forced to confront the issue of racism through the explicit content of the works in the show. Some of the paintings contained in "Queloides" bluntly denounced discrimination and racism in Cuban society. Two of them, "Cuidado, hay negro" (Look Out, There Is a Black Man) and "Carné de identidad" (Identity Card), by Manuel Arenas, portrayed the persistent association of blacks with crime and their selective targeting by the police. Another racist fear and stereotype—that of the sexually voracious black rapist—was ridiculed in René Peña's photograph of the nude torso of a black man in which the penis is replaced by a prominent sharp knife.

Racism and racist stereotypes are also denounced in the work of Juan Roberto Diago, a young black painter from Havana. His 2002 exhibit "Comiendo cuchillo" (literally, Eating Knife), proudly proclaims the centrality of Africa and of Afro-Cubans to Cuban history and culture while exposing ingrained stereotypes about blacks. For example, one of his paintings deals with the widespread racist cliché that blacks have bad hair. Titled "Autorretrato" (Self-portrait), it contains the following text: "Mi pelo también es bueno," or "My hair too is good." Another piece, "España devuélveme a mis dioses" (Spain Give Me My Gods Back), displays an equally explicit text: "Difícil no es ser hombre, es ser negro" (The Hard Thing Is Not to Be a Man, But to Be Black). As poet Nancy Morejón has stated, Diago's work is full of ancestral pain and fury.

What visual artists have expressed through their photographs and canvases, some black and mulatto youths have transmitted through their lyrics and music. Just as the American soul music movement enjoyed considerable popularity among young Afro-Brazilians in the 1970s, American hip hop, and particularly rap music, made it into Cuba in the 1990s. Both musical movements are linked to processes of racial assertiveness and to voicing the social and political concerns of underprivileged groups. Cuban rappers have gained significant visibility since 1995, when they managed to organize the island's first rap festival, which eventually became an annual event. While these festivals, and the creation of a special state agency to promote rap music, are likely to enlarge the control of the government over this cultural expression, they also allow for a larger circulation of rap and its politically charged messages in Cuban society. In these festivals, many important voices of the movement have been heard, including some that are fairly critical of the government.

As one would expect, Cuban rappers refer to a multiplicity of themes, but issues of race and discrimination figure prominently among them. For instance, some rappers have addressed the question of racial profiling by the police in terms very similar to those used by the painters mentioned above. "*Policía, policía tú no eres mi amigo, para la juventud cubana eres la peor pesadilla*" ("Policeman, policeman, you're not my friend, for young people in Cuba you're the worst nightmare"), sings the group Papá Humbertico. "*Mi color te trae todos los días . . . a toda hora, la misma persecución*" ("My color brings you every day, always, the same harassment"), concurs Alto Voltaje. Yet another example, this time by Anónimo Consejo: "*Cada paso en la calle es una preocupación. Extranjero en busca de comunicación con la población. Cinco minutos de conversación ¡policía en acción!*" ("Every step in the street is cause for trepidation. A foreigner looking for communication with the population. Five minutes of conversation, the police take you to the station!").

Young rappers have also used their music to raise more general questions about the persistence of racism and racial discrimination in Cuban society. A paradigmatic song by Hermanos de Causa exemplifies this discourse well. It is titled "Tengo" ("I Have"). This is, of course a parody of Nicolás Guillén's famous 1964 poem with the same title. Guillén's "Tengo" was a chant to the achievements of the revolutionary government in the area of racial equality, written by one of the most accredited voices of the Afro-Cuban intelligentsia, a poet who had been deeply involved in the struggles for racial equality before 1959. The poem listed all that blacks "had" under the revolution, from access to beaches and hotels to jobs and education. "I have," concluded Guillén's poem, "what I had to have." Thirty-five years later, Hermanos de Causa begged to disagree. Their portrayal of what Afro-Cubans have is very different: "*Tengo una raza oscura y discriminada. Tengo una jornada que me exige y no da nada. Tengo tantas cosas que no puedo ni tocarlas. Tengo instalaciones que no puedo ni pisarlas . . . Tengo lo que tengo sin tener lo que he tenido*" ("I have a race that is dark and discriminated against. I have a workday that's exhausting and pays nothing. I have so many things that I can't even touch. I have so many places where I can't even go. I have what I have without getting what I've had").

Rap and other Afro-Cuban cultural expressions such as the Rastafarian movement are important not simply because they exalt blackness and show Afro-Cuban culture to be a living process that cannot be encapsulated within the traditional parameters of folklore. They also create avenues for protest and dissent in an environment characterized by the lack of formal spaces for such purposes. Other areas of cultural activism that have contributed to channeling the resistance of Afro-Cubans include projects of black theater, grassroots centers for the study and promotion of Yoruba culture and religion, popular courses on the social history of blacks in Cuba and, of course, the spectacular growth that Santería and other Afro-Cuban religions experienced in the 1990s.

Parallel to this growing cultural activism, academics and social scientists inside and outside the country have begun to study the problem of race. This growing body of scholarship has underlined the continuing importance of race in Cuban society, studied Afro-Cubans' traditions of mobilization, and explained the processes by which their cultural expressions have become part of the national heritage. As it happened in Brazil in the late 1970s, researchers in Cuba are beginning to document race differences in a number of important areas and to disseminate their findings within the public. Some of their work has been published on the island, in journals such as *Temas* and *Catauro: Revista Cubana de Antropología*. The first issue of *La Gaceta de Cuba* in 2005 was devoted entirely to discussing questions of race in Cuban contemporary society. These experts may play an important role in shaping policy in the future.

The development of this cultural movement has had no parallel in the political arena, and conditions for the creation of independent political organizations remain much more hostile. In the Brazilian case, black political organizations emerged only during the state-sponsored democratic opening of the late 1970s, along with many other political groups seeking to participate in the democratic life of the country. Such an opening has not taken place in Cuba. Yet at least two organizations were created in the 1990s with the express goal of combating racism and racial discrimination. They are the Cofradía de la Negritud (Brotherhood of Blackness) and the Movimiento de Integración Racial "Juan Gualberto Gómez" (Movement of Racial Integration, or MIR). These movements seek to denounce the resurgence of racism in Cuban society, the exclusion of blacks and mulattos from the most lucrative economic activities, and the over-representation of Afro-Cubans among inmates. They seek to pressure the state into enacting concrete policies to eliminate the growing racial gap and call for a national campaign against racism and prejudice.

These organizations do not define themselves as political parties geared to obtain local or national power but as social movements that seek to implement change through public campaigns and influencing authorities. Staying away from formal politics in the current environment has clear advantages. Defining themselves as political parties with a racial agenda would make them easier targets of state repression. It would also open them to the charge that they represent an affront to Cuba's racial democracy and a threat to the integrity of a racially harmonious nation. As a result, these organizations have appealed not exclusively to blacks and mulattos. They present themselves as cross-racial movements that advocate the effective, equal integration of all Cubans, regardless of race, into a single national project. It is no coincidence that both the Cofradía and the MIR claim Juan Gualberto Gómez, the great Afro-Cuban advocate of racial integration and collaborator of Martí, as their main patriotic symbol.

Yet the agendas of these organizations have, as the program of the Cofradía openly acknowledges, clear political overtones. Political power is required to influence state policies and implement social changes. In the current political context, the activities of these organizations are seriously circumscribed, and their ability to access the press and educate the public on the problem of racial discrimination is rather limited.

Since state power is required to combat racism and to systematically reduce racial inequality, a transition that does not result in a process of political democratization is bound to have a limited effect on race relations on the island. In fact, as Cuba's own experience in the 1990s demonstrates, economic liberalization that is not accompanied by political opening may exacerbate race differentials. In the absence of organizations devoted specifically to combating racism, state policies that appear to be racially neutral can lead to growing racial disparities. By contrast, as in Brazil, a democratically elected government may be sensitive to pressures from within and without that may result in the adoption of policies against racial discrimination.

Building these pressures will largely depend, internally, on the formation of a black movement and on its ability to pressure political parties or to mobilize large sectors of the population and bring voters to the polls. Although in the past some cross-racial organizations (such as the Cuban Communist Party) played a leading role in the struggle against racism, black social, cultural, and political organizations were always at the forefront of this struggle. Besides, given the current situation, and given what we know from Cuba's own history and from the Brazilian transition, the eventual formation of a black political organization is to be expected. Such efforts will likely be led by members of the expanded black middle class, the same young professionals, intellectuals, and artists who have begun to voice their critique of Cuba's racial democracy through cultural means. There is in fact some evidence that young blacks and mulattos may be more inclined than other groups to pursue racially defined forms of mobilization. According to a nonscientific survey on racial attitudes conducted on the island in 1994, one-sixth of younger black and mulatto respondents advocated the need for a racially defined organization. By contrast, this statement drew almost no support among whites of any age or among older blacks. The size of the black and mulatto middle class in Cuba, which has grown considerably as a proportion of the total population since 1959, will also contribute to the viability of a black movement. Although this proportion is likely to decline once the inflated public sector is reduced, the relatively large sector of black and mulatto professionals created by the Cuban socialist education system is a potential base of support and a source of leadership for such a movement in the future.

Once created, however, how successful would this organization be? The answer depends on how we define success. If we mean the ability of this group to create a strong following, one that will translate into strength at the polls, then I suspect that a racially defined organization may have little success. If Cuba's past is any indication, and I believe it is, a racially defined organization will have great difficulties appealing to large sectors of the Afro-Cuban population. As in Brazil, racial mobilization in Cuba will immediately encounter the formidable obstacle of a pervasive ideology of racial fraternity. Despite the well-documented persistence of racial stereotyping among white Cubans, most of them approve of equal opportunities for blacks and whites and many believe that, although discrimination does exist, racism is not a major problem in Cuban society. In other words, race is still experienced by many Cubans, including many blacks and mulattos, through the prism of racial democracy. These conditions are not propitious for a racially defined political movement to prosper, as the Brazilian case shows all too well.

The viability and growth of a mass-based black political movement may be hindered further by social differentiation. To date, black political organizations in Cuba, Brazil, and even in the United States after the civil rights era, have represented mostly the problems and aspirations of the black middle class. As better-educated, upwardly mobile individuals seek to enter the ranks of the middle class, they typically face racial barriers that are of less relevance to poorer blacks and mulattos. Afro-Brazilian senator and community leader Benedita da Silva has experienced this problem: "The more elevated the social position of the black in Brazil is, the more uncomfortable this black feels." Historically, both in pre-revolutionary Cuba and Brazil, most black and mulatto workers have given their support to cross-racial unions and political parties, frequently in exchange for concrete and immediate benefits that the black movement can seldom provide. These cross-racial movements have been a much more effective vehicle for black workers to effect change than racially defined organizations.

But the Brazilian case also shows that, particularly under favorable circumstances, even a relatively small black movement can achieve considerable political success. Indeed, despite its poor electoral showing, black activism in Brazil forced the question of race onto the agenda of political parties, promoted an unprecedented scrutiny of the Brazilian racial democracy, managed to include a strengthened antidiscrimination provision in the federal Constitution, and pressed for the creation of state institutions whose main function is to combat racial discrimination. Several federal and state agencies have even begun to implement quotas for black employees. Although limited, these achievements are nonetheless astonishing.

In the Brazilian case, those favorable circumstances refer to two main factors: international influences and the leadership of President Cardoso, who governed from 1995 to 2002 and was unusually sensitive to the problem of racism. It is, of course, impossible to speculate about the roles that Cuba's future presidents will play, but a note on international influences is in order. Groups combating racism in a post-transition Cuba will benefit from an encouraging international context—a situation that differentiates this transition from earlier ones. As in Brazil, or other countries in Latin America for that matter, a black movement in Cuba will be able to seek support and resources from outside sources, including international agencies and human rights organizations. Indeed, international actors have already begun to influence the politics of race in Cuba. In response to questions raised by delegations of African Americans who have visited the island since the mid 1990s, for instance, Cuban government officials have acknowledged that racism continues to be a problem in the country. American rappers have raised money for their Cuban colleagues, providing them with options and sources of income outside the control of the state. Contacts and exchanges of this sort will only intensify in a post-transition Cuba, and a democratically elected government will likely be attentive to this sort of international scrutiny.

These influences may come at a price, however, because they tend to promote North American conceptions of race and to favor strategies of mobilization and activism that resemble the important—but by no means universal—lessons of the African American struggle for equality. They may contribute to reifying white-black dichotomies that are to some degree extraneous to the Cuban environment and add nationalistic fuel to racist responses, further exacerbating racial polarization.

The potential for racial conflict, however, should not be exaggerated. Although efforts to denounce racism and discrimination are likely to result in patriotic diatribes and other racist reactions (as in previous transitions in Cuba or in Brazil in the 1990s), it is important to note that most political actors in a democratic Cuba, including those living outside the country, will likely endorse the notion of a racially integrated and egalitarian nation, so dear to the Cuban imagery. This may be critically important. As the most recent research on Brazil shows, the ideology of racial democracy may in fact strongly *facilitate* the adoption of antidiscrimination policies, including the most extreme forms of state intervention such as racial quotas in universities and good jobs. Besides, in Cuba the struggle against racial inequality starts from a vantage point that is much better than Brazil's was. Despite the negative effects of the economic policies implemented in the 1990s, white-nonwhite inequalities continue to be much greater in Brazil than in Cuba. The Afro-Brazilian movement has pursued goals that are a given in the Cuban case. For instance, in Cuba the constitutions have explicitly condemned racial discrimination since 1940. The current Constitution characterizes racial discrimination as a crime, and the Penal Code prescribes imprisonment and fines for it. These laws will eventually be modified after a transition, but it is hard to envision a regression in these areas. Also, although low, the percentage of blacks and mulattos in Cuba's National Assembly has been consistently much higher (around 20 percent) than in the national congress in Brazil. The rates of illiteracy among Afro-Brazilians are high even in comparison to pre-revolutionary Cuba.

What seems clear is that, whatever form they adopt, there will be a need for specific antidiscrimination policies in a post-transition Cuba. These policies should build on some of the achievements of the current government (such as equal access to education) and address its shortcomings. The goal is to prevent the firing of workers because of the color of their skin, or at least to ensure that such workers find redress, support, and justice in state institutions.

SEVEN

Strategy for a Cuban Economic Transition

JORGE F. PÉREZ-LÓPEZ

In the early 1990s, Cuba's economy collapsed. For nearly three decades, the island's economy had depended on the former Soviet Union and Central and Eastern Europe for trade, credits, and aid. With the end of socialism in the former Soviet Union and Central and Eastern Europe, and the dissolution of the socialist economic bloc, Cuba lost its main trade and financial partners and entered a deep economic crisis. Between 1989 and 1993, Cuba's gross domestic product (GDP) contracted by about one-third and its foreign trade by about three-fourths. While the situation improved in the second half of the 1990s and early 2000s, the standard of living of the average Cuban citizen in 2004 was likely still below that of 1989.

The Cuban government dealt with the economic crisis by instituting an emergency economic program that did not threaten the political status quo. The program—a handful of market-oriented measures of limited scope—consisted of stopgap, shallow initiatives rather than a systematic blueprint for economic restructuring. The Cuban leadership proclaimed a "special period in time of peace," an austerity program that only recently is being relaxed.

Since the start of their transition toward democracy and free markets in the early 1990s, Central and Eastern Europe and the former Soviet Union have undergone a remarkable transformation. Despite bumps on the political and economic roads, the Czech Republic, Estonia, Hungary, Latvia, Lithuania, Poland, Slovakia, and Slovenia made so much progress that they joined the European Union on May 1, 2004. Bulgaria and Romania entered the EU on January 1, 2007. In order to join the European Union, a country must fulfill the economic and political conditions under the Copenhagen criteria, which prescribe that a prospective member must be a stable democracy, respect human rights, enact the rule of law, and protect minorities; have a functioning market economy; and adopt the common rules, standards, and policies that make up the body of EU law. That so many formerly socialist countries have met these criteria in a relatively short period of time is, indeed, an extraordinary accomplishment.

Cuba has chosen to remain on the sidelines of the transitions toward democracy and free markets that have swept the world. But when it moves beyond the sidelines, Cuban leaders will have to decide on strategies that will guide a transition to a free market.

INTERNATIONAL TRANSITION EXPERIENCES

The market transformations of the centrally planned economies of Central and Eastern Europe and the former Soviet Union have provided a living laboratory for economists and social scientists in which to analyze transition strategies and assess the performance of various policy prescriptions. Although differences remain regarding nuances in designing a transition strategy, economists have reached the consensus that it requires concentrated policy actions in three areas: macroeconomic stabilization, microeconomic restructuring, and institutional reform. Table 7.1 lists some specific measures associated with each of these policy areas.

TABLE 7.1   Elements of a Transition Strategy

Macroeconomic Stabilization
Eliminate fiscal deficit
Eliminate subsidies

Microeconomic Restructuring
Price and market reform
  Reform domestic prices
  Liberalize foreign trade
  Create or strengthen competitive factor markets
Enterprise reform
  Create legal framework
  Create institutions that support legality (e.g., property rights, commercial code, tax code, accounting and auditing functions, labor and capital market regulations, economic information systems)
  Allocate property rights to prepare for privatization
  Prepare state enterprises for privatization and develop methods for valuing assets
  Commence privatization

Institutional Reform
Formalize and deepen the legal environment
Formalize and deepen institutions that support legality
Create social safety net
Educate the public on market behavior

Macroeconomic Stabilization

Economies in transition—whether centrally planned economies transitioning toward the market or market economies seeking to reduce their public sectors—tend to be in a state of macroeconomic disequilibrium. In fact, a chaotic macroeconomic situation has often provided the principal impetus for undertaking painful reforms. Moreover, the reform process itself generates disequilibria in centrally planned economies—for example, inflation as prices are freed from controls and fiscal deficits as privatization reduces revenues from state enterprises. These issues need to be addressed before meaningful policy reforms can be implemented.

Thus, macroeconomic stabilization is a necessary but not sufficient condition for structural reforms. In essence, redressing macroeconomic imbalances requires ending production subsidies and tightening fiscal and credit policies to eliminate deficits and reduce inflationary pressures. Macroeconomic stabilization means austerity and, thus, it is politically unpopular. Reduced government expenditures translate into rolling back services and state employment. Tightening credit policies and eliminating production subsidies also reduce output, decrease employment, and disrupt enterprises, workers, and communities.

While the basic elements of all macroeconomic stabilization programs are similar, certain features of centrally planned economies (CPEs) call for special approaches. In market economies, when credit is reduced via interest rate increases, production scales down and eventually unprofitable enterprises close. In CPEs, where enterprises cover their deficits from the budget, the response to tighter credit at higher interest rates is to pass the higher costs on to the budget, unless a hard budget constraint prevents this from happening. Without a hard budget constraint and credible bankruptcy rules, in-the-red enterprises in CPEs continue to operate indefinitely, and credit expansion continues unabated.

Microeconomic Restructuring

There are two major areas of microeconomic restructuring: price and market reforms, and enterprise reform. Price and market reforms refer to the removal of price controls, liberalization of domestic and international trade, and the initial stages of the creation of labor and capital markets. Enterprise reform refers to the creation of a legal framework that supports private property, allows the creation and dissolution of firms, and facilitates the privatization of state enterprises.

Price and Market Reform

An essential feature of the classic CPE is state control over prices at the farm, factory, wholesale, and retail levels. Supply and demand do not determine prices and thus resources are not allocated optimally. This is true not only for product markets but also for markets for labor, capital, and other factors of production.

While different techniques can be used to adjust prices so that they approximate market prices, the most expeditious is to liberalize foreign trade so that domestic prices float and adjust to world-market prices. To be sure, the elimination or reduction of tariff and nontariff barriers that protected domestic producers from import competition results in short-term disruptions, particularly for inefficient producers. Over time, however, foreign trade liberalization leads to more efficient allocation of resources and enhances the competitiveness of those sectors that produce goods demanded by foreign customers.

The liberalization of domestic prices and foreign trade needs to be accompanied by the creation or strengthening of competitive labor and capital markets. In CPEs, the supply side of the labor market operates relatively well in the sense that individuals are generally able to make their own employment decisions, even if constrained by housing shortages, restrictions on internal migration, and limited mobility. In contrast, the demand side is severely distorted by institutional rigidities: virtual full employment and job security, centrally-set wages, enterprise incentives that encourage redundant employment (overstaffing), and ineffective union organizations. Labor-market reform requires easing restrictions on hiring, reassigning, and dismissing workers; abolishing centralized wage regulation; and creating mechanisms such as employment agencies that encourage labor mobility. In short, market-oriented restructuring cannot tolerate staffing that does not directly contribute to expansion of the output of a good or service in demand.

The capital markets of CPEs are severely underdeveloped. The state budget serves as the main instrument of fiscal policy, and investment resources are allocated centrally without regard for financial viability. Interest rates are kept artificially low so the cost of capital is often zero or negative. International capital flows are strictly regulated. Capital market reform involves the development of financial markets as well as private and public sector financial institutions such as banks. Functioning capital markets promote savings, raise capital, and allocate it efficiently. That is, they direct capital toward sectors with higher returns and increase efficiency by imposing financial discipline on firms. A competitive capital market is also essential to determine the true value of property to be privatized, which facilitates the transfer to new owners.

Enterprise Reform

Enterprise reform has two main components: restructuring and privatization. Its objective is to create and nurture a private sector that can act independently and serve as the long-term engine for economic growth.

A successful economic transition largely depends on a private sector that generates growth, creates new employment, and broadens the tax base. In former CPEs, an inconsistent legal framework inhibits the development of a private sector, so institutions that support a new legal framework—such as protection of property rights, rules to govern commerce and regulate bankruptcy, and a tax code—are essential for flexible economic relations. This is also true for key functions such as accounting, auditing, and management information systems. While a new private sector is being established, it is essential to restructure state enterprises to prepare for privatization. Management reforms must be put in place to reward efficiency and profitability and to do away with remnants of behavior typical of CPEs, such as labor hoarding.

A key element in management reform is the introduction of information systems that support the evaluation of enterprise performance in terms of profitability (rather than in terms of physical output targets as is customary in CPEs) and verification of performance via audits. Management reform can be spurred by setting clear, succinct rules and procedures for the creation of new firms, the dissolution of enterprises, and the breakup of monopolies.

There is broad consensus among economists that privatization is the cornerstone of creating a market economy. There is also consensus on the key elements of a privatization strategy: establishing the principle and legal reality of private ownership; quick privatization of small commercial and industrial firms either by selling shares to individuals or groups, or selling or leasing assets after liquidation of unviable enterprises; and beginning the restructuring of large industrial and commercial enterprises prior to their actual privatization. But there is still substantial disagreement on many specific aspects of privatization, including how to carry it out, at what stage and through what means; whether state assets should be sold or ownership shares distributed equally to all citizens; whether current employees should have special ownership rights; how claims from previous owners (i.e., where the state acquired the assets via nationalization or expropriation) should be treated; and what the role of foreign investors should be.

Institutional Reform

Economists also broadly agree that dismantling the economic institutions of CPEs—principally, state ownership of the means of production and central planning—and replacing them with institutions that support free markets are crucial elements of a transition strategy. The experiences of Central and Eastern Europe and the former Soviet Union have shown that eliminating CPE institutions is relatively easy; it is much harder and more time consuming to build the institutions that support and nurture the market.

And it is, indeed, a daunting task. The breadth of institutions that are needed is very great and, moreover, institution-building is a slow process. Institutional reform entails deepening microeconomic restructuring, such as legal protection for property rights; codes for commercial contracts and credit policies; rules regulating banking, bankruptcies, and investment; and a fair, efficient tax code.

As the transformation to market economies proceeded and resources were shifted to their most productive use, significant economic dislocations occurred. Some enterprises ceased operations temporarily or, in many cases, permanently, which naturally affected workers and communities. Macroeconomic disequilibrium at the outset of the transition could be corrected only by austerity measures that rendered these dislocations particularly severe.

Since full employment is the norm in CPEs, and often housing, education, health services, and even recreation are linked to employment, unemployment means not only losing wages but also losing access to many services. A corollary to the full-employment policy is that social safety nets are thin and not equipped to deal with unemployment. A successful transition, therefore, needs to develop institutions that provide unemployment benefits, pensions, and basic income support to carry workers over until they find new employment.

Findings from Transition Experiences

Transitions in Central and Eastern Europe and the former Soviet Union turned out to be more painful and slower than originally anticipated. These countries experienced significant output contractions that lasted until market-oriented reforms were sufficiently established to generate growth. In Central and Eastern Europe, economies contracted an average of 20 percent and resumed positive growth after about three years. In the former Soviet Union, the contraction averaged more than 40 percent, and a return to growth took significantly longer—about seven years.

How fast to reform was one of the most heated controversies of the early 1990s. Radical reformers favored the so-called Big Bang, or shock therapy approach, which sought the broadest and quickest transformation of the economy by undertaking simultaneous reforms in many areas. Gradual reformers argued for a slower approach that started with specific reforms and expanded to others as the policies took hold and showed positive results. In practice, the debate over the pace of reforms turned out to have been overblown. Early on, most transition countries undertook macroeconomic stabilization (reducing fiscal deficits and inflation, and stabilizing exchange rates) and microeconomic restructuring (liberalizing consumer prices and deregulating imports). In fact, one solid consensus finding on transitions is that macroeconomic stabilization is a necessary condition for the recovery of output. The main practical distinction between so-called radical and gradual reforms seems to have been timing and strategy for enterprise and institutional reform. Gradual reformers took a more deliberate approach to reform, building into their strategies some time for new institutions to take hold and begin to operate before tackling a new area of reform.

A second significant finding is the importance of initial conditions in shaping economic outcomes. Characteristics of countries at the start of the transition—such as geography, years spent under central planning, the nature of economic development under socialism, overall financial situation—tend to explain most differences across countries regarding depth and length of the economic contraction. Moreover, the impact of initial conditions on performance varies over time. It is strongest early on in the transition and tends to weaken as market-oriented policy reforms begin to take hold.

A final key finding is the central role of institutions in promoting the return to positive economic growth. Institutions that support the market are not just critical to the reform process, they also matter more as the transition progresses. Even in the absence of institutional development, empirical studies have shown that macroeconomic stabilization and liberalization can stimulate growth early in a transition. As time goes by, however, sustainable economic growth requires continuous institutional improvement. The enormous challenge, then, is to create institutions that protect property rights, ensure contract enforcement, deal with costs and benefits not reflected in the cost or price of a good or service (such as the cost of unregulated pollution), provide social protection and insurance, manage redistribution, and contend with conflict. This requires a major societal change that by nature is slow, gradual, and cannot be significantly hurried.

CUBAN ECONOMIC REFORMS IN THE 1990S

In mid-1993, the Cuban government instituted some market-oriented reforms to revitalize the economy, which was then at its weakest point. Additional measures were introduced in 1994. In the second half of the 1990s, the economy's relative recovery strengthened the hand of hard liners within the ruling elite who favored the status quo. Consequently, the reform process ground to a halt as the government postponed essential but politically sensitive changes—such as restructuring state enterprises, legalizing small businesses, and freeing prices and labor markets—and only made a few changes affecting the external sector (see table 7.2). No significant reforms have been adopted since 1997. Thus, Cuban leaders opted for continued economic inefficiency, lower output, and state control rather than risk worker dislocations, economic growth derived

TABLE 7.2.   Chronology of Cuban Economic Reforms

1993

June–August	Dollarization
September–October	Expansion of self-employment
September	Creation of agricultural cooperatives (*unidades básicas de producción cooperativa*)

1994

August	Tax code
September	Establishment of agricultural markets
October	Establishment of artisan markets
December	Convertible peso
December	Mining law

1995

September	Foreign-investment law

1996

June	Free-trade zones

1997

February	Banking-sector reform

from the private sector, and greater autonomy by citizens in procuring their livelihood.

Dollarization

The first market-oriented economic reform undertaken in the summer of 1993 was to decriminalize the holding and use of hard currency. The objective was to stimulate hard currency remittances to Cuban citizens from relatives and friends living abroad and to stem a booming black market for hard currency.

To further encourage remittances, the government established special hard-currency stores where Cuban consumers could purchase, with dollars, goods and services generally unavailable in the peso economy. Moreover, in December 1994, the government created a new form of domestic currency, the convertible peso, valued at par with the U.S. dollar, to increase the number of "dollars" in circulation and facilitate transactions at hard-currency stores. Two other actions that stimulated remittances were the decision by the Cuban National Bank in September 1995 to accept hard-currency deposits from individuals and the creation in October 1995 of foreign-currency-exchange houses where Cuban citizens could buy and sell hard currencies at rates competitive with black-market rates.

Self-Employment

The second reform was the authorization of self-employment in 114 occupations, primarily in the transportation, home repair, and personal services sectors. Subsequently, the number of occupations was expanded to more than 160. This action—which the government had little choice in taking because of the marked increase in unemployment and underemployment—essentially ended the state's monopoly on nonagricultural employment. Self-employment was subject to severe restrictions: self-employed workers could not hire others, were required to pay high fees and taxes, and were subject to strict rules on the purchase of raw materials and the sale of goods and services. Nevertheless, the number of self-employed workers increased rapidly in the mid-1990s, surpassing 208,500 workers by the end of 1995.

Agricultural Cooperatives

The third reform implemented in 1993 pertained to the creation of a new form of agricultural cooperatives called *unidades básicas de producción cooperativa* (basic units of cooperative production), or UBPCs, by breaking up large state farms. Cuban state farms, modeled after those of the Soviet Union, covered large spreads of land and made extensive use of machinery and chemical fertilizers. Workers on these farms were state employees with no ownership rights to the land they worked; production plans were determined by the central authorities, and all output had to be sold to the state. In contrast, the new cooperatives have indefinite use of the land they work and, after meeting a certain threshold level of sales to the state, can sell their output to third parties. They also elect their own leadership, manage their own financial affairs, and have their own bank accounts. The establishment of these cooperatives reduced government expenditures (in the form of salaries and agricultural input costs of the state farms) and gave workers greater incentives to increase production.

Tax Code

In August 1994, the National Assembly approved a broad tax code. The new system levied taxes on enterprise income, property, sales, consumption of tobacco, beverages and other luxury goods, utilities, transportation, inheritance, and the use of natural resources. The system also foresaw the establishment of road tolls, airport taxes, and employer contributions to social security. The Cuban revenue system thus would no longer rely mostly on payments and transfers from public enterprises to the central government. The tax code introduced a nexus between government revenue and level of economic activity.

Agricultural and Artisan Markets

In late September 1994, the Cuban government authorized the opening of farmers' markets, where producers could sell a variety of agricultural products at market-determined prices. Before an agricultural producer—whether a private farmer, a cooperative member, or even a state enterprise—could use the new markets, it had to meet sales obligations to the state procurement system. Vendors using the agricultural markets had to rent stalls and pay sales taxes. In most respects, the agricultural markets were similar to the farmers' free markets launched in 1980 and scuttled in 1986 when a series of market-socialist measures were retrenched as part of the so-called rectification process. In October

1994, the Cuban government also authorized the creation of markets for artisans and artists to sell their crafts to the public.

Foreign Investment and Export-Processing Zones

Although legislation to allow foreign investment had existed since 1982, little foreign investment materialized until the 1990s. After the collapse of communism, Cuba loosened the legal framework governing foreign investment and mounted an aggressive campaign to attract it.

In 1992, the National Assembly amended the Constitution to clarify the concept of private property and provide a legal basis for transferring state property to joint ventures with foreign investors. Two years later, a new mining law facilitated foreign investment in the exploration and production of oil and minerals. In September 1995, a comprehensive foreign-investment law eliminated the ceiling of 49 percent for foreign ownership in any given enterprise, simplified the screening and approval system, and allowed foreign investment in real estate. In June 1996, Cuba enacted complementary legislation that created export processing zones where foreign investors could locate their facilities.

At the same time, the Cuban government launched an offensive to attract foreign investment, sending missions to foreign countries, organizing seminars for potential investors, and holding auctions to lure foreign oil companies. Similarly, the government signed over four dozen bilateral investment promotion and protection agreements that provided additional guarantees to foreign companies considering investing in the country.

Banking-Sector Reform

To support foreign investors, Cuba began licensing branch offices of foreign banks in 1994 and created several semiautonomous enterprises such as the International Bank of Commerce and the Investment Bank. In May 1997, new legislation reformed the banking sector. A restructured Cuban National Bank would now supervise commercial banks and financial institutions involved in foreign trade and investment. A Cuban

Central Bank was created to carry out the functions formerly carried out by the Cuban National Bank.

Assessment of Reforms

Cuba's economic reforms were piecemeal, tardy, limited in number and scope, and implemented shallowly. As a result, these reforms do not constitute a solid foundation for a future transition to a market economy.

Countries in Central and Eastern Europe and the former Soviet Union began to implement market-oriented reforms in the 1980s. China and Vietnam have also engaged in profound market-oriented restructuring since 1978 and 1986, respectively. In contrast, only in 1993 did Cuba begin to take tentative steps toward reform, and only when the economic crisis threatened the survival of the regime. In the second half of the 1980s, during the rectification process, Cuba moved in the opposite direction of Central and Eastern Europe, the former Soviet Union, China, and Vietnam, dismantling the few market-oriented mechanisms that had been established in the 1970s and early 1980s.

In the 1990s, the Cuban leadership rejected reforms such as enterprise restructuring, legalization of small businesses, and liberalization of the labor market even though transitions in former CPEs, sympathetic foreign economists, and thoughtful Cuban economists indicated the wisdom of these measures. Thus, Cuba's economic morass does not stem from the lack of a conceptual framework to set the economy on a sustainable economic growth path. It is rather due to the leadership's unwillingness to undertake profound reforms that would improve living standards but might undermine the political status quo.

The Cuban government has also lacked the commitment to allow its modest reforms to settle and mature. Through action or inaction, it has undermined the economic effect of reforms. For example:

- Home-based restaurants (*paladares*) boomed after the liberalization of self-employment. Shortly thereafter, the government banned them and then recanted, but limiting their size to twelve customers at a time and imposing heavy fees ($850 per month), which compromised their economic viability and long-term prospects. The number of *paladares* fell from some 600 in 1995 to 150 in 2003.

- Onerous new fees and taxes on self-employed workers (a 300 percent increase in the cost of licenses and a 650 percent increase in fees) coupled with strict enforcement of rules regarding sources of inputs through aggressive inspections (to ensure that raw materials are not stolen from state enterprises) have severely hampered the economic viability of self-employment. Fines for violations are prohibitively high, for example $1,000 to $1,800 for each instance involving rentals to tourists. The government has also prohibited licensed private taxi operators to offer their services to tourists and closed down independent private art galleries.

- As a result of these actions, the number of self-employed workers fell from a peak of about 208,500 in 1995 to 152,900 in 2002 and to an estimated 150,000 in 2004. That number is expected to continue to decrease. Under a government decree that became effective on October 1, 2004, self-employment licenses will no longer be issued for 40 occupations; for another 118 occupations, licenses will be limited to two years, with the possibility of renewal.

- A law drafted in 1995 that would complement self-employment by allowing the creation of small businesses has been dormant for over a decade.

- Many obstacles to foreign investment remain, including time-consuming screening of all proposals and arbitrary decisions that affect profitability. Incoming foreign investment has slowed down in recent years, with the number of joint ventures with foreign investors actually declining.

- A moratorium on the construction of luxury condominiums and apartments financed with foreign capital was declared in May 2000. The government took over the sale or lease of units that were already completed.

- A decree in 2003 banned the use of hard-currency transactions among state enterprises and joint ventures, dictating instead the use of convertible pesos, which put into question the long-term convertibility of profits and assets of joint ventures.

In retrospect, the legalization of foreign currencies was the most successful reform undertaken in the 1990s: by mid-decade, hard-currency remittances had become the island's largest single source of foreign exchange, surpassing revenues from sugar exports and net revenue from tourism. In 2002, remittances reportedly amounted to about $1 billion. Dollarization has had a darker side, however, creating a dual economy—a dynamic sector that uses the dollar as a means of exchange, and a stagnant, or even contracting, sector that uses the peso—and exacerbating income and consumption inequalities.

LOOKING FORWARD

The transition experiences of Central and Eastern Europe and the former Soviet Union are relevant to the design of Cuba's transition strategy. Among the key findings from those experiences are: the need to manage the inevitable economic contraction carefully so as to avoid an anti-market backlash; the importance of sequencing reforms properly; the critical, long-term role of institutions in shaping the transition; and the potential for special treatment, corruption, and other pitfalls of privatization to derail the transition.

Another important finding from these transition experiences is that there is no one-size-fits-all economic transition strategy. Instead, each country must ground its economic transition strategy on its own special circumstances: geographic setting, natural-resource endowment, culture, economic structure, production possibilities, and overall economic conditions at the time of the transition. Foreign experiences can inform policy makers about key issues and help to identify concerns that may require special attention. But the architects of the Cuban transition will have to design a strategy to fit the nation's circumstances when the moment to do so arrives.

In the areas of macroeconomic stabilization, microeconomic restructuring, and institutional reforms, two scenarios may offer useful strategies: In the first, Cuba experiences a full transition to a market economy and a pluralistic democracy along the lines of the transitions in Central and Eastern Europe, the Baltic States, and some of the republics of the former Soviet Union. And in the second, Cuba experiences limited economic reforms and no change in political relations along the lines of the China-Vietnam socialist market model.

While the areas that require policy action under the two scenarios are the same, the specific actions that constitute the reform strategy will differ because under the China-Vietnam model, the political leadership will reject those economic reforms that would empower citizens in the economic arena or would create institutions that eventually could lead to political pluralism and democracy.

Macroeconomic Stabilization

After undergoing a period of severe macroeconomic instability in the early 1990s—when the budget deficit ballooned to about a third of GDP and inflation was rampant—Cuba successfully stabilized its economy, bringing down the budget deficit/GDP ratio to 2–3 percent of GDP and inflation to about the same annual rate by the second half of the 1990s. In the absence of financial support from international financial institutions (Cuba is not a member of the International Monetary Fund or the World Bank), Cuba stabilized its economy through across-the-board cuts in government expenditures—including reduction or elimination of price subsidies for certain consumer goods, cutbacks in military expenditures, reorganization of government ministries that eliminated some organizations, and overall reductions in the government's payroll—and targeted increases in government revenues, mostly hikes in prices of some nonessential goods, charges for goods and services that were formerly free, and income taxes.

Some macroeconomic instability returned in 2002, with the budget deficit climbing to about 3.5 percent of GDP and inflation jumping to 7 percent—both higher than the targets set by the central authorities. High prices for oil imports, relatively weak international prices for sugar and nickel, and shocks to the tourism sector—from recession in developed countries and the aftermath of the September 11, 2001 terrorist attacks in the United States—adversely affected the hard-currency balance of payments and created added instability in the external sector. By 2003, Cuba had defaulted on foreign debts incurred with developed and developing countries and was essentially shut out from international credit markets, with the exception of short-term loans to finance specific purchases. While the official exchange rate remains at one peso to one U.S. dollar, currency exchange outlets run by the government converted at the rate of twenty-five pesos to one U.S. dollar.

A transition strategy for Cuba would have to recognize the very difficult economic situation that the country faces, particularly with regard to external sector imbalances, and it might include the following stabilization actions:

- Institute a hard budget constraint to avoid unlimited extensions of government credit to unprofitable enterprises.
- Cut government expenditures, particularly by reducing subsidies to unprofitable state enterprises.
- Reduce the size of the government bureaucracy and eliminate over-staffing in state enterprises.
- Strengthen tax revenue collection and conduct public education programs to encourage individuals to pay taxes.
- Begin to collect social security contributions from individuals, consistent with the tax reform of 1994 but waived by the government.
- Seek expedited membership in the international financial institutions to gain access to technical assistance and financial support from these institutions.
- Seek to renegotiate the foreign debt (including seeking a certain measure of debt forgiveness) in order to regain access to international credit markets.

In addition, under the full-transition scenario, additional actions in the area of stabilization might be:

- Eliminate politically motivated foreign assistance programs (e.g., free medical school for students from foreign countries) that the country cannot afford.
- Eliminate costly special health and social security programs for members of the armed forces, the internal security services, and the political leadership, and consolidate these programs with those available to the general public.

- Eliminate government financial support for the Communist Party and its affiliated entities.
- Encourage the Cuban community abroad to increase remittances and financial flows to the island.
- Appeal to the international community, particularly the United States, for emergency assistance, including food and balance-of-payments assistance, to overcome the initial economic hardships.

Microeconomic Restructuring

Price and Market Reform

In the 1990s, Cuba made some feeble attempts at liberalizing consumer, foreign trade, and factor markets. Although prices of most rationed goods at the consumer level remain fixed, in the 1990s Cuba permitted the establishment of agricultural markets where prices are largely set by supply and demand. It also set up government-run stores that sell consumer goods—including imported goods—for hard currency, although at very high prices in comparison with the earning capacity of the average Cuban worker. Foreign trade—the ability to export and import—was formerly the exclusive purview of the state. In the 1990s, Cuba created *sociedades anónimas* (semi-autonomous enterprises) authorized to engage directly in international trade and gave joint ventures between Cuban enterprises and foreign partners the same ability to engage directly in foreign trade. Despite these developments, retail and wholesale prices in Cuba continue to be controlled by the state (except for those that prevail at farmers' and artisan markets); foreign trade remains largely under state control; and there are no operating markets for intermediate goods, labor, and credit.

A transition strategy under either of the two scenarios might contain the following policy actions regarding price and market reform:

- Eliminate the government's monopoly over foreign trade and allow enterprises to export freely and to manage their hard-currency transactions subject to government oversight.
- Eliminate barriers to importing and allow enterprises and individuals to import subject to government oversight.

- Eliminate price controls on traded goods and services, and allow domestic prices of such goods to adjust to international market prices.
- Abolish the artificial official parity of the peso with the U.S. dollar, and set an exchange rate that approximates the market-clearing exchange rate.
- Relax rules regarding self-employment.
- Remove impediments to the establishment of small businesses.

In addition, under the full-transition scenario, the following policy actions, which would be incompatible with the China-Vietnam model's priority of maintaining political control, might be part of the transition strategy:

- Eliminate domestic price controls and allow intermediate and consumer prices to be determined by the interplay of supply and demand.
- Lift restrictions on employment and worker mobility.
- Eliminate restrictions on foreign investors regarding direct hiring of Cuban workers and allow these employers to set wages for their workers.
- Provide labor market intermediation and employment services to facilitate labor market adaptability.
- Provide incentives for the creation of small businesses.
- Begin establishment of the legal framework for creating financial markets and their regulation.

Enterprise Reform

In order for markets to operate in Cuba, a base line of legal, economic, and financial institutions that support them must be in place. In 1994, Cuba enacted a tax code and more recently created some financial control and audit entities, primarily to try to stem a wave of corruption associated with joint ventures with foreign investors, mostly in the tourism sector. When the transition comes, however, Cuba will need to develop a legal framework to support market behavior, pursue policies that promote competition, and nurture the establishment of a private sector. Meaningful changes in these areas are largely incompatible with the

China-Vietnam model and can only be envisioned within a full-transition scenario. Among the specific policy actions might be:

- Create or further the legal framework for the market, including clearly established property rights, a commercial code, a tax code, banking and finance rules, clear rules for entry and exit of firms into and from the market (i.e., bankruptcy rules), transparency rules, accounting and auditing standards and regulations (including setting accounting, disclosure, and reporting standards) and regulations for labor and capital markets.
- Break up state monopolies and provide incentives for the establishment of small and medium-size enterprises.
- Create specialized credit institutions to support small and medium-sized enterprises (e.g., commercial banks, savings and loan institutions, and credit unions) and specific economic needs (e.g., agricultural credit and home loans).
- Revise the foreign-investment framework to bring it up to international standards and aggressively seek foreign investment that transfers technology and creates good jobs.
- Engage in a national campaign to educate the public about the operation and benefits of a market economy.
- Educate consumers about the benefits of competition.
- Establish clear rules on property rights as a precursor to privatization, including the possibility of developing special rules for dealing with residential property.
- Begin the privatization process, starting with small and medium-size state enterprises. (The privatization of large enterprises should be delayed until the legal framework is sufficiently advanced to handle complex transactions, and accounting and audit systems are in place to value properties to be privatized.)

Three very significant issues that will need to be addressed in designing a privatization strategy for Cuba are:

- how to handle claims by former property owners—individuals or corporations, domestic or foreign—whose assets were taken over by the Cuban state during the waves of nationalization in the 1960s (failure to adequately address these claims could result in very lengthy legal proceedings that in practice could thwart privatization and moot its positive impact for the transition);

- how to deal with foreign interests in purchasing privatized assets and, in particular, the role the Cuban community abroad might play in acquiring privatized assets; and
- how to avoid corruption from erupting during the privatization process (adopting strong transparency requirements and clear accountability rules would be essential).

As is discussed in chapter 9, corruption has undermined transitions in several former socialist countries, and Cuba may be particularly prone to a similar fate unless anticorruption measures are made an integral part of the transition strategy. A disturbing development that might presage corruption in a Cuba in transition is the "spontaneous privatization" that has already occurred, as Communist Party kingpins have become managers/owners of *sociedades anónimas,* appropriating state assets for their private gain.

Institutional Reform

Creating an institutional framework to support the market will be difficult and time consuming. The architects of the Cuban transition will be challenged to create, strengthen, and make operational formal institutions that provide the foundation for market behavior and support legality: protection of private property rights, contracts, commercial and credit practices, banking, bankruptcies, investment (including foreign investment), taxation, and economic management and control.

During the output contraction that is likely to accompany the early transition and the enterprise-restructuring process that will follow, numerous workplaces will shut down permanently, and many workers will face unemployment. Important for these workers will be the creation or strengthening of a social safety net that might include temporary income support and employment services to assist them until they are able to obtain productive employment. Some of these policies are discussed in more detail in chapter 8.

The institutions that Cuba will require in the medium and long term to foster economic development and improve the standard of living of its citizens are not compatible with the limited reforms of the China-Vietnam model. These can only be achieved under a full-transition scenario that implies strong market orientation and democracy. Among the specific policy actions in this regard are:

- Strengthen the legal framework that recognizes and protects private ownership, including a commercial code that, among other things, sets bankruptcy rules and establishes policies that regulate trade, investment, banking, and taxation and promote competition and economic growth.
- Strengthen institutions (e.g., accounting and auditing rules, and management information systems) that will permit the valuation of assets prior to their privatization and develop transparent bidding rules for privatization.
- Start the privatization of large state enterprises.
- Strengthen the social safety net, with emphasis on measures to assist dislocated workers.

The Central and Eastern European countries that aspired to enter the European Union made more progress in developing an institutional framework for a market economy than other countries in transition. This suggests that the incentive of joining the European Union and integrating their economies with the wealthier Europeans provided additional impetus for their reform. When Bulgaria, the Czech Republic, Estonia, Hungary, Latvia, Lithuania, Poland, Romania, Slovakia, and Slovenia joined the European Union, they adopted, in whole, its legal and economic institutions and therefore locked in place a legal system that has proven it can support a market economy. A bilateral free-trade agreement with the United States, possibly other free-trade agreements with Western nations, and inclusion in the Free Trade Area of the Americas might provide opportunities for Cuba to leapfrog some individual changes and adopt the state-of-the-art trade and investment regimes embodied in these agreements, thereby saving precious time on the road toward integration into the global economy.

CONCLUDING REMARKS

Cuba recorded four consecutive years of decline in GDP per capita between 1990 and 1993, not unlike the transition recessions experienced by Central and Eastern Europe and the former Soviet Union. While Cuba suffered the pain of severe output contraction in the early 1990s, it did not undertake the reforms that are necessary to achieve lasting economic gain. It is entirely possible that when Cuba ultimately does launch its transition, it may suffer a second output contraction—this one associated with transition rather than with external shocks. Such a scenario would be extremely painful for the Cuban people, who have already experienced significant belt tightening since the beginning of the Special Period, which began in 1991.

Cuba could soften this potential blow with aggressive policy reform, the time-tested way for economies to regain positive economic growth after a transition contraction. If the political will to undertake a full transition to democracy and free markets were present, Cuba could begin its path to sustained economic growth and development as other successful reformers in Central and Eastern Europe and the former Soviet Union have done. Cuba could improve its access to foreign markets by immediately seeking membership in regional trade agreements. Through these agreements, Cuba would adopt state-of-the-art international trade and investment practices that would jump-start the economy and serve its citizens well in meeting the challenges of the world economy in the twenty-first century.

EIGHT

Social Policy and Social Welfare

CARMELO MESA-LAGO

Social policy involves the provision of social services—health care, education, social insurance pensions, social assistance, and poverty reduction—as well as the promotion of employment and a fair income distribution. Social policies that are conducted in a financially sustainable manner promote social welfare. In Cuba, all social services are provided, financed, and administered by the state, while in market economies the market and the state share these three functions.

Cuba's economic crisis of 1990–2002 followed the collapse of communism in Central and Eastern Europe and the Soviet Union. To cope with the resulting changes, the government enacted moderate market reforms that produced positive but modest results, but in 1996 these reforms were halted. The transition from the present regime to the market economy, therefore, is yet to be, and it may happen under one of three scenarios: a resumption of the reforms halted in 1996, a socialist market economy as in China and Vietnam, or a full-fledged market economy as in Central and Eastern Europe and the Commonwealth of Independent States (CIS).

THE TRANSITION IN FORMER AND CURRENT SOCIALIST COUNTRIES

There are thirty former and current socialist countries. Twelve former socialist countries are in the Commonwealth of Independent States, twelve in Central and Eastern Europe, and three in the Baltic Sea. The current socialist countries are China and Vietnam (which have a socialist market economy), and Cuba, which halted its modest reform process.

During the 1990s, former socialist countries suffered a sharp economic decline brought on by their transition to market economies and the disintegration of the socialist bloc. Combined with crucial changes in social policy, the economic crisis in these countries led to adverse social effects. The market-socialist reform in China, and to a lesser extent in Vietnam, rapidly led to a very strong economic recovery. Previous to the reform, social policies were not as developed in these two socialist countries as in the others, although such policies were also harmed by the reform. Another important difference is that in China and Vietnam the Communist Party has retained full political power, and the state has continued to guide the economy, keeping part of the ownership of the means of production and economic control. Four adverse social effects have been precipitated by the transition in former and current socialist countries: increased unemployment, deterioration in social services, the growth of poverty, and the expansion of inequalities.

Increased Unemployment

Between 1990 and 2001, open unemployment increased in all former socialist countries, averaging 16 percent in Central and Eastern Europe, 10 percent in the Baltic states, and 6 percent in the Commonwealth of Independent States. Increasing competition among enterprises and the creation of private farms led to cuts in government jobs and the shut-down of state enterprises. Thus, redundant jobs, or disguised unemployment, which are so prevalent in centrally planned economies, were eliminated. Moreover, labor reforms made it easier to dismiss redundant employees. In most countries, the private jobs created did not immediately offset the cuts in public jobs. In China and Vietnam, land transfers from communes and cooperatives to village, family, and individual ownership reduced redundant labor. Some of China's rural unemployed were absorbed by town and village enterprises; others migrated to the cities. In 2004, China had about 5 percent unemployment; in Vietnam, it was closer to 6 percent.

Small enterprises and self-employment (part of the so-called informal sector) have created private jobs in all twenty-nine countries in question. Largely hidden and unreported, these sectors do not pay taxes nor make social insurance contributions. Particularly affected by open unemployment are youths, women, and residents of underdeveloped regions. Most countries took measures to protect employment, though not all did so equally—Russia did so much more than Hungary or Poland, for example. Initially generous, unemployment benefits were cut or eligibility rules tightened as the number of jobless increased and costs escalated. In countries with liberal programs such as the Czech Republic and Estonia, workers quickly learned that they were better off collecting compensation than working for relatively low wages. In Vietnam, dismissed workers receive compensation for twelve months, four times longer than workers in Russia; Chinese workers receive one month's salary for every year of employment.

Cuba's open unemployment allegedly fell from 7.5 percent in the early 1990s to 4.5 percent in 2001—lower than in fifteen former socialist countries and higher than in eight countries in the Commonwealth of Independent States and China. The CIS countries with low open unemployment are the least developed and poorest: between 48 and 72 percent of their populations live in rural areas where redundant labor is still the norm. These countries have chosen to protect jobs in state enterprises and agriculture instead of promoting market reforms. China and Vietnam's rural populations are 64 and 76 percent, respectively, but their agricultural sectors have been liberalized, and new private-sector jobs

created. In contrast, between 58 and 74 percent of the populations in virtually all countries of Central and Eastern Europe and the Baltic region
are urban; rural labor redundancy, therefore, is less common. Democratically elected governments in these countries have emphasized labor
productivity and economic growth over job protection.

Deterioration in Social Services

Prior to 1989, most former socialist countries had social services comparable or better than those offered by countries with market economies
at the same level of development. Services were free and universal. Educational facilities were owned by the state and centrally financed, although managed at lower levels. With few exceptions, these countries had
achieved, or were close to, full literacy. Health services emphasized primary care, access to water and sanitation, attention to pregnant women
and children, and control of infectious diseases. In some former socialist countries, hospital and medical services were provided by large urban
enterprises as an extra benefit for their workers. Low infant mortality
and higher life expectancy were the outcomes of a universal health care
system. In Central and Eastern Europe and the former Soviet Union,
social insurance provided pensions for retired or disabled employees
and their dependents. Conditions for access to benefits—for instance, a
lower retirement age—were more generous than in market economies;
workers made low or no contributions into the state-financed system.
In China and Vietnam, social insurance pensions were largely limited
to and financed by urban state enterprises, which also provided health
insurance. Rural citizens were protected by the cooperatives' pension
system as well as by a tradition of strong ties between members of the
extended family who cared for each other. Communal systems serviced
basic health care in rural areas. Water supply and sanitation were funded
by the central government.

These advances were not exempt from flaws. Despite central government transfers, considerable differences existed in the access to and
quality of services among regions, provinces, and municipalities, particularly in the least developed countries. With the highest rural populations,

China and Vietnam endured the broadest disparities. Aging populations and the increase in deaths from cancer and cardiovascular diseases rather than from contagious diseases led to higher health care costs. Pensions lacked the reserves to finance long-term benefits; in China and Vietnam, pensions covered only a small percentage of the population at a high cost. Finally, there was inefficiency in the allocation of resources.

During the transition in current and former socialist countries, access to and quality of social services deteriorated. The decline in gross domestic product (GDP) and government revenue forced cuts to reduce the fiscal deficit, balance the state budget, and curtail inflation. Partial or total privatization shifted social services to the market and introduced means-tested user fees in some countries, all of which limited access. Adverse social effects varied depending on the scope, depth, and velocity of the reforms; the GDP decline and its duration; and whether a social safety net was introduced. After the worst of the transition was over, one-third of the countries saw some social indicators advance; in most countries, these stagnated.

In former socialist countries, severe cuts in the education budget had harmful effects, from sinking expenditures on supplies and school maintenance to stagnation in the path to universal primary-level coverage and limits in the ability to train workers for the growing private sector, particularly in the poorest countries. In addition, there was serious deterioration in education in rural areas and the poorest regions, and families were made responsible for covering the costs of school maintenance, supplies, and teacher salaries.

In China, the target of nine years of compulsory education by 2000 was not met. In Vietnam, enrollments in preschool through secondary levels have declined, and parents now pay user fees.

Cuts in public health budgets have also forced payments from some users, which has often led underpaid health workers to ask patients for side payments. As many as one-third of all users in the poorest countries borrow money to pay for inpatient care or forgo health care; 41 percent of Russians, for instance, cannot buy medicine. In several countries, the growing number of private health providers is unregulated. In China, the central government has drastically cut subsidies and transfers, forcing local communities to become "self-reliant"; urban enterprises now cover only half of their employees; and privatization sharply curtailed the services of rural health cooperatives. Provinces and municipalities, now starved for resources, are still responsible for the health care of workers and the self-employed in towns and villages. In Vietnam, only 20 percent of all health workers are in the public sector. User fees are charged for public medical services and, naturally, by private clinics and private-practice doctors. Communal health center budgets have plummeted while those of private providers tripled. The end result is that inequalities in health care are rising in these countries, where large sectors of the population lack access to health care.

In former socialist countries, pension costs increased to an average 9 percent of GDP; in Croatia, Poland, Slovakia, and Slovenia, these costs climbed to 13 percent, twice the level before the transition. Pensions were totally privatized in Kazakhstan and partially privatized in Bulgaria, Croatia, Czech Republic, Estonia, Hungary, Latvia, and Poland, shifting the burden of contributions from employers to employees. The experience of Latin America—a pioneer in pension privatization—indicates that these reforms may create significant problems in the future, such as decline in population coverage, increasing percentage of affiliates who do not pay their contributions, lack or poor competition between administrators of pension funds and high administrative costs, and excessive concentration of the fund investment portfolio on state debt paper. In China and Vietnam, state enterprise reforms and the reduction of state subsidies drastically curtailed pensions, which are now financed by employers, workers, and, in China's case, the government.

Growth of Poverty

Before 1990, there were few published statistics on poverty in most former and current socialist countries. After the transition, poverty has increased sharply, and much more than expected. Causes include the decline in inflation-adjusted wages and pensions, the increase in prices of consumer goods, higher costs for housing and public utilities, the user fees charged for education and health care services, and the increase in open unemployment and informal sector employment.

Between 1990 and 1998, poverty in former socialist countries rose considerably, although it varied greatly among countries. Poverty now tends to be lower in the most developed countries in Central and Eastern Europe and the Baltic than in the CIS region: between 9 and 24 percent in Hungary, Estonia, Romania, and Poland; between 31 and 36 percent in Russia, Ukraine, Kazakhstan, and Moldova; and between 40 and 68 percent in Armenia, Belarus, Kyrgyzstan, and Tajikistan. Despite lower poverty rates, Central and Eastern Europe and the Baltic countries allocate more resources to social assistance to the poor than the Commonwealth of Independent States, which has been slower in implementing market reforms. In general, social assistance programs do not reach a majority of the poor.

Expansion of Inequalities

Prior to 1989, socialist countries had some of the lowest levels of inequality in the world. During the transition, inequality in income distribution began to rise, and it has continued to grow, though in varying magnitudes. Broadening inequalities were to be expected as privatization expanded and the state sector contracted. The income of investors, rent seekers, entrepreneurs, and technocrats grew; so did poverty and unemployment. In Central and Eastern Europe and the Baltic countries, a competitive environment has rewarded educated people and entrepreneurs for their skills and risk taking. In the CIS, market reforms have been less encompassing and competition weaker, thus allowing a small elite to monopolize power in pursuit of its own interests through corruption. Self-employment and subsistence agriculture have persisted, and wages have drastically decreased.

The Gini coefficient is the standard gauge for inequality in income distribution: a value of 1.0 indicates the highest inequality, therefore, 0.61 reflects high inequality and 0.25 indicates low inequality. Between 1996 and 1998, the average Gini coefficient in Central and Eastern Europe and the Baltic countries ranged from 0.25 in the Czech Republic to 0.37 in Estonia, which was considerably lower than in most Commonwealth of Independent States countries, where the value spanned from 0.35 in Kazakhstan to 0.61 in Armenia.

SOCIAL POLICY AND SOCIAL WELFARE IN CUBA, 1990–2002

In 1989, Cuba led the socialist and former socialist countries in health indicators, ranking at the midpoint in education. Both health care and education were universal and free. Pensions covered almost all the labor force, eligibility rules were generous, and the state fully financed the system. Open unemployment was lower than in twelve socialist countries. The collapse of communism in the Soviet Union and Central and Eastern Europe led to a 75 percent cut in Cuban trade and the termination of all economic aid. Almost immediately, Cubans felt the adverse effects on social services.

During the 1990s, the Cuban government continued to administer, finance, and provide free social services, but with the crisis, the quality of these services severely deteriorated. In 2000, Cuba was behind most socialist and former socialist countries in two key education indicators: the illiteracy rate, which at 3 percent put Cuba in a twenty-first place tie with Azerbaijan and Kyrgyzstan (only Albania, China, and Vietnam had higher rates), and a combined enrollment (primary, secondary, and university) of 76 percent, which tied it with Slovakia and Uzbekistan for thirteenth place. Conversely, Cuba's infant mortality rate was 7 per 1,000, the third lowest in the group, below Slovenia and the Czech Republic, and life expectancy at birth was 76 years, the highest. In terms of basic infrastructure, Cuba also failed to measure up: it registered eighth in access to potable water among fourteen countries providing that data and ninth in access to sanitation among eleven countries; the poorest countries had better access than Cuba. Pension costs, at 7 percent of GDP, were still below the average in former socialist countries, in part because of a relatively younger population and the plummeting real value of pensions. The burden is nonetheless rising as Cuba's population becomes the oldest in Latin America while the retirement age of its workers remains very low and life expectancy very high.

Modest economic reform prompted a partial recovery after the mid 1990s, which redressed some of these effects. In 2002, however, some social indicators were still below their 1989 level. Contrary to other socialist and former socialist countries that undertook full restructuring, Cuba's minimalist and incomplete reforms had positive medium-term effects. When deeper reforms are introduced, social indicators are sure to deteriorate.

Unemployment

Cuba eliminated open unemployment by overstaffing state agencies, enterprises, and farms. Between 1991 and 1997, unemployment rose to 7.5 percent; by 2002, it had allegedly decreased to 3.3 percent. The government gave no explanation for how the 50 percent reduction was accomplished, and there are reasons to doubt the government's statistics. In 1995, for example, between 500,000 and 800,000 state workers were deemed redundant and therefore candidates for dismissal. The small private sector is stagnant, tightly regulated, and heavily taxed. Job creation depends largely on the state sector, which is already bloated. And in 2002, 100,000 state sugar workers lost their jobs when the government closed nearly half of all sugar mills.

According to the Economic Commission for Latin America and the Caribbean, equivalent unemployment in Cuba (measured by adding open unemployment and displaced workers receiving compensation) peaked at 35 percent in 1993 and decreased to 25 percent in 1998. The commission has stopped publishing those figures. The official 3.3 percent open unemployment rate in 2002, moreover, did not include dismissed sugar workers who were paid to go to school, or 320,000 persons raising vegetables part-time in small urban plots, a limited private sector that does not generate full-time employment. The real open unemployment rate then was close to 11.9 percent. Like the Commonwealth of Independent States, Cuba has opted for protecting jobs in state enterprises and agriculture and therefore having lower productivity, rather than creating productive private-sector jobs—as did Central and Eastern Europe and the Baltic countries.

Social Services

Education

From 1959 to 1989, Cuba made continuous advances in education: illiteracy declined from 21 to 6 percent, primary school became universal, secondary education enrollment rose from 20 to 90 percent, and higher-education enrollment increased from 3 to 23 percent. The education system is fully state owned and financed and operated by the Ministry of Education, which also hires and pays all teachers. All services are provided for free.

The crisis of the early 1990s hurt education. A jump in inflation (26 percent in 1994 compared to 0.5 percent in 1989) and in the fiscal deficit (34 percent of GDP in 1993 compared to 7 percent in 1989) forced the government to enforce an adjustment program, the "special period in time of peace." Between 1989 and 1997, the education budget in real pesos was cut 38 percent, which—as in other socialist and former socialist countries—resulted in a scarcity of books, pencils, and paper; retrenchment of investment and maintenance; deterioration of equipment; reduction in student transportation and meals; and decline in the quality of services. Between 1989 and 1999, enrollment in primary education fell from 100 to 99 percent and in secondary education from 90 to 79 percent, and at the university level it shrank from 23 to 12 percent between 1987 and 1997.

Transportation difficulties, cuts in school meals, and the devaluing of higher education degrees explain the decrease in secondary education enrollment. Dramatic shrinkage in university enrollment reflects the difficulties graduates face in finding state-sector jobs that, in any case, are poorly paid. Before 1989, university professors and physicians earned the highest salaries, and teachers had adequate wages. Now, private farmers, transporters, owners of home-based restaurants, domestic servants, and prostitutes top the income ladder. Sadly, many professionals have abandoned their careers to pursue better-paid occupations. Though authorized in 1993, the right to self-employment was not extended to university graduates. The impact of the decline in university enrollment will not be felt immediately because there is a glut in certain professions such as doctors and teachers, but in the long term it will result in a shortage of professionals and thus harm economic growth.

Health Care

Before 1959, Cuba had a relatively developed health care system, which accounted for health indicators that were among the best in Latin America. After the revolution, a new national health system established universal, free health care and greatly reduced the urban-rural gap in facilities, personnel, and health standards. The health care system is capital intensive, placing emphasis on hospitals, equipment, and physicians. The family doctor program created in 1984, although positive in terms of giving patients closer access to physicians, is also very expensive. In the context of scarce resources and other more urgent needs, these programs are wasteful. Between 1959 and 1989, the number of physicians rose from 9.2 to 33.1 per 10,000 inhabitants, hospital beds from 4.2 to 5.3 per 1,000 inhabitants, and real expenditures per capita by 162 percent. Infant mortality declined from 33.4 to 11.1 per 1,000; maternal mortality dropped from 125.3 to 26.1 per 100,000, and the mortality rate of the population 65 and above decreased from 52.9 to 46.3 per 1,000. Most contagious diseases were eradicated, although a few, such as tuberculosis (which reappeared), chicken pox, and AIDS, increased.

Between 1991 and 1995, health indicators deteriorated. They have improved somewhat, but by 2000 some had still not recovered to 1989 levels. Hospital bed rates fell from 5.3 to 4.7, maternal mortality rose from 26.1 to 55.7, and the 65-and-over mortality rate increased first from 48.4 to 55.7, then dropped to 49.7. Most eradicated diseases did not make a comeback, but those exhibiting a rising trend before the crisis continued to do so. Conversely, the rates of physicians jumped two-fold between 1989 and 2001, to 60 physicians per 10,000 inhabitants, the highest among socialist and former socialist countries and in Latin America, and infant mortality was almost halved to 6.5 per 1,000 (the lowest in both regions). These achievements are a financial drain. Expensively trained physicians, many of whom have left the profession in pursuit of better-paying jobs, and the continued reduction of an already low infant mortality rate absorbs scarce resources that could be used to meet more pressing needs, such as the badly deteriorated infrastructure for potable water and sewage.

Multiple factors explain the deterioration of health care. Real health expenditures per capita shrank 75 percent between 1989 and 1993; in 1999, they were still 21 percent below the 1989 level. Reduced budgets and a drastic decline in imports combined to create a severe shortage of medicine, spare parts, materials for medical tests, anesthesia, and the like. Badly neglected before the crisis, the potable water and sewerage infrastructure broke down, which largely explains the growth of acute diarrhea and hepatitis. The lack of prophylactics and the increase in prostitution have led to a higher rate of venereal diseases, and the reduction in vaccinations accounts for increases in chicken pox and tuberculosis. Between 1990 and 2000, undernourishment increased from 5 to 13 percent. Hospital occupancy decreased from 83.9 to 69.4 percent. Amid extreme scarcity, Cuba's public health system is plagued by widespread inefficiency.

Members of the armed forces and state security, as well as high level officials in the government and the Communist Party, are serviced by a separate health care network. Similarly, the government has established a dollar-based health care system for foreigners. Both provide a higher quality, more efficient, and better stocked health care system than that of the general population.

Social Insurance Pensions

After 1959, the Cuban government unified the fifty-four existing social insurance funds for retirement, disability, and survivors and standardized their entitlement conditions. Coverage increased from 63 to 91 percent of the labor force; independent farmers, the self-employed, and unpaid family workers could join voluntarily. Retirement ages—fifty-five for women and sixty for men—were set unusually low. By 1989, Cuba's pension system was among the most extended, liberal, and costly in Latin America. Employees did not pay into the system, and state enterprises paid only 12 percent of the payroll. (In the former socialist countries, by comparison, employers contributed 36 percent.) Although meager, pensions were supplemented by a safety net that offered subsidized prices for consumer goods, free health care, free or cheap housing, and low-cost public utilities.

The economic crisis and a rapidly aging population undermined the pension system's positive features. Between 1989 and 2001, the private sector grew from 4 to 15 percent of the labor force, which means more people are privately employed and not covered by a pension plan.

The trend will deepen if the private sector expands. The system allows self-employed workers and private farmers to join by paying 12 percent of their income. A 1994 tax law mandating worker contributions was suspended for sociopolitical reasons, so that only employees in a pilot program that operates in 12 percent of all enterprises are paying into the pension plan.

Low retirement ages and rising life expectancy have created a mountain of problems. The average length of retirement increased to twenty years for men and twenty-six years for women (the longest in any socialist or former socialist countries and the second longest in Latin America). By 2025, Cuba will have the oldest population in Latin America: 25 percent of the total population will be over fifty-five (women) or over sixty (men) and retired, and there will be only 1.5 active workers per pensioner. The real average pension shrank 42 percent between 1989 and 1998. Moreover, the supplementary safety net is badly frayed because the ration of subsidized goods has shrunk to about a week's worth of supplies per month, transportation difficulties mount, and health care continues to deteriorate. In 2001, 1.5 million pensioners received an average monthly stipend of 110 pesos, which covered one-half the cost of essential food items and one-fourth the cost of total basic needs including clothing and utilities. Most senior citizens need foreign remittances to get by. In mid-2003, pensioners in Old Havana and four provinces staged protests over delayed or canceled payments. Even so, between 1986 and 2000, pension costs rose from 4.6 to 6.5 percent of GDP and generated an expanding fiscal deficit from 26 to 40 percent of total pension expenditures. If expenses are to be covered, the combined contribution (employer and employee) must be raised to at least 20 percent, keeping open the option of future increases.

As with health care, members of the armed forces and state security are covered by a separate pension system that is more generous than that of the general population. A man who joined the armed forces at age seventeen can retire after twenty-five years, at age forty-two, and collect a pension equal to his last year's salary for an average of thirty-seven years. In 1995, the armed forces pension costs equaled the entire deficit accrued by the general system.

Poverty

The Cuban government has never published poverty statistics and claims that poverty is not widespread. Two studies carried out around 1995, however, measured poverty among different population groups and arrived at divergent results. The first, conducted by the Ministry of Economics and Planning, estimated that 15 percent of the urban population was "at risk of not covering some essential need," meaning that their income was insufficient to buy basic food; it also showed that Havana's poor increased from 4 to 20 percent between 1988 and 1995. The second study, done at the University of Havana, estimated that 61 to 67 percent of the country's population was poor. Not surprisingly, children and women, people with only a primary education or living in households with more than six members, and the unemployed were most at risk. Furthermore, beggars have reappeared on Havana streets asking for money and goods from tourists, and the government struggles to control them. The safety net is much worn, and rationing no longer covers monthly needs.

In spite of increasing poverty, the state budget assigned to social assistance averaged 0.6 percent of GDP between 1990 and 2001, the lowest share among all social services, while real social assistance expenses shrank 29 percent between 1989 and 1998. In 2002, the monthly pension under this program was 40 pesos ($1.53 at the exchange rate of 1 U.S. dollar for 26 pesos), hardly sufficient to buy even a day's supply of unsubsidized food items.

Inequalities

Similarly, Cuba has never published income distribution statistics. The Gini coefficient has been estimated to have increased from 0.22 in 1986 to 0.55 in 1995, the latter being comparable to the pre-revolutionary level. Average real wages in the state sector declined 44 percent between 1989 and 1998, while the income of private farmers, artists, owners of home-based restaurants, private taxi drivers, other self-employed workers, and black-market speculators rose dramatically. In 1989, the maximum wage difference was 4.5 to 1; in 1995, the ratio between the highest income earner and the average wage was 829 to 1, while by 2002 it had expanded to 12,500 to 1. Monthly wages ranged from $4 for a janitor to $23 for a cabinet minister (at the exchange rate of 26 pesos per 1 dollar). In the private sector, the range was from $40 for a well-paid domestic servant to $15,000 for a home-based restaurant owner.

In 2002, the government began paying an average monthly bonus of $19 to 1.2 million workers (25 percent of the labor force) and awarding in-kind goods to an additional 1.5 million. The incentives were intended to deter workers from leaving strategic sectors in favor of self-employment. Armed forces personnel also receive monthly allocations of food and can purchase other goods at reduced prices. Top officials at the Export-Import Bank are fully paid in dollars. Employees in foreign-operated enterprises or joint ventures have better salaries and benefits than those in the state sector and often receive under-the-table additional monthly sums. Salespersons may receive $250 in salary; managers get as much as $700 a month plus sales commissions, an enterprise car, and 200 liters of gasoline.

Foreign hard-currency remittances are another source of inequality. In 2000, as much as 62 percent of the population received an estimated annual average of $103. Most recipients of remittances live in Havana and are white; blacks get about one-third of the average. Remittances are thus generating a more regressive income distribution and providing disincentives to work in the state sector.

The concentration of savings accounts is yet another indicator of inequality. In 1997, 66 percent of those with bank deposits had up to 200 pesos (2 percent of total savings), while 0.1 percent had deposits above 50,000 pesos (5 percent of total savings). In addition, in 2000 there were $200 million deposited in bank accounts. After the 1994 reform, taxes shifted from direct to indirect: in 2001, 56 percent of tax revenue came from indirect taxes (sales, public utilities, alcohol, and tobacco) and 44 percent from direct taxes on personal income, profits, fees, and payroll (only 2.6 percent from personal income). Indirect taxes are usually regressive. Regional inequalities have also become more marked. Havana has better living standards than the three poorest provinces (Las Tunas, Guantanamo, and Granma), which endure higher poverty and unemployment, less access to water and sanitation, and a lower proportion of physicians and hospital beds.

ALTERNATIVE POLICIES FOR THE PENDING TRANSITION

Proposed policies for coping with current social problems and those
that would occur in a transition are based on three scenarios that posit
varying degrees of economic restructuring.

Under the first scenario, the current political regime continues in
power but resumes the reforms it halted in 1996, reinstates policies that
were reversed, and implements others that were planned but not exe-
cuted. Such moves would indicate that the leadership has partly overcome fears of market reforms as detrimental to regime control. Even a
modest resumption would reflect a commitment to improving living
standards as a means of bolstering political legitimacy. As Cuban economists have argued, economic growth is imperative, and only further reforms will promote it. By 2001–2003, plummeting prices for sugar and
nickel, the effects of September 11, 2001, on tourism, and rising oil prices
combined with lagging domestic reforms had resulted in a slowdown
reminiscent of the early 1990s. This is a logical scenario for the current
regime to embrace, but the political will has been missing.

The second scenario is a socialist market economy similar to that
developed in China and Vietnam, where the impressive economic performance under Communist Party control is a win-win proposition.
Fidel Castro, however, has dismissed this model, arguing that there are
major differences between Cuba and China in terms of size, distance
from the United States, and ability to trade worldwide, considering that
Cuba is burdened by the embargo. His arguments, however, are not as
applicable to Vietnam. It is more likely that the real roots of his opposition have to do with fears that the population might develop a sense of
autonomy that could weaken or transform the regime in unacceptable
ways. The socialist market (China-Vietnam) scenario is not likely to ma-
terialize while Castro is alive and in control. After his death, it might be
the best road map for a successor regime.

The third scenario is a full-fledged transition to a market economy
and democracy similar to what took place in Central and Eastern Europe, the Baltic region, and the Commonwealth of Independent States.
Social policies and outcomes in the first two groups of former socialist
countries would be more appropriate to Cuba than those in the Com-

monwealth of Independent States. In any case, under a full-fledged market scenario, policies must be carefully designed to ameliorate the likely adverse social effects on unemployment, social services, and poverty.

Whatever the scenario, Cuba will not be able to cope with social problems, now or in the future, without macroeconomic reforms that increase GDP, output, jobs, real wages, and fiscal revenue (see chapter 7). In order to design proper policies, identify the vulnerable population, and estimate costs, the Cuban government would need to collect and analyze statistics on open and disguised unemployment, poverty and inequality, and real access to and costs of social services. The full-fledged market scenario especially should take a humane approach, balancing growth and equity, while spreading the costs of restructuring among all sectors of the population. The public needs to be engaged in an informed discussion of fair alternative social policies and their consequences, a process essential to forging consensus and building democracy.

Employment Creation and Help for the Unemployed

Under the first scenario of resumption of modest reform, employment policy is unlikely to change significantly. If the crisis worsens, the leadership would avoid open unemployment by sticking to the current policy of overstaffing, offering subsidies to redundant workers, and compensation for those who must be dismissed (as happened in the sugar sector). It could allow the private sector to expand somewhat by authorizing more occupations for self-employment, relieving some tax burdens, and easing tight regulations. Licenses and fees would almost certainly continue, and small businesses would not be authorized. Strictly regulated, cooperatives outside of agriculture might be allowed in specific activities.

In a socialist-market scenario, more substantive changes would be feasible. They would include

- expansion of productive and service activities in the private, cooperative, and mixed sectors, and introduction of competition in the state sector;
- elimination of current restrictions on self-employment, allowing university graduates to practice their professions as well as approving

small and medium-sized businesses managed by cooperatives, groups
of workers, and individuals;

- gradual reduction of state employment as the private sector creates
  jobs to absorb redundant workers;
- full autonomy for agricultural cooperatives on matters of production, distribution, and prices;
- granting more land parcels to individuals and families;
- authorization to invest foreign remittances in small businesses; and
- allowing mixed enterprises and joint ventures to hire workers directly and reward them in salaries, fringe benefits, and promotions.

All of these measures would create productive jobs, increase output and
services, and promote better living standards.

A full-fledged market scenario would embrace the above measures
and enact more radical changes, including privatization of state enterprises, setting most prices by supply and demand, establishing more
flexible rules to attract foreign investment, and granting freedom to
practice privately for all professions and occupations. Though necessary
for job creation, economic growth does not automatically assure it.
Cuba should avoid the example of CIS countries, which protected jobs
in overstaffed state enterprises, cooperatives, and public agencies; instead,
it should follow the Central and Eastern European and Baltic countries'
model of placing priority on labor productivity, the reduction of redundant labor, and the promotion of small and medium-sized enterprises—
all of which lead to higher growth. Cuba, however, would need to put
more emphasis on social policies to address the huge open unemployment that would follow the streamlining of state enterprises. Labor legislation should be amended to strengthen trade unions, empowering
them to defend workers' rights and engage in collective bargaining. Privatized enterprises should be encouraged to transfer ancillary activities
to small enterprises and thus generate new jobs and higher productivity.
Dismissals should be more flexible in order to facilitate workforce adjustment in large enterprises. A well-funded public employment service
must be established to help displaced workers, match the unemployed
with labor demand, and facilitate transportation to new locations. While
highly educated, Cuba's labor force needs retraining in view of new tech-

nologies and demand. Adult and vocational education must be expanded, and large enterprises must be given tax incentives to train their workforce.

All scenarios require special programs to keep the unemployed from falling into poverty. Unemployment insurance—a benefit paid for a set number of weeks that is based on wage level and years of work—is typical of high-income Central and Eastern European and Baltic countries. Unemployment assistance—an equal, universal benefit paid for a given period—and severance—a lump sum paid at dismissal—are found in middle- and low-income former and current socialist countries. The latter are more sensible for Cuba to start, shifting to the unemployment insurance when economic conditions improve. Whatever the program, benefits cannot be too generous or they would become financially unsustainable, and they must be made contingent on worker retraining and quick re-employment.

Coping with the Deterioration of Social Services

Since 1991, the social safety net has deteriorated noticeably in Cuba. A transition will need to cement legitimacy by mending and preserving essential social services without wavering from a commitment to finance them properly.

Education

In a 1999 survey of recent Cuban immigrants to the United States, 67 percent of respondents believed that the Revolution had improved education, 93 percent praising its being free, and 72 percent its availability for all regardless of race. Although 88 percent favored the reintroduction of private schools, 60 percent supported public education under a new government. At the same time, 84 percent considered that current education emphasizes ideology over knowledge, and 50 percent noted the drawbacks of limited classroom resources and poor job prospects after graduation. A strong public education system should be a top priority. It should be knowledge centered, devoid of political bias, efficient, competitive with private schools, financially solvent, and attuned to the labor needs of the economy. Under the modest reform scenario, no significant change in educational policies would happen, except for the incorporation of new technological demands and the allocation of more resources to vocational education. Under the socialist-market and full-fledged market scenarios, the following policies would be feasible:

- Target educational resources to favor the most vulnerable sectors of the population and the poorest provinces.
- Develop education programs that respond to economic needs and demand.
- Rationalize resources at the primary school level. Low student-teacher ratios and declining birth rates justify shifting resources to other areas in need. For example, establish an adequate wage structure for teachers in secondary and higher education.
- Make vocational education a priority.
- Improve educational efficiency, reduce drop-out rates, and establish rigorous quality standards.
- Introduce proper incentives for training technicians, agronomists, managers, bankers, and other professionals. Establish schools of business administration.
- Allow full participation of private schools at all levels under general rules set by the state.
- Establish tuition in public higher education, exempting capable poor and low-income applicants who have taken a means test.

Health Care

In the 1999 survey, 53 percent of all respondents and 72 percent of blacks credited the Revolution with improving health care. Ninety percent of all surveyed considered the health care system a great accomplishment, and 89 percent favored its preservation under a new government. A financially solvent, more efficient public health care system that provides better quality of services is, therefore, an imperative in all scenarios.

Under the modest reform scenario, the government could adopt a few measures to cut costs and improve efficiency. Low-income groups and the poorest provinces should be favored. A sustainable health care system must curb expenditures and increase revenues. Plausible measures are:

- Give priority to improving the badly deteriorated infrastructure for potable water and sanitation.
- Establish entry quotas in schools of medicine until the current glut of physicians abates; promote instead the training of nurses and other paramedics.
- Cut the overhead of the Ministry of Public Health, which is high by international standards.
- Stop investing in new physical plants and give priority to maintaining buildings and equipment.
- Convert unneeded hospitals (particularly gynecology and pediatrics units, which are the most underutilized) into old-age homes for those in need.
- Make the pharmaceutical and biotechnological industries efficient, competitive, and profitable.
- Raise revenues by taxing the salaries of physicians and other medical personnel who work under contract abroad.

The socialist-market and full-fledged market scenarios would allow the above policies, and even more daring ones. For instance, to further reduce expenditures:

- Cut the number of doctors in the public sector, authorize their private practice, and encourage the creation of cooperatives, private clinics, and hospitals.
- Reallocate scarce resources to areas in urgent need, such as basic infrastructure, prevention of contagious diseases, and import of essential medicines and prophylactics. (Funds invested in reducing the already low infant mortality, as well as in the costly and low efficient family doctor program, are prime targets for reallocation.)
- Terminate the free overseas medical aid program and fellowships for foreign students in Cuba.

- Integrate the costly, privileged scheme for the armed forces, state personnel, and top leaders of the party and the government into the general health system.

Health care services that are free, universal, and not means-tested increase costs, subsidize high-income groups, reduce the quality of services, and are financially unsustainable.

The following policies could be implemented to increase income from health care services:

- Introduce means-tested user fees and copayments for hospitals and laboratories in curative care, though not in preventive and primary care.
- Charge the full cost of private rooms to high income groups that want better quality of service (e.g., better food and air conditioning) and can afford to pay.
- Attract retired Cubans living abroad to move back and receive health care, negotiating the transfer of insurance costs with foreign governments.
- Offer large enterprises tax incentives to provide primary health care to their employees.
- Allow the private sector to offer paid services to foreigners in competition with the state sector.

Social Insurance Pensions

Whatever the scenario, the most important measure on the expenditure side is to increase the retirement age (fifty-five for women, sixty for men). One reform proposed in the first few years of the twenty-first century gradually increased the retirement age five years for both men and women over twenty years. Timid as it is, the government has yet to accept this change, and the most recent proposal does not increase the age of retirement. In the socialist-market and full-fledged-market scenarios, the retirement age could be increased to sixty-five years for both sexes, over the course of twenty years for women and ten years for men. An even more problematic cost-cutting measure would be the integration of the privileged schemes for members of the armed forces and state security into the general pension system.

Although they would reduce costs, these measures would be insufficient to meet the pension needs of a rapidly aging population. The modest reform scenario may gradually enforce the suspended worker contributions included in the 1994 tax law. In the other two scenarios, contributions should be established in all firms having a minimum number of employees: workers would contribute between 3 and 8 percent of their salaries, enterprises between 12 and 17 percent of payrolls. An alternative is to close the current pension system, make the state responsible for ongoing pensions, and create a mandatory system for younger workers, at lower costs and financed by employer and worker contributions. A voluntary supplementary pension program could be opened for high- and upper-middle income groups. Private-sector employees—formal and informal—should also be covered, some under special conditions and benefits. The minimum pension should be gradually raised, as the economy improves and fiscal resources allow.

Anti-Poverty Policies

Anti-poverty policies would reflect the tenor of means testing. Targeted social assistance to the poor—not indiscriminate subsidies to all—would be more just, improve income distribution inequality, and correct current price distortions. The modest reform scenario could, indeed, take such a step—reformist economists suggested it in the early 1990s. In 2001, the Communist Youth proposed that recipients of remittances be denied free access to education, health care, and subsidized consumer goods. Market forces would operate more freely in the other two scenarios, and thus prices for basic needs would increase significantly—all the more reason for a strong social assistance program.

The most adequate type of social assistance program for a post-transition Cuba would be those applied by the more developed countries in Central and Eastern Europe and the Baltic region. A social safety net would provide temporary income supplements to the poor that guarantee a subsistence minimum under a simple, decentralized administration. Free health care and education would also be available for the population in need.

Equilibrium between Incentives and Extreme Inequalities

Whatever the scenario, balancing growth and equity should be at the heart of economic transformation. Even in the modest reform scenario, adequate economic incentives are indispensable for promoting savings, growth, and employment. The socialist-market and full-fledged market scenarios would strongly emphasize economic efficiency and rationality; consequently, even greater inequalities would ensue. Central and Eastern European and Baltic incentives for rewarding education and risk-taking should prevail over CIS practices that encourage corruption and graft (see chapter 9). Several measures discussed above would help to reach an optimal equilibrium between the unavoidable inequalities and the pursuit of equity. Changes in tax policies would also promote such equilibrium.

Currently, indirect taxes make up 56 percent of Cuba's tax revenue and have a regressive effect on distribution. The share of sales taxes is 30 percent; they are a heavy burden on the lowest income groups and aggravate income inequalities. Taxes on alcohol and tobacco generate another 21 percent and should be kept because of their additional positive health effects. The remaining 5 percent comes from taxes on electricity, water, and phone utilities, and the first two have regressive effects. Sales and public utility taxes should be limited to the minimum necessary and replaced by a combination of a progressive personal income tax and a corporate tax. Total taxes on enterprises generate more than 35 percent of fiscal revenue: 15 percent on profits and 20 percent for social security. The tax law of 1994 failed to include a general income tax but introduced progressive taxes on inheritance and income earned abroad. And yet, less than 3 percent of tax revenue is generated by direct personal income because the enormous restrictions on wealth buildup make a sizable inheritance and the corresponding tax revenue miniscule, and the same is true for real estate taxes. Taxes on income earned abroad— mostly by famous artists and musicians—is not a significant source of revenue either. Conversely, heavy taxes imposed on self-employment, home-based restaurants, and house rentals for tourists, rather than increasing tax revenue by promoting those positive activities, have provoked their reduction. All of these activities and others not authorized today should be promoted instead of discouraged and their income taxed properly.

In the three scenarios, all residents as well as those who earn income abroad must pay income tax; it should have few rates and exemptions (those below a minimum income) and be withheld on salaries, interest, and dividends. The income tax would tackle bank savings properly by taxing interest income. Taxing remittances will be difficult due to the informal channels used, although part of that income is currently taxed in the state dollar shops at a very high rate. In the socialist-market and full-fledged market scenarios, as more consumer goods are available and private shops established, the sales tax rate should be reduced because the increase in sales volume should offset that cut. Finally, in the full-fledged market scenario, citizens could be made owners of part of the national productive capacity, in order that the privatization process achieves some degree of distributive equity.

NINE

Escaping the Corruption Curse

DANIEL P. ERIKSON

Corruption poses an insidious challenge to political legitimacy and economic growth in countries across the world. In many new democracies, the transition away from authoritarian rule has failed to end corrupt practices and even created new opportunities to harness public resources for private enrichment. Similarly, Cuba's success or failure in controlling corruption will quickly emerge as a central test for the legitimacy of any democratic government that takes root after Fidel Castro. The historical precedents are not reassuring. More than fifteen years since the fall of the Berlin Wall, Eastern Europe is still awash in graft, and Russia's economy remains distorted by the fraudulent privatization schemes that followed the collapse of the Soviet Union. Meanwhile, corruption continues to undermine democratic consolidation in Latin America and the Caribbean, and even the East Asian tigers remain mired in crony capitalism. In this context, Cuba will face formidable challenges in enforcing the rule of law during a transition period, and the legacy of misrule left by Castro and his predecessors will conspire against easy success.

Corruption has played a crucial role in Cuba's past and will remain a feature of the island's political and economic landscape in the near future. While the battle against corruption will be marked by slow progress and frequent setbacks, it need not be in vain. Cuba's chance to achieve political legitimacy and economic prosperity is inextricably linked with how deftly future policy makers can outmaneuver corrupting influences and work to strengthen institutions over time. The question facing Cuba, therefore, is not whether corruption can be quickly eliminated under a new government, but rather how to ensure that the country's future democracy is not severely or even mortally wounded by the breakdown of existing institutions, an explosion of theft of state assets, or a surge in organized crime. After more than half a century of authoritarian rule, Cuba will require new and revitalized strategies to ensure that extreme levels of corruption do not eclipse the island's democratic prospects.

CORRUPTION AND NEW DEMOCRACIES

Corruption is defined as the misuse of public office for private gain, and it occurs in all types of governments in both the developed and developing world. In countries with low levels of development and high degrees of inequality, corruption can take the form of bribery, graft, and state capture that skews state and private resources away from the poor and toward those with political or bureaucratic influence. In centrally planned economies like China, Vietnam, and members of the former Soviet Union, individuals connected with the ruling party are often positioned to reap ill-gotten gains without risking deep public scrutiny. Corruption tends to be most prevalent in countries where the government exercises greater control over economic resources, but even democratic societies often witness abuse of public property by political and private elites. It is a cruel irony that newly democratic regimes often prove no better at controlling corruption than the authoritarian and centralized governments that they replaced.

Why do new democracies struggle with corruption? While there is no single cause—or set of causes—that explains the high incidence of corruption in the developing world, corruption typically flourishes in countries with large power disparities, ineffective institutions, a weak civil society, and low levels of social capital. In theory, democratic procedures and greater transparency should curb the abuse of public office and lay the groundwork for more honest government. But the reality is not so simple. The dispersion of power within a democracy reduces the absolute authority of the state, but it also opens up opportunities for graft within a much broader range of actors, including citizens who have spent decades being disenfranchised by authoritarian governments.

Although widely recognized as a key obstacle to development, corruption remains a frustrating and elusive topic: hard to quantify, difficult to control and with relatively few quick solutions. Existing research offers great insight into the negative effects of corruption and sets forth sensible goals such as building strong institutions, establishing an effective legal and judicial system, encouraging transparency, empowering civil society, and cultivating honest political leadership. But these goals are hard to achieve, and the process of strengthening political norms and democratic accountability has been filled with setbacks, surprises, and dead ends. In many countries, the cyclical nature of anticorruption campaigns fuels public cynicism; dozens of leaders have come into high office pledging to fight corruption, only to leave tainted by their failure to make progress, or, worse, accused of corruption themselves. In Latin America, it is hardly unusual for former presidents to watch their legacies dissolve amid corruption allegations, yet even disgraced leaders often retain support and influence over the political process.

Corruption in new democracies typically takes two forms: administrative corruption and state capture. Administrative corruption, such as bribery, can occur at all levels of government, ranging from the small fee paid to expedite paperwork to multimillion-dollar kickbacks to help secure government contracts. State capture is an even more pernicious phenomenon. It allows officials and party leaders to shape the legal and regulatory environment to favor their own interests. While this was common practice in Central and Eastern Europe and the former Soviet Union when the legal system was in flux during the post-communist transition, it also occurs in developing countries in Africa, Asia, and Latin America. When the democratization process is accompanied by a visible rise in corruption, this can cut deeply into support for democratic politics and market economics and provoke nostalgia for the defunct policies of authoritarian governments. When considering corruption in post-Castro Cuba, the most relevant examples are the post-communist governments in Central and Eastern Europe and the former Soviet Union that emerged in the early 1990s, and the democratic governments that replaced military dictatorships in Latin America. Despite very different circumstances, these experiences offer important insights into the challenges that will confront Cuban democracy.

Smash and Grab: The Experience of Russia and Eastern Europe

The collapse of the Soviet Union in 1991, followed by the subsequent emergence of fifteen successor republics, ranks as one of the most significant democratic transitions in the last century. But it also demonstrates the degree to which corruption can pose deep challenges to democratic consolidation and impede economic performance. Although the transition irrevocably ruptured the fusion between public and private interests that had existed under communism, the new boundary lines between the state and the economy were often murky or poorly defined. High-level party officials—known as the *nomenklatura*—quickly moved to retain their positions of privilege and influence as the ruling oligarchs in the new system. The sudden lurch toward capitalism allowed them to ensconce important advantages for vested interests in the reformed rules and institutions. State capture in the former Soviet republics privileged key groups in both the public and private sectors through new laws, decrees, and regulatory policies.

Russia therefore presents a cautionary tale for Cuba that should not be taken lightly. Both countries share the characteristics of highly concentrated economic power, underdeveloped political systems, and a weak civil society. Today, Russian democracy continues to live in the shadow of widespread state theft and asset stripping that constituted the original sin of the region's new capitalism. In particular, Russia's experience with privatization had devastating long-term repercussions. The government of Boris Yeltsin implemented the initial stage of enterprise privatization in 1992, distributing 150 million privatization vouchers to the population for investment in state-owned enterprises at public auction. Within five years, about 130,000 enterprises had become privately-owned or stock corporations, representing nearly half of all nonagricultural entities. Yet ordinary citizens were largely excluded from the process, due to lack of information, limited transparency, and insufficient knowledge about how to pursue their ownership rights. By contrast, wily enterprise managers quickly moved to buy controlling shares in pretransition enterprises, often at far below the actual value.

Russia's second wave of privatization only deepened corruption-fueled inequality through the loans-for-shares scandal that allowed giant Russian companies to be turned over to private investors for bargain-basement prices. As collateral for bank loans, Russia auctioned off major enterprises at low prices to a limited number of bidders. When the government defaulted on the loans in 1996, a handful of oligarchs claimed the assets and were transformed into instant billionaires despite having paid only a tiny fraction of the actual value of enterprises in important sectors like oil, natural gas, and telecommunications. The Russian parliament later concluded that potential revenues for this stage of privatization were undercollected by a factor of 280. The result was that several of Yeltsin's associates became billionaires, but the country was unable to afford paying pensioners their $15 a month.

Russia's explosion of corruption produced potent disappointment with democracy, and citizens used the popular saying "the fish rots from the head" to sum up their disgust with the high-level graft that occurred. The massive enrichment of a few seemed even crueler because it coincided with a steep drop in economic output and sharply rising poverty and inequality. The poor thus suffered twice over—once when their existing safety nets disappeared and again when public resources were stolen and international assistance was misdirected. In addition, privatization was rushed because there was a total breakdown in discipline that forced rapidly assembled programs to be implemented as pre-emptive action against so-called spontaneous privatization by greedy bureaucrats. In fact, asset stripping began shortly before the fall of communism. Once the Soviet Union broke apart, the theft of state assets by enterprise managers, politicians, and bureaucrats began to unfold at an intolerable rate. Although rushed and poorly designed, state-run privatization programs quickly emerged as the only alternative to allowing state-owned enterprises to succumb to wholesale theft. While the process became somewhat more transparent and participatory, privatization ultimately failed to direct state assets toward positive social and economic goals.

In this view, Russia's roughshod privatization process served as a last-ditch measure to prevent the outright dismantling of state enterprises for no compensation whatsoever. Nevertheless, there is little question that the legacy of Russia's shock therapy has seriously undermined that country's subsequent democracy, which has faced further setbacks during the rule of Vladimir Putin since 2000. According to the Washington-based nongovernmental organization Freedom House, Russia today is "at least as corrupt as its communist predecessor," with 72 percent of Russians citing a positive view of the old regime, compared to a 47 percent favorable rating for the current government.

Central and Eastern Europe experienced a less severe economic collapse than the Soviet Union did (the region's gross domestic product, or GDP, dropped by 15 percent compared to Russia's nearly 50 percent plunge) but these new democracies suffered a similar pattern. The French novelist Honoré de Balzac coined the phrase that "behind every great fortune there is a crime," but Eastern Europeans prefer to say "never ask a man where he made his first million." In addition to flawed privatization processes, the region's corrupt and poorly managed banking system provided the lifeblood for the kleptocracies that later emerged. In its 2004 Corruption Perceptions Index, anticorruption watchdog Transparency International consistently ranked Eastern European nations at levels equivalent with many lesser-developed countries in Africa, Asia, and Latin America. For example, the Czech Republic shares fifty-first place with El Salvador and Trinidad and Tobago, and Poland and Croatia share a four-way tie for sixty-seventh with Peru and Sri Lanka. Based on surveys of international and private institutions, these measures reveal that perceived levels of corruption in Central and Eastern Europe continue to lag behind those of the developed world.

This conclusion is supported by closer analysis. In a 2001 survey of ten countries negotiating accession to the European Union—a group

that included Bulgaria, Hungary, Poland, the Czech Republic, and Slovakia, among others—trust in public institutions was dismally low. The
police were trusted by only 28 percent of the population, and that number fell to 25 percent for the courts, 14 percent for parliament, and 12 percent for political parties. Beyond profits from state capture, the World
Bank has estimated that administrative corruption accounts for 3.7 percent of firm revenues in the successor republics of the Soviet Union and
2.2 percent of revenues in Central and Eastern Europe. In countries with
the highest levels of corruption, that figure can account for 25 percent of
annual firm profits.

Indeed, the plague of corruption continues to haunt even the Central and Eastern European countries considered to have managed the
most successful transitions. In the Czech Republic, nearly three-quarters
of the population considers itself to be victims of illicit schemes perpetrated by the rich and powerful, and Freedom House reports that "receiving a government contract is considered impossible without paying
a bribe or having political connections." Slovakia, its sister republic, generally scores even worse despite increased anticorruption measures, including reforming public administration and passing criminal statutes
against racketeering, bribery, and fraud. Poland ranks lower still, notwithstanding progress in cutting red tape and raising civil-service salaries,
coupled with more aggressive investigations into government wrongdoing and new legislation against money laundering and bribery. Hungary emerges as one of the countries where corruption has been held to a
medium level, where bribes are not uncommon but not a prerequisite to
doing business. Nevertheless, Hungary's ten-person privatization agency
saw the forced resignation of eight members during the mid-1990s due
to corruption allegations in the sale of state-owned enterprises. Only tiny
Estonia and Slovenia have managed to keep corruption to more manageable levels, in part because these countries had fewer vested interests
and more developed civil societies at the time of transition.

Of course, corruption in the former Soviet bloc was widespread
long before the region moved toward a market economy, and it would
be disingenuous to blame the persistence of the problem entirely on how
the transition was managed. Under the Soviet system, midlevel bureaucrats generally benefited from the system of patronage that provided

better schooling, private houses, and greater access to food and medi-cine. Still, to many citizens the comparatively discrete corruption of the Soviet era seems almost quaint compared to the ostentatious windfalls that materialized for the oligarchs during the transition. The wave of de-mocratization provoked multiple changes with contradictory effects on corruption levels, but the shift toward a market-oriented economy in-disputably created lucrative new opportunities for graft. The very process of reducing state intervention in the economic sphere was managed by a state controlled by the very vested interests that it was supposedly seek-ing to extirpate. The experiences of the former Soviet Union and Central and Eastern Europe demonstrate how failure to control corruption can leave lasting scars on the democracies that emerge from the ashes.

A Crisis of Trust: Latin America's Captured States

Latin American democracy emerges from very different political and social roots than the former Soviet bloc, but endemic corruption con-tinues to pose a major problem for democratic governance. Of course, there are important distinctions. Central and Eastern Europe and the former Soviet Union have been indelibly marked by the massive wave of corruption that accompanied the collapse of communism because it distorted the foundations of their new societies during a time of great hope and expectation. By contrast, Latin American societies have expe-rienced greater continuity between the corruption that existed under authoritarian governments and what persists in new democracies. In Mexico, for example, corruption has been described as "the oil and the glue" that provides a useful way of bridging the gap between idealistic laws and the management of daily life. Today, conflicting views of cor-ruption are evident throughout the region; according to the United Na-tions Development Programme, nearly 42 percent of Latin Americans say they would be willing to tolerate a certain degree of corruption "pro-vided things work." In 2002, however, the respected Chile-based Latino-barómetro polling organization found that citizens ranked corruption only behind unemployment as the region's most pressing problem. Worse, 80 percent of Latin Americans believed that corruption had risen over the previous year, and 71 percent regarded civil servants as corrupt.

While many Latin American leaders have pledged to combat corruption, few see this as a central challenge for strengthening democracy. Instead, corruption is primarily viewed as an economic or legal problem. When the United Nations Development Programme conducted round-table discussions with regional leaders in Latin America for an influential 2004 report on democracy, corruption ranked at the bottom of issues they felt had to be tackled in order to strengthen democracy. Only social policy was seen to be less important to democracy, while nearly half selected either political reform or party-related institutions as the top priorities. Still, concern about illegal practices and the criminal influences of drug trafficking, money laundering, and contraband remained high, and one high-level official commented that "drug traffickers buy off everyone and everything—judges, border guards, police, entire institutions. It is an aggressive, anti-democratic and terrible power that even succeeds in electing its own representatives to Congress and other bodies."

In fact, Latin Americans appear to feel that corruption will be an ongoing feature of the political landscape. In the 2004 Latinobarómetro poll, more than half of all respondents believed that corruption would either never be eliminated from their countries or it would take much longer than twenty years to disappear. More than 20 percent of those polled said they experienced corruption directly during the previous year, despite the fact that only 16 percent said they would pay or negotiate a bribe to expedite an important procedure—and 60 percent said they would denounce an official who requested a bribe. In every Latin American country surveyed, at least 20 percent of respondents thought that it was possible to buy off a police officer, judge, or ministry official, and this belief was expressed at levels approaching or exceeding 50 percent in Mexico, Paraguay, Argentina, and Ecuador. Other regional studies have shown that the negative effects of corruption can be especially pernicious for the poor. In surveys of Bolivian and Honduran citizens, exposure to corruption has been found to be much more widespread in urban than in rural areas. This is a general trend throughout Latin America, and it reflects the fact that government is often more present in the cities than in the countryside.

But Latin American corruption extends far beyond administrative graft to include levels of state capture that in some cases rival post-communist countries. In a survey of international executives conducted by the World Economic Forum in 2003, Latin America ranked second out of nine regions—ahead of Eastern Europe and behind only the former Soviet Union—in terms of perceived state capture as defined by excessive or illegal influence of powerful firms and individuals on state policy making. As the World Bank noted in a 2004 study, state capture has long represented a pernicious trend in Latin American countries. Prominent examples have included the personalistic rule of the Somoza dynasty in Nicaragua or Alfredo Stroessner in Paraguay, and the corrupt *partidocracia* (partyarchy) that ruled Venezuela until the end of the 1990s. Although these powerful cliques and families have given way to electoral democracy in every country in the hemisphere except Cuba, their legacy of concentrated wealth and influence continue to hinder democratic governance.

Indeed, any examination of corruption in Latin America and the Caribbean yields a litany of woes. In Argentina, former President Carlos Menem faced charges that he approved the illegal sale of arms to Croatia and Ecuador in the 1990s in violations of UN weapons bans, and the U.S. Commerce Department has reported that "government corruption and private sector business fraud are common complaints [and are] a significant problem for trade and investment." Brazil witnessed the resignation of former President Fernando Collor de Mello amid corruption charges in the early 1990s, and more recently President Luiz Inacio Lula da Silva weathered a corruption scandal that erupted in 2005, shaking his ruling Workers' Party to its foundations and imperiling his presidency. Mexico's deep-rooted graft continues to be a significant factor in that country's politics. The government of Vicente Fox investigated the apparent transfer of $170 million from the state-run oil company Pemex to the former ruling party during the 2000 election. In addition, the brother of former President Carlos Salinas was prosecuted on corruption and murder charges.

In Transparency International's 2006 global survey of 163 countries, only Chile, Barbados, and Uruguay cracked the top 50 least corrupt countries, while Ecuador, Venezuela, and Haiti all ranked with the bottom 30 most corrupt countries. In addition, the Latin American and Caribbean region boasts three of the ten most corrupt leaders worldwide based on their estimated stolen wealth. Jean-Claude Duvalier of Haiti is estimated to have stolen $300 to $800 million from 1971 to 1986, and he is joined by Alberto Fujimori, who allegedly took $600 million during his ten-year reign in Peru, and Arnoldo Alemán, who emptied $100 million from Nicaragua's treasury between 1997 and 2000.

Despite notable democratic progress, Latin American societies are haunted by a lack of trust that fuels corruption and depletes the collective value of all social networks in a given society that would otherwise facilitate improved governance—known as social capital. As in much of East Asia and Africa, social capital in Latin America primarily exists within a narrow circle of family and personal contacts instead of extending more broadly to other citizens, as occurs in the more developed societies of Europe and the United States. Far from transgressing social rules, corrupt officials in many countries are responding to societal expectations that helping family and friends takes precedence over protecting the general public interest. An unhealthy byproduct is that stealing from public officials on behalf of one's family—or abusing the public trust to steal from strangers—is culturally reinforced because a lower standard of behavior is required in the public sphere. In this sense, the *doble moral*—or double moral standard— that permeates Cuban society is an extreme version of a common cultural malady in Latin America.

The negative economic effects of corruption have been widely documented, but the shift from authoritarian regimes to democracies has contradictory effects that can expand opportunities for corruption in some areas while reducing it in others. Furthermore, institutional reforms that do not help to reshape underlying cultural patterns are unlikely to achieve much progress. The economist and Nobel Prize laureate Amartya Sen argues that without building a new standard of behavioral norms, organizational reforms are not enough to eliminate corruption. He sees corruption as part of a cyclical pattern that can be either reinforced or reversed through a combination of political institutions and leadership. "Just as the presence of corrupt behavior encourages other corrupt behavior, the diminution of the hold of corruption can weaken it further. In trying to alter a climate of conduct, it is encouraging to bear in mind the fact that each vicious circle entails a virtuous circle if the direction is reversed." In Central and Eastern Europe, Russia, and Latin

America, newly democratic societies are still struggling to overcome the political and economic distortions sown by corruption.

THE CHINA EXAMPLE: HIGH CRIMES AND MISDEMEANORS

Concern about Cuba's potential loss of state authority sometimes prompts analysts to argue that Cuba should follow China's path toward economic reform in the hope that this will lead to greater political liberalization. While this prescription may have some merits when compared to the damaging privatization reforms that were carried out in Central and Eastern Europe and the former Soviet Union, a closer assessment reveals that China is hardly a model worthy of emulation in the sphere of anticorruption. Instead, China's market socialism has failed to erect proper boundaries between official power and private markets, leaving the government unable to address corruption except by mobilizing the repressive instruments of the state. Before China started down the path of market reform, corruption did occur, but party apparatchiks also held themselves in check to avoid a crackdown by party authorities. Official power could be withdrawn at the leadership's discretion, and civil servants were hesitant about overreaching and perhaps losing access to the system of perks and preferences. But that level of discipline has broken down over the last decade, allowing corruption in China to soar to previously inconceivable levels.

At China's Fifteenth Party Congress in October 1997, Chinese Premier Jiang Zemin declared that the "fight against corruption is a grave political struggle vital to the very existence of the party and the state." In 1998, the People's Liberation Army was stripped of its commercial operations by the ruling party. The military's participation in economic affairs had simply become too worrisome for high officials; the divestiture was apparently prompted by the disproportionate corruption of a half-dozen military-controlled companies, including pervasive oil smuggling that was debilitating China's oil monopolies. While the army was allowed to continue engaging in some productive activities, it was prohibited from any commercial activities such as trade, tourism, and telecommunications. According to one China analyst, the move resulted in the transfer of almost three thousand firms owned by the People's Liberation Army and People's Armed Police to local governments, while nearly another four thousand were shut down. Yet the army continued to work in vital sectors, including civil aviation and railways. The divestiture did incur political costs, including bruising conflicts over the disciplinary measures to be taken for cadres alleged to be involved with profiteering and smuggling. According to the *Far Eastern Economic Review,* at least twenty-three company executives at the rank of major general or above fled the country following the divestiture. The anticorruption charges have deepened a rift between China's military and civilian leadership. Military corruption has moved from an extremely dangerous problem to a serious but manageable matter of discipline.

Rather than attempting to eliminate corruption entirely, China's cyclical anticorruption campaigns appear intended to control it at an acceptable level. While the revealed rate of corruption appears to have leveled off, available data indicate that the intensity of corruption rose dramatically in the 1990s. For example, while only 652 cadres at or above the county level were charged with economic crimes in China in 1992, that number rose to 2,670 in 2001. At the same time, cases of ordinary corruption appeared to decrease over that same period. Thus, China's levels of corruption experienced a qualitative shift during the 1990s, during which time more high-level cases involving much greater sums of money proliferated, even as reported instances of lower-level corruption remained static or even decreased.

China has attempted to address these developments through periodic anticorruption campaigns, but these have proven a weak substitute for regular policing. Instead, they represent an attempt to control corruption using fear and uncertainty, generated through random arrests, humiliation, and public denunciation. Instead of striving to implement the rule of law on a regular basis, China appears to have a chosen episodic anticorruption crackdowns as the cornerstone of its efforts to contain corruption.

The inadequacy of these measures recalls the ancient Chinese saying that "the mightiest dragon cannot crush the local snake." In early 2005, China was hit by a wave of bank robberies carried off by branch managers and corrupt company executives. At the Bank of China, a branch manager embezzled $100 million and subsequently vanished. Other commercial banks suffered from a rash of insider theft, including $8 million that was stolen from the China Construction Bank and a conspiracy discovered at another commercial bank to steal nearly $1 billion. The head of China Construction Bank resigned after it was discovered that he accepted a bribe of $1 million from Alltel Information Services. Government investigations have found that billions of dollars have been robbed from state-owned companies. The country's banking and financial systems have simply been unable to impose enough financial safeguards and controls to ensure that the investment fueling the country's growth does not get illicitly siphoned off by corrupt parties. The consulting firm McKinsey & Company estimates that China's state-run banks had bad loans of $204 billion in 2004. Chinese officials estimate about $8 billion was pilfered from state-owned enterprises in 2003, and at least two dozen government officials in China have been sentenced to death for corruption in recent years. In the final analysis, China's plague of corruption will worsen as long as the rule of individuals trumps the rule of law, and personal connections are the only available antidote to the hidebound communist bureaucracy.

CUBA AND CORRUPTION: DEFINING THE PROBLEM

Corruption in contemporary Cuba shares some characteristics that exist in centrally planned economies and throughout Latin America and the Caribbean. During the first thirty years of Fidel Castro's regime, Cuba exhibited many of the dysfunctions evident in the old Soviet Union—such as a complex web of patronage and negligible economic liberalization—combined with some of the small-scale bribery and graft that exists throughout Latin America. But Cuba differed from the rest of the region in that the 1959 Revolution permitted Castro to evict the island's previous oligarchs and rule in their place. This system remained intact until the early 1990s, when the dissolution of the Soviet Union forced a new economic reality onto Cuba. Faced with a collapse in its international trading partners and a resulting 35 percent drop in GDP, the Castro government was forced to make several economic changes with far-reaching consequences for Cuban society. As the Cuban government orchestrates the inevitable transition away from Castro's rule, effectively combating corruption will remain essential to the legitimacy of the new regime.

In 1993, the legalization of U.S. dollar holdings in Cuba created a dual currency system that fueled previously unheard-of levels of income inequality in the communist system. The search for foreign direct investment and the subsequent opening of the tourism industry dramatically increased the levels of foreign currency that were entering the state-owned enterprises. Self-employment was allowed in a limited number of categories such as personal services and private restaurants, but severe scarcity forced much of the Cuban population into the underground economy to earn dollars illegally in both traditional activities and illicit behavior such as prostitution. These changes inverted the supposedly socialist norms of Cuban society, transforming Cuba's "normal" if regrettable socialist-style corruption into a deeper cultural and economic malaise.

In today's Cuba, survival for much of the population entails living outside the law. This creates multiple obstacles to any useful discussion of corruption because the very term inserts the type of stealing, trading, and "inventing" prevalent in Cuba into a moral context that its citizens would not recognize. Hewing closely to the political and economic explanations that define corruption in the developing world, there are several areas where Cuba is more corrupt and others where it is less so. Cuba suffers from two extreme maladies: abuse of power and state capture. After nearly fifty years at the helm of Cuba's political system, Fidel Castro and the Cuban Communist Party retain near total control, thereby limiting the possibility of citizen appeal against arbitrary or unjust government action. In addition, the Cuban government's command over economic resources has transformed the island into the most captured state in Latin America. In recent years, even Cuba's tiny private sector has become increasingly besieged by higher taxes, stricter licensing requirements, and more punitive fines for small infractions. On the political level, of course, this power manifests itself in the iron-fisted efforts to ensure that Cuba's independent political movements are divided and weakened and, in many cases, their leaders incarcerated. In Castro's fiefdom, the state and party tolerates no economic or political rivals, but it is permitting a system of special advantages to evolve for the country's ruling elites.

The prevalence of abuse of power and state capture in Cuba leads to a third area of corruption: the theft of public goods and the creation of thriving black markets that many Cubans depend on for access to basic resources. Faced with low salaries paid in Cuban pesos and the high costs of goods available in dollar stores, many Cubans engage in prohibited entrepreneurial activities that would be legal in most market-oriented countries. By the late 1990s, the stark disparities introduced by the legalization of the U.S. dollar had shattered the egalitarianism that had existed in Cuba's society during the Soviet bloc years, when the basic relationships among wages, incomes, and prices were the same for the majority of citizens. In the aftermath of this adjustment, corruption in Cuba metastasized from a primarily government-driven phenomenon into a societal affliction that forced ordinarily law-abiding citizens to steal, buy, and sell goods in the island's black markets as a means of survival. For example, when Cuba's fisheries reported a 10 percent drop in their 2002 catch from the previous year, large-scale mismanagement, corruption, and petty theft were cited as the main factors. Similarly, the president of the Cuban Postal Company, Juan Marañón Depestra, has conceded that mail from abroad is regularly subject to theft. At present, this type of corruption in Cuba has become so routine that the public is becoming immune to scandal. Interestingly, early in his tenure as the provisional president of Cuba, Raúl Castro permitted the official state publication *Juventud Rebelde* to undertake an investigation of corruption in Cuba in the fall of 2006 that opened a limited public debate on how systemic corruption is undermining the island's socialist ideals.

It is tempting to aggregate these facts into an indictment of the Cuban system as hopelessly and irretrievably corrupt, but not all the evidence points in this direction. According to the Transparency International index of corruption, for example, Cuba consistently ranks in the top half of all countries worldwide and in the middle of the pack for Latin America and the Caribbean. In the 2006 Corruption Perceptions Index, Cuba ranked sixty-sixth out of 163 countries—tied with Belize and Grenada and ahead of Brazil, Mexico, Peru, the Dominican Republic,

FIGURE 9.1   Changes in Cuba's Governance Indicators

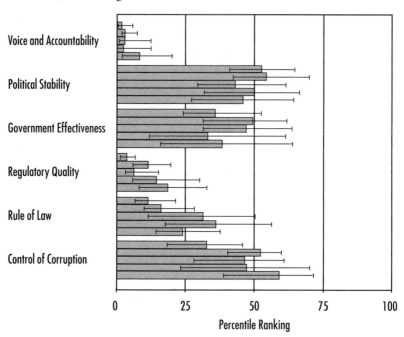

Source: World Bank Governance Research Indicators Database. The data are from 2004, 2002, 2000, 1998, and 1996 in order from top to bottom.

and fourteen other countries in the region. Officials from development agencies in Canada, the European Union, and the United Nations consistently rate Cuba as an effective partner for implementing foreign aid programs, despite the fact that Castro's pugnacious diplomacy has made several countries reconsider their assistance. European governments have also praised Cuba for its counternarcotics efforts, and even U.S. officials have grudgingly admitted that the Castro government has been a useful partner in stemming the flow of drugs through the Caribbean. While administrative corruption in Cuba is not uncommon, it has hardly reached the heights seen in China.

Figure 9.1 shows that the comprehensive World Bank Governance Research Indicators have charted a significant drop in Cuba's quality of governance between 1996 and 2004. Trend lines since 2002 are negative in all six measurable categories, but the eight-year comparisons demonstrate a net improvement in political stability and government effectiveness accompanied by a decrease in regulatory quality, rule of law, and control of corruption. The voice and accountability category, which measures political and civil rights, also declined from its already low 1996 levels.

Cuba's downward shift in governance is noteworthy because the global data for this period reveal no discernible trend in the quality of governance worldwide; the island ranks among the mere 10 percent of countries that showed a statistically significant change during those eight years. Interestingly, Cuba's apparent deterioration occurred at a time when the Castro government has demonstrated an increasing preoccupation with controlling corruption within its ranks. Of course, corruption has been a feature of life in Cuba throughout the twentieth century, including the years since the Cuban Revolution. Cuba's First Party Congress in 1975 discussed the problem of small-scale corruption at the municipal level, and in 1989 Cuba witnessed the execution of the once-respected General Arnaldo Ochoa for alleged corruption and drug trafficking. In the mid-1990s, Cuba organized a special commission to fight corruption, headed by General Armando Quiñones of the Ministry of the Interior. But Cuba's limited economic liberalization during the 1990s produced a new set of challenges that have fueled reports of internal graft, especially through the sectors open to foreign direct investment and in the cash-flush tourist industry. It is unclear whether Cuba's recent anticorruption measures reflect a real concern for eliminating corruption, the Cuban leadership's desire to tightly control the country's finances, or the micromanaging tendencies of the Comandante. Whatever the motivation, Cuba's focus on controlling internal corruption has generated new policies and institutions to limit the authority of state-owned enterprises over their hard-currency accounts.

Since 2001, Cuba has taken a number of steps to strengthen internal financial oversight of state-owned enterprises and the larger population. In 2001, the government established a Ministry for Auditing and Control to oversee enterprise transactions. The following year, the new minister, Lina Pedraza, remarked that "there are cases of corruption . . . that occurred because officials managed economic operations and others because they managed resources," and she pledged to help maintain discipline over the island's inventories and crack down on practices such as double-billing and false contracts. In 2002, the Cuban government confiscated nearly 250 houses, imposed 1,900 fines, and removed more than 30 public officials from office to crack down on illegal activities in the housing sector, including unsupervised house swaps and home purchases, and improvements made without authorization. In July 2003, the government prohibited state-owned enterprises from conducting dollar transactions domestically and instituted new controls for all international purchases exceeding $5,000. By the summer of 2004, the Cuban Politburo was reported to be visiting local branches and warning against corruption within the government. At the time, a video was circulated that quoted Raúl Castro warning against corruption in the tourist sector, saying, "Corruption will always be with us, but we must keep it at our ankles and never let it rise to our necks." According to Western news sources, an internal report showed that 219 of 593 audits found serious instances of corruption, especially in the tourist sector.

In October 2004, Cuba's Central Bank passed Resolution 80 stipulating that all cash transactions must now be performed using convertible pesos, commonly referred to as *chavitos*. Shortly after the dollar-exchange deadline was announced, Cubans lined up in surprising numbers to trade-in hard-earned dollars and cherished cash gifts from relatives in the United States. Within two weeks, an estimated half a billion dollars poured into the Cuban government's coffers. Although a devaluation of the convertible peso was widely feared, Central Bank President Francisco Soberón declared, "It would be extremely unwise to change the one-to-one exchange rate after the Cuban people have shown such confidence in the Cuban government." But Cuba also stopped short of criminalizing private U.S. dollar holdings, as was the case prior to 1993, and it later raised the value of the peso by 7 percent against the dollar.

Potentially destabilizing corruption scandals have been nipping at the government's heels for some time. In late 2003, one such episode at the major state-run tourism agency Cubanacán led to the ouster of its president and several high-level managers. Shortly thereafter, Cuba's Council of State summarily dismissed Minister of Tourism Ibrahim Ferradaz García, installing a younger military colonel to oversee the island's main cash-earning sector. In the summer of 2004, responsibility for tourism was shifted from economic czar Carlos Lage to Raúl Castro,

Fidel's brother and loyal deputy who heads the armed forces. Raúl Castro explained the move by declaring that the tourism industry was like "a tree born twisted that must be uprooted and planted anew." In October 2004, Castro fired Marcos Portal, the Minister of Basic Industries who had been one of the closest members of his inner circle. Portal frequently negotiated crucial investment deals with European and Canadian multinationals, and he was one of the leading figures of Cuba's "capitalism." Dismissed shortly before the dollar phase-out, Portal was publicly reprimanded for disagreeing with "more experienced colleagues." The purges continued in 2006 when Juan Carlos Robinson, a leading figure in the Politburo, was fired for abuse of power.

Cuba's dollar crackdown appeared to be an effort to rein in the capitalist impulses of the government. Since 2005, the Cuban regime has become increasingly aware of high-level corruption within its own ranks, fueled by the large amounts of U.S. currency funneling through the island's more than four hundred state-owned enterprises. Reasserting central authority over the dollar sectors within the Cuban government has emerged as a leading concern for Fidel Castro. Additional mechanisms were installed to monitor all overseas trade, and dollar payments have been centralized into a single account in Cuba's Central Bank. In January 2005, Cuba's Central Bank established a sole account for all dollar revenues and formed a Hard Currency Approval Committee to monitor all cash transfers involving state-owned companies. The heady days of wheeling and dealing in large dollar sums between Cuban enterprises have effectively ended, and now all significant transactions occur under the watchful eyes of the Castro brothers. At an economics conference in February 2005, Castro blasted "self-financing in foreign currency," the now-forbidden practice of allowing Cuba's state enterprises to manage large dollar accounts. It had to end, he declared, because "A great many middle managers came up, and began committing serious enterprise mistakes and errors. Some very good people ended up in bad conditions when we had nearly 3,000 people working with funds and foreign currency." In other words, corruption had rooted inside the Cuban government, and draconian measures had to be taken.

As a result, the Cuban military has taken on an increasingly prominent role in the island's economic affairs, with important implications for the future. In 2005, Castro increased the military budget to $1.5 billion, which represents 6.5 percent of total government expenditures. The Cuban Armed Forces have moved aggressively into the tourism industry, and this has provided access to needed hard currency. Military-operated agricultural enterprises do give soldiers access to greater levels of food distribution than is available to the population as a whole. There is little question that the military has benefited disproportionately from market reforms, but this has left the Cuban army increasingly vulnerable to charges of corruption and resulted in a corresponding loss of prestige.

Other institutional practices could be perceived as corrupt. For example, Cuba appears to be seeking greater knowledge about the free-market system, and many officials and academics have worked or studied in capitalist parts of the world. Government agencies like Cubatécnica have initiated the practice of exporting hundreds of business managers to work in capitalist firms abroad, although such training is limited to top intelligence officers and individuals with strong ties to senior members of the government. This is consistent with Cuba's widespread patronage system, whereby Communist Party linkages are required for ascending professionally in Cuba's institutions, and connections also facilitate access to housing, televisions, automobiles, and travel abroad. At the local level, citizens who volunteer for the neighborhood watch groups called Committees for the Defense of the Revolution sometimes receive Panda-brand televisions assembled in China or other imported items that may not otherwise be accessible.

Cuba's anticorruption measures highlight the challenges facing the country's eventual democratic transition. Until his failing health forced him to surrender power on a provisional basis in July 2006, Fidel Castro had become accustomed to arbitrarily setting the boundary between what kind of corruption is allowed and what kind merits official rebuke. High-level party officials who attempted to straddle that line often found that it could shift suddenly and without warning. In order to preserve their privileges and their status, those who manage power within the Cuban government have had to cultivate a sense of where that line is headed. Nevertheless, corruption in the upper echelons of the party is believed to have moved beyond merely mitigating shortages to achieving levels of wealth that far surpass the average of Cuba's ruling elites. Although the underground economy remains a significant factor in Cuba, the external sector has become the nexus for access to massive revenues. Fidel Castro, not surprisingly, has invoked comparisons with the United States as a defense against corruption, stating, "None of our leaders is a millionaire like the president of the United States, whose monthly wage is almost twice that of all the members of the Council of State and Council of Ministers in a year." Castro has also denounced his neighbors in the region as "neoliberal friends in Latin America who are Olympic champions of misappropriation and theft since the few who do not steal from the public coffers and state taxes steal from the poor and the hungry." In the meantime, fueled by high nickel prices, a booming tourism sector and new investment by China and Venezuela, the Cuban economy is clawing its way out of the abyss that followed the Soviet Union's demise in the early 1990s. Yet Cuba's paradigm of excessive government intervention, widespread low-level corruption and severe internal controls will pose a paradox for a successor regime.

NEW REGIME, NEW THREATS

While the task of minimizing corruption will be central for any post-Castro government in Cuba, in many ways the potential for a democratic transition will multiply the unknowns. If the Cuban government plots a managed transition from above, Cuba could avoid some of the problems that plagued the privatization process in post-communist countries, but it could also encounter the more extensive problems being experienced today in the market-oriented socialist regimes of China and Vietnam. Democratization by definition disperses power within a much wider range of groups and can extend the range of actors who can demand payment for their role in the decision-making process. At the same time, the possibility that Cuba's communist government will quickly devolve into a weak state unable to maintain control over its territory raises the specter of institutional breakdown at a moment when large sums of foreign assistance will be entering the country.

Another concern is that Cuba is at the hub of a major drug-transit route through the Caribbean that could fuel new problems such as

narcotics-related corruption and money laundering. Cuba's geographi-
cal position will inevitably force the island to confront the same threats
of transnational crime that affect many of its neighbors. Cuba is located
in a direct air and maritime path from South America to Florida, and
speedboats from Jamaica frequently transport hundreds of kilograms
of marijuana through Cuban and Bahamian waters to the United States.
Indeed, the Caribbean region as a whole remains particularly vulnerable
to corruption according to Transparency International, and Belize, the
Dominican Republic, Jamaica, Trinidad, and Tobago were among a small
group of countries with a recent perceived increase in corruption. Significant amounts of cocaine continue to enter the United States from the
Caribbean, estimated at 160 metric tons in 2001. Although this is less
than half of the amount that entered annually during the 1980s, traffickers
have increasingly penetrated the Caribbean, and the percentage of cocaine exports from the region to the United States rose from 29 percent
in 1990 to 48 percent in 2001. The total trade balance for drugs in the
Caribbean is estimated at $3.45 billion, which represents about 3.4 per-
cent of the region's GDP—a greater proportion than that of other drug
source and transit countries in the Western Hemisphere. But Cuba is
thought to play a far less significant role in the drug trade than its neighbors. For example, in the 1998–99 fiscal year, the U.S. Drug Enforcement
Agency estimated that only 1.85 metric tons of cocaine entered the United
States via Cuba. By contrast, the Dominican Republic's estimated cocaine flow was greater by a factor of three, and Jamaica's was larger by
a factor of eight. The Bahamas and Haiti ranked by far as the largest
transit countries in the Caribbean, with an estimated 32 metric tons and
53.9 metric tons respectively.

Money laundering—the process of hiding, transferring, and investing the revenues from criminal activities—is another powerful source of
corruption that often accompanies the drug trade. The Organization for
Economic Cooperation and Development–sponsored Financial Action
Task Force on Money Laundering estimates that global money laundering accounts for 2 to 5 percent of world economic output. Money is
easiest to catch when it first enters the banking system, but it is harder to
trace over time or as revenues are funneled through multiple accounts.

Criminal enterprises also utilize shell companies, which have no operations except to produce invoices. Though far from the dominant force in money laundering, offshore financial centers, such as the Bahamas or Cayman Islands, have tax structures that favor illicit transactions. Tracking money laundering will become more complicated as the rise of the euro provides an alternative for illegal dollar holdings.

In 1999, an estimated $50 billion in criminal revenues was funneled through Caribbean financial institutions. Money launderers increasingly target the Caribbean, taking advantage of its proximity to major U.S. and Latin American markets, the relative sophistication of its financial industry, and the presence of the booming drug trade. In a 2004 report, the Inter-American Development Bank estimated that money-laundering transactions accounted for between 2.5 and 6.3 percent of the GDP of Latin America and the Caribbean. Six of the top ten countries for money laundering through both bank and nonbank channels are located in Latin America: Argentina, Colombia, Haiti, Paraguay, Nicaragua, and Bolivia.

Cuba has been perceived as an effective counternarcotics partner and has implemented agreements with the Bahamas, Colombia, Mexico, and Venezuela, as well as the United Kingdom and some other European governments. In 2005, the U.S. State Department released a counternarcotics strategy document reporting that the Cuban Central Bank has regulations in place to investigate suspicious transactions and trace large deposits. The Cuban government has also requested training in combating money laundering from Canada and European governments including England, France, and Spain. In 1999, its National Assembly criminalized money laundering related to arms smuggling and drug trafficking; it criminalized terrorist financing in 2001. Not surprisingly, the island's tight currency reporting requirements and state-run banking sector provide a powerful deterrent to money laundering, and the Cuban government's strict internal surveillance has also kept the narcotics trade significantly at bay when compared to other countries in the region. But maintaining this discipline will be a difficult task for a democratic government unless the capacity of the existing institutions can be maintained under the rubric of a free political system.

COMBATING CORRUPTION: THE QUEST FOR GOOD GOVERNANCE

Given the enormous stakes for the future of Cuban democracy, controlling corruption will inevitably emerge as a central priority for the country's future leaders. Yet the available evidence on corruption offers few quick solutions for countries that are transitioning to a more pluralistic political system. The World Bank has estimated that corruption costs the global economy about $1.5 trillion a year—about 5 percent of its total value—but offers few concrete recommendations for reversing the pull of corruption. Popular ideas, such as improving civil service pay or establishing anticorruption watchdogs, often fail to achieve measurable results in practice. Wide-ranging media awareness campaigns have more often than not failed to curb corruption, and anticorruption workshops that focus on journalists or members of Congress similarly have little to show in the way of success. While strong political leadership at the top can help to curtail corrupt practices, there is no way to guarantee that these types of leaders will emerge through the democratic process. Even well-intentioned politicians are often thwarted by entrenched interests and the lack of tools at their disposal. State capture thrives where economic power is highly concentrated, social organization is weak, and the political system is not sufficiently developed to mediate competing interests in accordance with the law. In Cuba, where corruption has become a powerful social phenomenon, the task facing a democratic government will prove even more challenging.

The likely involvement of foreign donors will further complicate the picture. The United States has already promised a large amount of aid to a democratic government in Cuba and will encourage international financial institutions like the Inter-American Development Bank, the International Monetary Fund, and the World Bank to follow suit. The U.S. Agency for International Development (USAID) has begun to prioritize anticorruption efforts in its worldwide activities, dedicating $222 million to programs targeting corruption in 2002 and establishing anticorruption programs in two-thirds of USAID missions overseas. The resources diverted by corruption also threaten U.S. security interests by fueling illegal trafficking in people and goods, and terrorism and organized crime. Still, large levels of foreign aid can spur corruption, as competing social groups attempt to extract maximum benefits from the largesse of foreign donors. This occurred in Central and Eastern Europe and the former Soviet Union, and the Asian Development Bank estimates that more than one-third of all public sector investment in East Asia succumbs to corruption. Against this backdrop, Cuba will be hard-pressed to avoid repeating the cycle.

On the international level, the Cuban government should actively engage with the existing treaties and mechanisms that have evolved to fight corruption in the inter-American system and at the global level. The Organization of American States has developed the Inter-American Convention Against Corruption, first adopted in 1996, which calls for parties to reform their legal codes to combat bribery, promote interstate cooperation to fight corruption, and implement measures to register the assets of high-level public officials, monitor government procurement systems, and deter graft within publicly-owned companies. In 1997, this was followed by the Inter-American Program of Cooperation to Fight Corruption, and a follow-up mechanism was developed to monitor and review the countries' performance in April 2001. The UN Convention Against Corruption promulgated in December 2003 should also be joined by Cuba. While treaties alone are a poor substitute for wise domestic policy making, they will help Cuba to better enlist international support for the battle against corruption. Closer to home, Cuba's accession to the Caribbean Financial Action Task Force would allow it to work with its neighbors to limit money laundering and other types of financial corruption.

In the final analysis, however, the effort to contain corruption will only be successful if there is steady progress on improving Cuba's quality of governance across the board. Since corruption represents a failure of governance, a focus on adapting and strengthening government institutions will be essential. The democracies that suffer the most damaging levels of corruption are often the ones that opened the system politically while failing to address the regulatory, legal, and bureaucratic obstacles that fuel graft. Improved transparency and greater political freedom must be accompanied by judicious regulatory reforms and changes in the legal structure to permit the development of a market-oriented economy. The current Cuban government's efforts to impose strict financial oversight could provide an important advantage to a democratic government by creating systems that can help to monitor usage of funds and ensure that corruption is kept to a minimum. In a scenario where the communist government takes steps to reform itself out of existence, maintaining professional oversight of the enterprise and banking system can help forestall the asset stripping that occurred during transitions in other parts of the world. The process of political and economic decentralization will have to be well managed. In the case of Central and Eastern Europe and the former Soviet Union, short-term winners in the reform process are also able to leverage long-term political influence to maintain the distortions that enabled them to profit handsomely at the time of transition.

More difficult but equally important will be the tasks of rebuilding citizen confidence in the state and restoring the social capital that has become depleted since shortly after the 1959 Revolution. Cuba will require a viable tax system to help maintain social spending, but a distrustful population may result in high levels of tax evasion, as has occurred elsewhere in Latin America. Effective capitalism requires a legal structure to support it, and Cuba will need to substantially reform the legal sector, which is presently designed to settle disputes in ways that further the goals of socialism. Cuban democracy requires respect for judicial review, which gives judges the power to decide whether government actions are consistent with the country's Constitution. A strong judiciary can help combat corruption and abuse of power.

In the short term, it appears that Cuba will experience a communist succession after the passing of Fidel Castro, but the recent history of Latin America indicates that democratic forces cannot be forever kept at bay. When democracy eventually moves to the forefront of the island's political agenda, Cuba's future leaders can take comfort in the fact that, on balance, poor democracies are less corrupt and better governed than poor authoritarian regimes. Nevertheless, corruption cripples democracy, and it has to be addressed systematically, not merely tactically. Tackling corruption will require policies that target the underlying cause: a society that is thoroughly lacking in social trust. By proceeding wisely and with greater transparency, Cuba's policy makers can remove barriers to democratic freedom and market reform that can restore vital trust in public institutions. It would be optimistic to expect that a democratic Cuba could eliminate corruption in the short term. Strong political leadership and steadfast international support, however, can help the island to achieve better governance—an important antidote to corruption and a worthy goal in itself.

TEN

The Émigré Community and Cuba's Future

LISANDRO PÉREZ

The life and death of Jorge Mas Canosa provide a fitting symbol for the relationship between Cuban émigrés and their homeland. For nearly two decades, until his death in 1997, Mas Canosa was the most influential émigré leader, attaining a political stature that had no precedent and thus far has not been replicated in the exile community. He transformed from a foot soldier in the shadowy world of anti-Castro activism during the 1960s and 1970s to the undisputed leader of a political organization that took the struggle against the Cuban regime into the spheres of legitimate political action: campaign contributions, lobbying, information dissemination, and advertising. Mas Canosa's Cuban American National Foundation fought Fidel Castro the American way, following the playbook of organized single-issue constituencies that have long exerted inordinate influence in Washington, from the halls of Congress to the White House itself.

Mas Canosa cultivated the image of the exile who had the ear of members of Congress, Cabinet secretaries and even the president of the United States. His organization successfully lobbied for legislation and executive orders designed to tighten the U.S. embargo on Cuba and to create radio and television stations that would spread the antiregime message to the island. Mas Canosa's successes led many of his followers and sympathizers (both inside and outside the exile community) to elevate him to the rank of statesman, a sort of president-in-exile. Only half-heartedly would he disavow assertions that he would be the next president of Cuba.

The day after his death at the age of fifty-eight, a woman called in to a Miami Spanish-language radio program in honor of Mas Canosa and asked this rhetorical question: "How many Cuban exiles who longed for, and even struggled for, the liberation of their homeland, have died, as has Mas Canosa, in this foreign land without realizing their dream and setting foot once again in a free Cuba?" The answer is tens, if not hundreds, of thousands. But it is not the answer, but the question, that is important, for it expresses the unmet expectation that is at the heart of the ethos of Cuban exiles and of all exiles: the recovery of the homeland.

Mas Canosa's life and death bring together that ethos. He embodied the expectation of not only returning to the homeland but also of recovering it—indeed, of governing it. Even if many rejected his anointment as the next president of Cuba, the very expression of it was a reflection of the exiles' perception of their role in Cuba's future. On the other hand, his death was a sobering reminder of the unmet aspirations of exiles. In fact, stretching back to the nineteenth century, many Cuban émigrés have died in a foreign country without realizing the dream of recovering the homeland. This, too, has been a constant of the Cuban émigré experience.

In contemplating the future of Cuba and the many possible outcomes of a transition from socialism, one of the many factors to consider is the role that Cuba's émigré community may play in that transition. Are the exiles' aspirations of recovering the homeland likely to be realized? Will exiles play a role in Cuba's future? Or will the Cuban diaspora essentially fade away while Cuba undergoes a transition without them?

ÉMIGRÉS AND THE HOMELAND: THE CUBAN HISTORICAL TRADITION

Throughout the country's history, Cuba's émigré communities have played an influential role in the destiny of the homeland. Émigrés, especially those in the United States, lent a decisive hand in developing the foundations of the Cuban nation and launching the modern Cuban state. Their role became part of the island's political culture and serves as a legacy for contemporary Cuban exiles who seek to recover the homeland. It is a tradition that has shaped how those exiles define themselves and their role as players in the island's future. In considering a transition in Cuba, that historical tradition is perhaps more important than any foreign model of change.

The second half of the nineteenth century was the decisive period in the creation of the Cuban nation. Those decades saw the development of the intellectual, cultural, political, and military currents that led to the end of Spanish rule and the establishment of the Cuban republic in 1902. The leaders, texts, symbols, ethos, goals, traditions, and even legends of that long separatist movement became the core of the identity of the Cuban nation in the twentieth century. All subsequent political movements aspiring to legitimacy, including the one that resulted in the present government, have invariably claimed to be trustees of the values and purposes of that formative independence movement.

Except for military campaigns, the bulk of the separatist activity of the nineteenth century took place outside of Cuba, especially in the United States. Virtually all of its significant figures at one time or another lived in the United States—some for short periods, others for most of their adult lives. New York and Philadelphia became the centers of émigré intellectual and political leadership, with popular support from workers in the Florida cigar-making communities.

Even the military actions waged inside Cuba were usually organized, launched, and financed from outside the country. The outfitting of expeditions carrying arms and men to Cuba became the principal activity of the émigrés. In the end, Cubans who had lived abroad, some of them U.S. citizens, occupied most of the highest positions in the first administration of the Cuban republic.

Spanish rule and repression and the wars for independence that started in 1868 and 1895 created sizable émigré communities. The leaders who launched the rebellion of 1868 immediately sent representatives to the United States to raise funds among their compatriots, outfit expeditions, and lobby for a favorable U.S. stance toward the insurgents. Those representatives were elites, most of them scions of powerful and wealthy families who sacrificed everything for the homeland and typically died before returning home, never seeing their aspirations realized. They were active in the United States as spokespersons, lobbyists, and agents on behalf of the rebel army.

The final war for independence, which started in 1895, brought an even greater role for émigrés in the affairs of the homeland. In contrast to the previous conflict, this rebellion was launched not from within Cuba but from the United States as a result of the organizational efforts of one man, José Martí—the most important figure in the pantheon of Cuban heroes and nation builders. Martí lived in New York for fifteen years, and from there he painstakingly assembled a political party and an army, which he took to Cuba in 1895. He died on a battlefield shortly thereafter. In other words, the most influential figure—indeed, icon—of Cuban history, the man who successfully organized the most significant rebellion against an entrenched regime in Havana, was an émigré.

The importance of that example in establishing a model and tradition for émigré political action cannot be overstated. A successful replication of the model, of course, was carried out in 1956, when the rebels of the 26th of July Movement, led by Fidel Castro, launched an armed struggle from Mexico that was successful in toppling the regime of Fulgencio Batista three years later.

The leader of that 1956 expedition is still governing Cuba. As for the 1895 rebellion, those émigrés who survived it rose to the forefront of the political ranks after the departure of the Spanish. At least six of the nine appointees of Leonard Wood (the U.S. military governor of Cuba from 1900 to 1902) as members of his "Cuban Cabinet" were men who had lived in the United States and carried out much of their revolutionary activity outside of Cuba. Several, in fact, were U.S. citizens. When the United States ended its occupation on May 20, 1902, Wood turned over the administration of the island to a Cuban government headed by Tomás Estrada Palma, a U.S. citizen and Martí's successor as the head of the Partido Revolucionario Cubano in New York, who had been the headmaster of a school in the Hudson Valley for most of the previous three decades.

The post-1959 Cuban exiles who have spent decades struggling to recover their homeland are, therefore, drawing from a successful and venerable tradition of émigré activism. It is not surprising that after this much time, the dream of accomplishing a regime change and influencing Cuba's destiny remains alive. It is the historic Cuban émigré project. It is this autochthonous tradition, and not foreign models, that has been most decisive in shaping the role that Cuban émigrés assign to themselves in relation to their homeland.

THE POST-REVOLUTIONARY CUBAN DIASPORA

Approximately 1.4 million persons of Cuban origin or descent live outside the country. Of those, 1.2 million live in the United States. Nearly two-thirds of Cubans in the United States were born in Cuba. In other words, most Cuban Americans are first-generation immigrants, reflecting the fact that the largest waves of migration from Cuba have taken place since 1959. About 60 percent of all U.S. Cubans live in South Florida, despite the efforts of the Cuban Refugee Resettlement Program (CRRP) of the U.S. government. From 1961 to 1978, the CRRP, which sought to alleviate the pressures of the Cuban influx on Miami, resettled more than 300,000 persons away from southern Florida. Almost from the beginning of the program, however, many began making their way back to Miami, a city that is today the undisputed Cuban American capital and the main stage for the political activism of Cuban émigrés. Most of the analysis in this chapter is applicable primarily to Cubans in the United States and, especially to those in Miami, although it is recognized that the Cuban diaspora is not limited to those locations and populations.

The Dominant Political Tradition

Since the Revolution, the relationship between Cuban émigrés and the homeland has generally been characterized by distance and hostility. Lack of communication and contact, isolation, mutual suspicion, distrust, intransigence, and conflict have featured prominently. The leadership in both Havana and Miami has maintained and reinforced these problems, with the support of significant sectors of their constituencies. Although considerable and diverse contact between émigrés and the island has developed since the 1980s, these connections are still viewed, regardless of their magnitude, as the exception rather than the norm.

To understand how distance and hostility came to prevail in the relationship between Cuban émigrés and their homeland, one must go back to the early days of the Cuban Revolution. The leaders of the Revolution projected themselves as trustees of a tradition of social justice, nationalism, and anti-imperialism that predated the country's independence in 1902 and manifested itself in various nationalist movements that rose and fell throughout the first half of the twentieth century. Those movements, which were usually frustrated, sought to curtail the growing and pervasive U.S. influence in Cuba and to assure a better distribution of wealth, especially by closing the wide gap between urban and rural Cubans. The rise to power of the forces that opposed the Batista dictatorship was seen as a victory for this nationalist agenda, and the new government wasted little time in acting to fulfill those expectations.

From 1960 to 1964, Cuba underwent a radical transformation into a country with a centrally planned economy, no private sector, and a government ostensibly guided by Marxist-Leninist principles that had close ties with and was largely dependent on the Soviet bloc. The measures taken against U.S. economic interests, the implementation of a drastic wealth distribution program, and the emerging authoritarian character of the regime put the government of Fidel Castro on a collision course with both Washington and Cuba's upper socioeconomic sectors.

But early opposition to the revolutionary leadership did not come exclusively from the elites. The new order was seen by many Cubans as an intolerable overstepping of the traditional nationalist agenda. Consequently,

the United States and the elites were joined in their opposition to the
regime by other sectors of Cuban society (many of whom had earlier
supported the Revolution) such as students, organized labor, the Catholic
clergy and lay religious organizations, and anti-Communist and pro-
democracy groups.

The conflict was most intense between 1960 and 1962, during which
time the U.S. government and many Cubans cooperated in various
attempts (including the unsuccessful Bay of Pigs invasion) to overthrow
the Cuban government. During that period, many in the opposition opted
for exile. The approximately 300,000 Cubans who left during those years
were marked by the experience of having lost the struggle against the
new regime. Yet they have never abandoned the struggle and have maintained the goal of recovering the homeland. Émigrés who arrived in subsequent waves were not as evidently marked by that early struggle for
power. To this day, virtually all the political leaders of the Cuban American community, those involved in the leading émigré organizations, are
of that 1960–62 generation of Cuban emigrants.

That the émigrés have kept alive their struggle during all these years
should not be surprising, given that the basic outlines of that early conflict still remain in place: a socialist-inspired government headed by
Fidel Castro, a U.S. policy that seeks to topple the regime through hostility
and isolation, and an exile leadership—in collusion with Washington—
that continues to oppose the Cuban government.

The émigrés' opposition to the Castro regime has a number of political and ideological manifestations that have been at the center of the
political ethos of the contemporary Cuban diaspora. Among them are
the primacy of affairs of the homeland over domestic (U.S.) issues in
the émigrés' agenda; a tendency to use the Cuba issue as a litmus test in
evaluating candidates for local political office; an overwhelming preference for the Republican Party; and emotionalism and intransigence as
predominant features of the political discourse.

The strategies that Cuban émigrés have used to carry out the struggle
have varied over the years from outright violence and belligerence to
peaceful methods such as lobbying, informational campaigns, and electoral politics. Much of that activity is now carried out within the context
of U.S. policy toward the island, with efforts to maintain, and even

tighten, the measures taken by the United States to isolate the Cuban regime economically and politically. Lobbying by Cuban Americans, especially the Cuban American National Foundation (CANF), was largely responsible for the establishment of Radio Martí and TV Martí, which broadcast to Cuba. Cuban American efforts played a critical role in the passage of the 1992 Cuban Democracy Act (the "Torricelli Act") and the 1996 Cuban Liberty and Democratic Solidarity (Libertad) Act (the "Helms-Burton Act"), both of which tightened the U.S. embargo. In fact, the émigrés' increasing influence through the ballot box in the 1980s and 1990s, representation in Congress, and lobbying constitute the principal force that explains the lack of change in U.S. policy toward Cuba.

The influence of Cuban émigrés was further enhanced in recent years by the pivotal role of the Florida—and specifically the Cuban American—vote in the 2000 presidential elections. Bill Clinton had made significant inroads in capturing Cuban American support in the 1996 election, receiving about 36 percent of their vote—a high percentage for a Democratic candidate. But in 2000, the candidacy of Al Gore was hobbled in its effort to attract the Cuban American vote by the saga of Elián González. The well-known story of the little boy who was rescued near the Florida coast by the Coast Guard on Thanksgiving Day 1999 culminated less than seven months before the presidential election with the raid by U.S. immigration officials on the home of the child's Miami relatives. That forcible action, which returned the boy to his father and soon thereafter to Cuba, was carried out by the Clinton administration after an emotional struggle by many in the Cuban American community to keep the child in the United States. The entire Elián affair made clear that the legacy of the traditional exiles was very much alive. While the exiles lost the fight for Elián, they extracted a measure of retribution by voting overwhelmingly for George W. Bush in 2000, contributing to his narrow yet determining victory in Florida.

The results of that election led to an administration in which several Cuban Americans played prominent roles, from the Cabinet, where Mel Martínez was secretary of housing and urban development, to the State Department, where Otto Reich was chosen to be the administration's top official in Latin American matters. With the support from the traditional leadership of the Miami community, these influential Cuban Americans pushed the White House to take an even more aggressive and hostile stance toward the Castro regime in anticipation of the 2004 election. The result of their efforts was the Report of the Commission for Assistance to a Free Cuba (CAFC), or Powell Report, officially issued in 2004. It proposed a set of subsequently adopted regulations for reducing the flow of dollars to Cuba by restricting travel and remittances. These regulations primarily hurt post-1980 émigrés who—in contrast to those of the 1960s—have family on the island. The CAFC report also offered a blueprint for the future of Cuba, one that reflected the traditional exile aspiration of a profound change on the island, followed by externally directed reconstruction of its institutions and infrastructure. In the summer of 2006, just in time for the congressional mid-term elections, the White House issued its endorsement of a new installment of the CAFC report, this time coauthored by Secretary of State Condoleezza Rice and Commerce Secretary Carlos Gutierrez, a Cuban American. In this update of the 2004 report, the Bush administration announced a "Compact with the Cuban People" that reaffirms the commitment of the U.S. government to play an active role in a Cuban transition. It also pledged increased funding for "strengthening democratic movements."

Although it had been anticipated that the political tradition of hostility and isolation toward Cuba within the émigré community would start abating with the passing of the original exile generation of the 1960s, it is evident that this generation and its legacy continue to exercise a dominant force on U.S. policy. It has not, however, gone unchallenged. In the past decade, sectors of the community have exhibited more moderate positions and have sought greater contact with Cuba.

Changes within the Cuban Émigré Community: The Rise of Moderation and Contacts with the Island

The search for moderate émigré alternatives to the traditional exile vision of hostility and isolation began in the years when the Carter administration pursued a policy of cautious rapprochement toward the Cuban government. In 1978 and 1979, various individuals and groups within the community engaged in contacts with the Cuban government. Spearheaded by émigrés such as Lourdes Casal and Bernardo Benes, those efforts resulted in the beginning of family visits to the island by Cuban Americans. More intensive contacts were fomented by young Cuban Americans who returned to the island under the sponsorship of organizations such as the Brigada Antonio Maceo and the Institute of Cuban Studies, émigré groups that in different ways promoted the growth of cultural and intellectual ties between Cubans outside the country and those inside.

Years later, the fall of the Berlin Wall had a particular effect on the political landscape of the Cuban community in the United States. Cuban exiles who had long struggled to do what had not been done previously—overthrow an entrenched socialist regime—now had in Central and Eastern Europe an operational model of how such a feat might be accomplished. Rather than the overnight rupture scenario traditionally envisioned by the exiles, the new model involved an evolution that might be led by elements from within the system, a process that could be helped by openness, rather than hostility, from the outside. Consequently, some Cuban Americans, including some traditional hardliners, began to promote the relaxation of tensions with Havana and to engage elements within Cuba. The rise of this new orientation led in the 1990s to the establishment of several organizations that, in different ways, conceptualized anti-Castroism in more moderate terms, espousing an elimination of hostility and emphasizing constructive relations with the Cuban government. These new organizations were committed to a peaceful, gradual transition to democracy.

One of the first such organizations was Cambio Cubano (Cuban Change), which was led by Eloy Gutiérrez Menoyo, a veteran of the anti-Batista struggle who later organized military operations against the Castro government. Menoyo served a prison sentence of more than twenty years and moved to Miami after his release. His unimpeachable credentials in the anti-Castro struggle gave him high visibility and a measure of legitimacy when he started advocating peaceful political alternatives for Cuba in the 1990s. His initiative paved the way for other groups to advocate a similar line of constructive rapprochement. The Cuban Committee for Democracy is one such group. It has attempted to provide an alternative voice, especially in Washington, to the more conservative elements within the Cuban diaspora, even advocating for lifting the embargo.

With the broadening of the ideological spectrum of Cuban-exile politics, new voices rose to argue against a continuation of U.S. policy. Although they have thus far failed to gain predominance, they have served to challenge what had been a monolithic image of exile politics by providing support for initiatives that diverge from the traditional course of U.S.-Cuba relations.

Perhaps an even greater challenge to the continuation of a policy of isolation toward Cuba have been the visits of émigrés to the island and the increased immigration from Cuba to the United States. Cuban Americans whose only motivation is to visit and help family and friends on the island represent a major point of contact between the two countries. Remittances and family visits provide Cuba with more foreign exchange than its tourism industry, with estimates ranging between $500 million and $800 million annually.

The 1994 and 1995 migration accords between the United States and Cuba raised the ceiling for Cuban migration to the United States. Since then, some 20,000 Cubans have legally migrated to the United States each year; a smaller number enter the country in other ways. This new influx has served to increase the number of Cubans with an interest in sending remittances and returning to visit relatives. Unlike the earlier migration wave, which departed at the height of the Cold War and has sought to keep the anti-Castro struggle alive, newer arrivals are likely to place their priority on communicating with their families still in Cuba. Numerous polls have shown that newer arrivals and newer generations are more likely to favor softer approaches to dealing with Cuba in comparison to the earlier exiles, who are much less likely to have family there.

The threat posed by these new arrivals has not gone unnoticed by émigrés with a hard-line view. While the traditional discourse favored economic isolation, remittances from recent émigrés were becoming one of the island's leading sources of foreign revenue. The CAFC report is a response to that contradiction. Through their access to the White House, the more traditional émigrés have attempted to minimize the economic impact of the new arrivals on the island's economy. For their part, it is likely that many Cuban Americans will find a way around the new regulations in order to continue visiting and sending money to their family members in Cuba. One obvious corollary of this situation, however, is a greater fragmentation of the émigré community along the fault lines of class, ideology, and generation.

While there is a dominant discourse of hostility and isolation toward Cuba within the émigré community, there is evidence of increasing pluralism, moderation, and a growing number of personal contacts between exiles and the island, a trend that will continue despite efforts to curtail it. In assessing the role of that community in a transition, however, it is important to go beyond political dimensions and look also at the economic characteristics of the diaspora. Depending on the scenario of change, the émigrés may be more likely, at least initially, to have an economic role, rather than a political one, in the future of Cuba.

The Economics of the Cuban Émigré Community

It is a frequently repeated sentiment that although Cubans have been unsuccessful as exiles because they have failed to recover the homeland, they are very successful as immigrants. That is, they have succeeded in making an excellent economic adjustment in their new countries. Although the degree of that success has frequently been overstated—and little attention is paid to the growing income disparities within the Cuban diaspora, especially in the United States—it is the case that, overall, Cubans are an atypically successful population of immigrants, especially considering that they attained that success within the span of one generation.

The Cuban success story is the result of the emigration of much of the upper sectors of pre-revolutionary Cuban society, shortly after the triumph of the Revolution in 1959. This created a migrant population that was high in human capital, which translated into a competitive advantage that soon become most visible in Miami, where, by the late 1970s, Cubans were building one of the foremost examples anywhere of a true ethnic enclave. Characterized by highly differentiated entrepreneurial activities, enclaves further the social and economic position of members by providing dense networks for advancement, all within a familiar language and culture. In the case of Cuban Miami, many of the entrepreneurial activities have been in sectors of the local economy with high growth potential: professional services, international commerce, construction, and real estate development. In all those sectors, Cuban émigrés have accumulated both experience and capital as proprietors and managers.

The differences in wealth between the diaspora and the population of Cuba have already affected the island's economy through the remittances and visits of émigrés. This phenomenon, in virtually any transition scenario, is likely to become both more extensive and intensive. The émigré community, especially in Miami, is engaged in economic activities that will complement the needs of a Cuban economy moving in the direction of liberalization and market mechanisms.

These, then, are the highlights of the Cuban émigré experience in anticipation of a transition in Cuba:

- There is a rich historical tradition of émigré involvement in the homeland's affairs, including a role in changing the regime in Havana and in shaping the political destiny of the island.
- The post-1959 émigrés have maintained a deep and abiding interest in all matters related to Cuba and its future.
- That interest has been most evident in the pursuit of political strategies designed to isolate the Cuban government, thereby reducing the contact between the island and the United States and hence the contact between Cuba and its diaspora.
- Since the 1990s, the émigré community's distance from Cuba has been reduced significantly by family visits and remittances to the island, to the point that such contacts now represent important social and economic factors in Cuban society.
- Regardless of the transition scenario, it is likely that the wealth disparities between island and diaspora will lead to the expansion of the émigrés' economic influence in Cuba, especially in those sectors in which the exiles have accumulated significant business experience and capital.

It appears, therefore, that the émigré community is poised to exert a significant force on Cuba's destiny. The nature, manner, and extent of that force will be shaped by the dynamics of the transition process. Before exploring how different transition scenarios are likely to shape the role of Cuban émigrés, we should see whether the experience of other transitions may inform the Cuban case.

ÉMIGRÉS AND POST-SOCIALIST TRANSITIONS

In the transitions throughout Central and Eastern Europe during the early 1990s, it is difficult to find a case in which émigré communities wielded a significant influence. This is especially true if one is looking for evidence that émigrés played a role as catalysts for change. Without exception, and despite the various modes of transformation, the European transitions were not induced by any external pressures that were exerted directly or indirectly by their respective émigré populations. In fact, those transitions offer models that run counter to the scenario traditionally favored by Cuban émigrés. Rooted in Cuban history, that traditional model views émigrés as agents of change through strategies of hostility and isolation.

In the European transitions, the external pressures for change came instead from worldwide forces favoring political and economic liberalization from which regimes could not isolate themselves. In some cases, in fact, the governing elites *opened* their societies to such influences, sealing their own fate. In other words, across the spectrum of the transitions, change occurred in Soviet-controlled Europe through openness, not isolation, and it was led by internal political agents, not émigrés.

There is another possible dimension for émigré participation in a transition, and that is in building a post-socialist political, social, and economic order. But even in that process the record in Europe is spotty. The European transitions did not include organized efforts by émigrés to implement particular social, political, or economic programs. In other words, groups or communities of expatriates did not influence the direction of transitions through organized, concerted efforts. Individual émigrés who returned, or sought to return, to their homelands frequently were engaged in one of three types of activities: as candidates for, or appointees to, political or administrative offices; as entrepreneurs or investors in the nascent private sector; and in the recovery of assets lost at the time of the imposition of socialism. Generally, these efforts have had mixed results. In the political sector, for example, no returned ex-patriate has thus far reached the highest levels of public office.

Despite the paucity of examples in Europe in which émigré communities played a role in the transitions from socialism, there is one case that merits attention because of its many parallels with the Cuban case: German reunification. The divided German nation—one side a former socialist nation-state within the Soviet bloc, and the other side a democratic country with a prosperous market economy—faced the challenge of building a unified future. Cuban émigrés do not constitute a nation-state, but they have successful economic institutions and wield political influence in the United States, and their island compatriots will be facing challenges somewhat similar to those faced by the German Democratic Republic (GDR, East Germany).

The German experience during the 1990s holds a number of lessons that should be taken into account in anticipating the émigré factor in the Cuban transition. There was an overall lack of mutual understanding that led to miscues and conflicts. The West Germans operated from a superior economic position in relation to the East Germans. This led them to think that they would be in control of the reunification process, and their actions under that assumption were perceived by East Germans as arrogant and condescending. Polls showed that negative stereotypes abounded. The East Germans tended to view the "Wessies" as more confident and disciplined but as more self-centered, overindulgent, and smug, and also materially wealthy but spiritually impoverished. For their part, West Germans saw the "Ossies" or "Zonis" as lazy, unwilling to work hard, and preferring to have things "handed to them."

These stereotypes proved prickly in the reunification process. East Germans wanted to keep features of their former government such as full employment, income equality, subsidized housing, and utilities. West Germans were more than annoyed and were soon reeling from the costs of reunification, especially increased taxes. The resolve of many West Germans soon weakened, and an ambivalent approach-avoidance conflict with the East quickly spread. The passion for reunification had been lost.

Another contentious issue was that of properties confiscated since World War II by the GDR. East Germans were alarmed by the prospect of West Germans returning to claim their former homes. Uncertainty ensued, and the issue of confiscated properties represented one of the most important obstacles to the economic reconstruction of East Germany, stalling business creation and new investment. The property issue became much more complex than originally anticipated, involving also Polish concerns about possible German claims over the eastern lands Germany lost at the end of the war, as well as the prewar confiscations of Jewish properties by the Nazi Aryanization laws of the 1930s.

Resolution took a long time and failed to meet the expectations of all concerned parties. The basis for it was a 1990 compromise agreement between the two Germanys that was appended to the unification treaty. The pledge to return confiscated properties to their original owners was balanced with a determination to reach a "socially acceptable compromise" in settling conflicting claims. In the end, only a fraction of the more than a million claims for restitution actually resulted in the return of the properties to the claimants. Ultimately, the authorities involved in the adjudication of the claims were unwilling to take properties away from more recent owners who had legitimately acquired them under GDR laws many years before. Observers wondered if Germany's long-term interests would have been better served by bypassing the property issue altogether or taking a less conflictive approach such as compensation.

Despite its shortcomings, the attempt to deal with property issues in a just manner was part of a larger German commitment to resolve the concerns of the past in the reunification process. To that end, charges were brought against former East German officials for crimes committed during their time in office, especially the officials and collaborators of the Ministry of State Security (Stasi). Many of those brought to justice were convicted, but their sentences were relatively light or eventually reduced. For the Germans, the process of seeking justice was more important than the severity of the punishment.

Weighty political, economic, and justice issues were not the only concerns that threatened the delicate process of reunification. There were also social and cultural differences to be resolved between the two Germanys. For example, the debate in the Bundestag on the unification treaty turned acrimonious when East and West Germans tried to reach a compromise on different national traditions with respect to women's reproductive rights.

German reconciliation and reunification were achieved, but the process proved to be a conflictive and unpredictable one that holds lessons for the future relations between the "two Cubas."

There are at least two Asian experiences that merit a brief mention here. Arguably, both China and Vietnam qualify as post-socialist despite the absence of regime change because they have implemented sweeping market-oriented reforms. As was the case with post-socialist Europe, those reforms were not initiated by pressures or programs imported from their respective diasporas. Rather, the leadership made the decision to move toward market reforms. But once those countries opened up to foreign investment and entrepreneurship, émigrés capitalized on their familiarity with the language and culture of their homeland to initiate business ventures there. This has been more widely reported in the case of China than of Vietnam.

ÉMIGRÉS AND POLITICAL CHANGE IN POST-AUTHORITARIAN SOCIETIES

Are there any transitions from authoritarian regimes that can provide some clue as to the role émigrés could have in the future of Cuba?

One case that is close to Cuba, culturally and historically, is that of the émigrés from Francisco Franco's Spain, many of whom lived their exile years in Cuba and had to wait for decades until Franco's death to return to their country. The post-Franco democratic institutions permitted the participation of expatriates in national political life and many of them were instrumental in the establishment of the Socialist Party, which eventually took the reins of government. In the larger scheme of things, however, the expatriates' role was almost negligible.

Post-Sandinista Nicaragua offers yet another model. Like the Cubans, many Nicaraguan exiles settled in Miami. After the electoral transition from Sandinista rule, many returned home, though they maintained close ties with those who remained in Miami. In the post-Sandinista transition, the issue of confiscated properties became important and, as in the German case, was resolved to no one's satisfaction.

Two recent cases involving the end of authoritarian rule are also noteworthy because, though geographically and culturally far from Cuba, they are close to the Cuban historical experience of émigrés having a prominent role in homeland affairs. Unlike all the examples previously offered, the United States was involved militarily in ending the regimes in Afghanistan and Iraq and is now deeply engaged in shaping post-regime institutions. In both cases, expatriates returned riding American coattails and played prominent political roles in reconstruction administrations controlled by the United States.

LOOKING TO THE FUTURE

Predicted levels of émigré involvement according to various scenarios are presented in table 10.1. But first a word about the table itself and some of its assumptions. The labels in the last column on the right (letters A through F) are intended only for ease of reference. The table crosses economic and political scenarios with the nature of the transition (peaceful vs. conflictive) and the presence or absence of the embargo. Obviously, the table does not present all possible combinations of those factors. It only presents the plausible combinations of scenarios. For example, the model assumes that the minimum change required for a process of transition would be the onset of economic liberalization. Hence, all modalities in column 1, "economic scenarios," are "yes," which means, of course, that the model does not regard as plausible the onset of democratization prior to economic liberalization.

The model does allow for the possibility—perhaps unlikely, but nevertheless plausible—that during a peaceful transition the embargo could remain in effect for a meaningful period of time, depending on how the United States assesses the changes. The Helms-Burton Act of 1996, for example, has a detailed set of requirements that must be met before sanctions are lifted. Hence, the table allows for the possibility of a peaceful transition occurring while the embargo is in place.

A conflictive rupture scenario is understood as a sudden and drastic change in the political order that sweeps away the status quo and leads

TABLE 10.1 Probability of Émigré Involvement in Cuba's Future, according to Different Scenarios of Change

	Economic Scenarios	Political Scenarios		Probability of Émigré Involvement		
	Economic liberalization and market oriented-reforms	Establishment of democratic institutions	Direct U.S. involvement	Economic involvement	Political involvement	
Peaceful transition with embargo	yes	no	no	low	low	A
	yes	yes	no	low	medium	B
Peaceful transition without embargo	yes	no	no	medium	low	C
	yes	yes	no	high	medium	D
Conflict/rupture without embargo	yes	yes	no	high	medium	E
	yes	yes	yes	high	high	F

immediately to the start of economic liberalization and democratization. Political convulsions that do not lead to market reforms nor to a
transformation in the nature of the political system are not included
in the table. Because the break with the past would be clearly defined
(unlike a gradual transition), it is likely that the United States would not
delay in lifting sanctions. It is therefore assumed that the changes that
result from rupture will occur without the embargo.

Consequently, the rupture scenarios have only two modalities:
with or without direct U.S. involvement. The involvement of the United
States is defined as a military-administrative one, as in a protectorate, in
which the changes are largely under Washington's control. It could come
about either from a direct U.S. action that leads to the conflict, or an intervention after an internal conflict provided the opportunity of a U.S.
involvement—ostensibly to restore order. The cases of 1898 Cuba and
contemporary Iraq and Afghanistan are the prototypes of this model.

Émigré involvement can take two possible forms: economic and
political. Economic involvement is understood to be the participation
of émigrés in the island's economy as investors, entrepreneurs, venture
capitalists, and any other form of economic activity that would bring
them into the economic life of the country. The return of Chinese and
Central and Eastern European entrepreneurs to their respective countries are examples of how such involvement can occur. Political involvement, as happened in post-Sandinista Nicaragua and in the early Cuban
republic, is the rise of expatriate participation in governance at the highest levels.

Two major considerations influenced the judgments about the likely
level of émigré involvement under the various scenarios. One is that, of
course, émigré economic involvement will necessarily be low while the
embargo remains in effect. The other is that political involvement is seen
as less likely than economic involvement. This is based on the assumption that there will be greater resistance on the island to that type of
involvement than there will be to economic participation, especially in
those scenarios (A through E) that are initiated by Cubans living in
Cuba. Only in scenario F, with direct U.S. involvement, is there the high
probability of expatriates assuming significant political roles. On the other
hand, the probability of economic involvement is high in scenarios D

through F because they combine the absence of the embargo with economic liberalization and democratization.

A medium probability level reflects the uncertainties inherent in some of the scenarios more than anything. In scenario C, for example, the absence of democratic institutions, which implies the continuation of the present regime, is likely to lead to restrictions on, or at least make uncertain, the economic entry of expatriates, even with economic liberalization and the lifting of the embargo. Democratization, however, will not necessarily lead to a high probability of émigré political involvement, as reflected in the medium level for political involvement in scenarios B, D, and E, despite both economic liberalization and democratization. Expatriate political participation may be restricted or even disallowed by the very legal instruments that establish those democratic institutions.

Pessimism regarding émigré political involvement in Cuba's future is a major, and arguable, conclusion based on the factors discussed in this chapter. Only on the coattails of direct U.S. intervention is political involvement likely to happen. Under this scenario, the process of reconciliation would be long and difficult, especially in institutional terms. The German experience is not encouraging.

In the Cuban case, the long decades of hostility and isolation have served to drive a wedge of suspicion and incomprehension between the island and its diaspora. While it is true that the émigré community has always fought to recover the homeland and sees a role for itself in the island's future, it is also true that it has disassociated itself from the process of revolutionary change and has, therefore, not been involved in the island's development since 1959. On the contrary, with their support for policies of hostility and isolation, expatriates have largely been typecast as antagonists, eager to return only for the spoils, for the restitution or compensation of long-lost properties and, generally, for a return to the institutions that existed before the Revolution.

While such stereotypes may be unfair or simplistic, they will shape the climate of future contacts, particularly in scenarios of peaceful and gradual transition in which those on the island are likely to retain control. Suspicion of the motives of exiles and resentment over their role in maintaining Cuba's isolation during so many years may lead to restrictions on their degree of involvement in the future political and, to a lesser degree, economic systems of Cuba. A sliver of optimism, however, can be gleaned from the experience of contact and family visits that began in the 1990s. Those encounters have served to reduce the distance between island and diaspora and have contributed somewhat to dispelling the stereotypes about the émigrés. It is an experience that confirms the strength of Cuban society and culture in the area of interpersonal relations and therefore bodes well for the future once the barriers to isolation are removed and interpersonal contacts become pervasive. The flight time between Miami and Havana is only forty-five minutes.

ELEVEN

Ideology, Culture, and Memory

Symbolic Dilemmas of the Cuban Transition

RAFAEL ROJAS

Any approach to the history of contemporary Cuban culture must consider the great transformation produced by the revolutionary triumph of 1959 and the subsequent establishment of a Marxist-Leninist regime. That change produced not only a new social order and a new set of practices, values, discourses, and customs, it also marked a break with the island's intellectual framework, creating new attitudes of adherence, rejection, and other subtle forms of symbolically processing the conflict. Traditionally, the schism in Cuban society and culture in the second half of the twentieth century has been conceptualized according to dual opposing categories: Revolution vs. counterrevolution, Castroism vs. anti-Castroism, communism vs. anticommunism, nationalism vs. annexation, socialism vs. liberalism, totalitarianism vs. democracy. In a reflection of Cold War thinking, these identities—ideological, political, or sentimental—have been conceived as polarized camps, based on the assumption of two symmetrically divided and homogeneous sides.

After decades of fragmentation, it is only natural to expect the emergence of a range of intellectual and political strategies for resolving or managing the conflict. These strategies, whether more or less effective, must overcome not only the intransigence of the two opposing sides but also their tendency to gloss over or deny the schism. In this context, it is worth pointing out that complex theories for addressing the dilemmas of Cuban intellectual life from 1959 to the present have little chance of epistemological success if their goal is to sublimate or suppress those dilemmas. Since the early 1960s, Cuban culture has experienced a rupture, with ideological and political identities playing a decisive role in the break. It is an undeniable fact that at the conflict's symbolic level, Cuban cultural and political actors have mobilized themselves according to subjective realities: revolutionary and nationalist, liberal and socialist, democratic and authoritarian.

Instead of avoiding the dilemma, an attempt to displace it conceptually may allow us to understand the behavior of actors whose identities are less rooted in ideology. The notion of civil war could contribute to a recasting of the dilemma that may facilitate its conceptual displacement, even if it doesn't neutralize it. A civil war is the polarization of a community from the family through the nation and along multiple dimensions: military, political, ideological, diplomatic, and cultural.

From 1959 to 1967, when the last guerrilla outposts in the Escambray Mountains were eliminated, Cuba experienced a civil war between a revolutionary government and an armed opposition supported by the United States. The 1970s brought the consolidation of the socialist regime and its entry into the Soviet orbit, shifting opposition activity to the Cuban exile community in Miami. For three decades, exile groups, with few resources and little interest from Washington, tried to overthrow the Castro regime through sabotage, assassination attempts, and the infiltration of commando groups on the island. After the fall of the Berlin Wall and the disintegration of the Soviet Union in 1992, the Cuban opposition adopted new tactics, acting through the United States—and, to a lesser degree, Europe, Canada, and some Latin American countries—to pressure for democratization of the Cuban regime through trade, immigration, and diplomacy and to reinforce peaceful dissident movements on the island.

Throughout this long process, the civil war itself continued to express itself in different dimensions, militarily at first and then in politics, diplomacy, trade, and immigration. In the mid-1990s, however, the symbolic dimension of the conflict began to intensify, turning the civil war into a battle over memory between heirs to the opposing sides. The confrontation has not disappeared; the repressive apparatus of the Cuban government and the U.S. embargo continue to play their roles in fueling the conflict. Since the early 1990s, however, the spotlight has shifted to a dispute over national legacy, amounting to a quarrel over the country's symbolic heritage.

The case of Elián González and the "battle of ideas" launched by the Cuban government in 1999 are recent episodes in this symbolic war, but they are not the only ones. The great debates between intellectuals on the island and in the diaspora over three centennial commemorations—the hundred-year anniversaries of the death of José Martí in 1995, the first U.S. intervention and the fall of the Spanish colonial regime in 1998, and the founding of the republic in 2002—as well as constant disputes over the legacies of José María Heredia, Félix Varela, Gertrudis Gómez de Avellaneda, Fernando Ortiz, Lydia Cabrera, Jorge Mañach, Dulce María Loynaz, Gastón Baquero, Eugenio Florit, José Lezama Lima, or Virgilio Piñera—all major literary figures in the nineteenth and twentieth centuries—reflect this quarrel over heritage. At times, this war over memory—as in the case of the Varela Project, which proposes economic and political reforms and is the most celebrated Cuban opposition initiative in recent years—shifts to the sphere of politics.

OTHER TRANSITIONS AND EXPERIENCES

An ideal starting point for considering the roles of ideology, culture, and memory in any process of democratic transition is the theoretical distinction, developed by the Spanish political scientist Juan Linz, between a totalitarian and an authoritarian regime. This distinction is essential for describing the mechanisms of symbolic legitimization that characterize every political regime. In this sense, communist totalitarian regimes—the Soviet Union, Central and Eastern Europe, China, North Korea, and others—have a state ideology that manifests itself in different versions of Marxist-Leninism. In contrast, authoritarian regimes—Spain under Francisco Franco, Portugal under Antonio Salazar and Marcello Caetano, the Southern Cone military juntas, the Central American dictatorships, Mexico under the Institutional Revolutionary Party—lack a state ideology. Their discourse of power is limited to a regime doctrine based, to a greater or lesser degree, on nationalist values. State ideology tends to be more philosophically and morally dense than regime doctrine. Regime doctrine does not present a closed version of history, nor does it aspire to a cultural and educational regeneration of the citizenry. Both discourses may share messianic, teleological, and legitimizing elements, but while state ideology is transmitted in its entirety by way of the state ideological apparatus, transmission of regime doctrine is only partial. While totalitarian regimes aspire to an ideological indoctrination of society, authoritarian regimes settle for a mental construct that leads the masses toward certain collective actions.

The relationship between discourses and regimes with their national symbols is different as well. Authoritarian regime doctrine identifies national symbols with a *caudillo* (strongman) or government. That identification, however, refers to a condition that is nearly always exceptional or associated with a temporary state of emergency. In contrast, totalitarian state ideology—Stalinism, Maoism, North Korean *Juche*—reorders national symbols under a universal communism that is historically embodied in the bureaucratic-charismatic duality of party and leader and justifies annulling any other type of nationalism not amenable to the government.

The differences between regimes and discourses manifest themselves in complex ways during the transition to democracy. During transitions, authoritarian regimes—because they are capable of tolerating a controlled opposition and a certain level of public freedoms—have generally coexisted with peaceful and moderate dissident groups that question the official doctrine and re-establish the concept of ideological pluralism within the public. In contrast, the fall of totalitarian regimes in the Soviet Union and Central and Eastern Europe has been accompanied by the emergence of new political actors from within the power elite or subaltern (subordinate) sectors, such as labor unions and intellectuals, which confront the state's Marxist-Leninist ideology from a liberal, social democratic, Christian democratic, nationalist, or purely democratic standpoint.

All democratic transitions since the late 1970s have faced the symbolic problem of memory along with the criticism of official ideology or doctrine and the articulation of a pluralist public sphere. Memory in this sense is understood to be not only a form of cultural knowledge that permits the construction of historical, moral, and political narratives, but also a dimension of justice that encompasses conflicts related to the crimes and abuses of the past and national reconciliation among the actors involved in the democratic transition.

Democratic transitions, therefore, whether in communist totalitarian regimes or authoritarian ones, have made the official historical narrative more flexible by vindicating the losers and iconoclasts of the past, dismantling the legitimizing doctrinal apparatus of state power, and, above all, separating national symbols from government discourse.

Every transition handles the relationship between memory and justice differently. In former totalitarian regimes, such as the Soviet Union and Poland, as well as in former authoritarian regimes, such as Franco's Spain or the Institutional Revolutionary Party's Mexico, political actors have opted for varying expressions of "amnesty but not amnesia," the formula advocated by the Polish intellectual Adam Michnik. In addition to South Africa—an exceptional case given the institutionalized segregation of apartheid—other countries in transition, including some in South America, Central America, and the Andes, have chosen to establish truth and justice commissions, with strikingly dissimilar results.

Another historical point of comparison is the example of the reformed communist regimes in some Asian countries, among them China and Vietnam. In these cases, entrenched communist parties undergoing a process of generational renewal have launched social and economic liberalization programs—including certain capitalist elements, such as allowing small and medium-sized private enterprises and promoting the domestic market—while maintaining the system's one-party structure. The ideology, culture, and memory of these societies have also been transformed by a new diversity of legitimizing discourses that incorporates Eastern mystical, religious, nationalist, and cosmopolitan traditions and the effort to enter Western markets.

Where does the Cuban regime fall in the distinction between authoritarian and totalitarian regimes? Above all, how should we describe Cuba's symbolic transition? The debate over defining the existing political regime has intensified in recent years in light of the theory of democratic transition. From the time of its institutionalization (the early 1970s) through 1992, Cuba's political system exhibited the distinctive traits of a totalitarian communist regime: a single party, official Marxist-Leninist ideology, state ownership of the means of production, and corporativist integration of civil society. The regime functioned constitutionally between 1976 and 1992. But before its institutionalization the Cuban revolutionary process went through a series of nationalist, distributive, mobilizing, and charismatic phases that never entirely disappeared and that balanced the system's bureaucratic rationality.

Other factors, both external and internal, also contributed to the Cuban regime's singularity within the socialist camp. These include the confrontation between the Revolution and the United States (a relatively autonomous conflict in the Cold War context), the island's geographic location, the establishment of an opposition movement in Miami, and the Latin American and Caribbean cultural framework of Cuban society itself. This singularity was also reflected in the mechanisms of symbolic legitimization adopted by the Cuban regime. The Revolution's initial agrarian, anti-imperialist, redistributive ideology soon found its echo in the third-world anticolonialist movements. This third-world line was absorbed into nationalist revolutionary discourse, which Cuba's leaders emphasized over Marxist-Leninism. Until 1992, therefore, the regime's symbolic legitimization was based on two fundamental narratives: the doctrine of revolutionary nationalism and Marxist-Leninist ideology. In cultural and educational policy, these discourses merged or coexisted.

After the fall of the Berlin Wall and the disintegration of the Soviet Union, the Cuban regime tried to adapt, constitutionally, to the dangers presented by the absence of the socialist camp and the intensification of the conflict with Washington and Miami. Observers of the Cuban transition regard the 1992 constitutional reforms as a possible starting point toward regime change. For some, the reforms represent the transformation of the totalitarian communist regime into a merely authoritarian one. Others argue that they mark a shift toward a charismatic, post-totalitarian model because the communist system continues to be based on a single but not hegemonic party, and the opposition is repressed rather than controlled.

In the ideological sphere, however, the collapse of socialism and the Cuban economy's reinsertion into Western capitalism have had a decisive effect, as have the reforms of the 1990s—the 1992 constitutional reforms and other, no less significant ones that followed, such as the decriminalization of the dollar, the reopening of the agriculture and livestock markets, the authorization of self-employment, mixed foreign investment schemes, the reduction of the communist party's professional cadres, and the development of tourism and remittances as the national economy's first steps toward integration. All together, their effect has been the abandonment of Marxist-Leninism as the state ideology and the re-adoption of revolutionary nationalism as regime doctrine.

Some elements of the transformation of post-communism in Russia and Central and Eastern Europe are perceptible in the Cuban experience since 1992, such as the emergence of an entrepreneurial and monetary mentality among the technocratic elite, the articulation of dissident discourses grounded in civil society and human rights, or the intellectual debate over the notions of sacrifice, blame, and reconciliation. What makes the Cuban process distinctive, however, is that these symptoms of the post-communist phase have emerged alongside the political structures of a regime that is still capable of maintaining both the governability of a social majority and a consensus among the elite.

This readjustment of the regime's symbolic structure underlines the exceptional nature of the Cuban case in the context of democratic transitions from totalitarian regimes, such as those in the Soviet Union and Central and Eastern Europe, or authoritarian regimes like the Latin American dictatorships. Cuba has remained outside of the third wave of democratic transitions, but it has also, temporarily at least, begun to incorporate certain elements of those transitions, such as substituting a Marxist-Leninist state ideology with a nationalist revolutionary regime doctrine—within a very effective strategy of symbolic reproduction of power. Fidel Castro's government managed to survive late-twentieth-century democratization and to nourish itself symbolically on the failures of the new Latin American and third-world democracies.

The enduring strength of Fidel Castro's Cuba in the global environment of resistance to U.S. hegemony also differentiates the Cuban case from those of China and Vietnam. Although since 1992 Cuba has experienced ideological flexibility similar to that of the Asian countries, tense relations with the U.S. government and the Miami exile community, as well as the Communist Party's lack of institutional consistency and the timidity of its economic reforms, distinguish Cuba from the reformed socialisms and state capitalisms of Asia.

The singular relationship between time and democracy in the Cuban case suggests that the island's de-Sovietization since 1992 is a process of political change unconnected to democratic transition in any real sense. The drama of regime change shared by almost all of the third-wave transitions and the "heuristic metaphors" surrounding the fall of dictatorships described by Laurence Whitehead have no place in Cuban postcommunism. Since the early 1990s, the political drama on the island has been associated with social explosions such as the *balsero* (rafter) crisis of 1994, government campaigns like the 1999–2000 Elián case, or opposition campaigns such as the mobilization of European public opinion against the executions and incarcerations of spring 2003. This drama is not related to any change in the regime but rather to its persistence.

THE SYMBOLIC ADJUSTMENT

The transformation of the Cuban regime in the twelve years of the postcommunist period (1992–2004) can be observed in at least three areas: ideological policy, educational policy, and cultural policy. While relatively autonomous, particularly in terms of language and agency, these policies function as part of a discursive legitimization that originates from the center of power. The dilemmas of personal and collective memory and national reconciliation, so important in any democratic transition, are related to the modification of the ideology, politics, and culture of the Cuban regime.

Since the mid-1990s, the political ideology of the Cuban government—as reflected in the mass media, public propaganda, official Communist Party documents, National Assembly laws, the discourses of its leaders, and official journalism—has focused on the confrontation with the U.S. government, Cuban American exiles (referred to as the "Miami mafia") and the domestic opposition. Among intellectuals, signs of the shift toward revolutionary nationalism were visible as early as 1992–96, but political implementation of the trend accelerated after the downing by the Cuban Air Force of the Brothers to the Rescue planes in 1996 over the Straits of Florida, which cost four lives, and the Fifth Communist Party Congress a year later. It culminated in the campaigns for the return of the young *balsero* Elián (1999–2000) and for the release of the "five heroic prisoners of imperialism" (2001–2004) which molded the so-called battle of ideas that took place between 2000 and 2004. In 2004, the agenda for this battle—which was led by a new generation of Cuban politicians such as Hassán Pérez, Yadira García, Carlos Valenciaga, Carmen Rosa Báez, and Otto Rivero, whom the Comandante incorporated into his support staff at the start of their careers—became official government policy with the creation of a vice-presidential post in the Council of Ministers to implement it.

Evidence of the new emphasis on revolutionary nationalism can be found in legislation and in official pronouncements. Examples include Fidel Castro's Convocation and Report to the Fifth Cuban Communist Party Congress in 1997; the Declaration of the Mambises of the Twentieth Century issued the same year; Law 80 of 1997 (On Cuban Dignity and Sovereignty) and Law 88 of 1999 (On Protecting the Independence and Economy of the Cuban Nation), both conceived as antidotes to the Helms-Burton Act (1996) and the domestic opposition; the propaganda offensive in favor of the return of Elián González, including the installation of a special protest stage a few meters from the U.S. Interests Section; and finally, the wave of repression in the spring of 2003 and the propaganda machinery that accompanied it.

Another dimension of the battle of ideas beyond its direct ideological function relates to what the Cuban government calls the "educational revolution." From a quantitative point of view, this "revolution" is a function of the state's efforts to compensate for a teacher shortage by turning out young instructors with only a few months of training, all the while recalling the epic literacy campaigns of the 1960s. From a qualitative point of view, the new educational strategy envisions a virtual ideological re-education of the citizenry, promoting a "political culture" based on a heroic nationalist narrative—from the nineteenth-century wars of independence, the ideas of José Martí, the struggles against neocolonialism in the twentieth century, the 1933 and 1959 revolutions to today's resistance to U.S. imperialism—rather than a Marxist-Leninist reading of Cuban history.

Although post-communist cultural policy is the symbolic sphere least caught up in the battle of ideas, it also reflects the shift from Marxist-Leninism to revolutionary nationalism. The two main themes of the Ministry of Culture's new strategy under Abel Prieto—defense of "Cuban cultural identity," a principle introduced by the 1992 constitutional reforms; and "openness," a policy that combines looser political and ideological controls on creativity, a rediscovery of the intellectuals of the republican *ancien régime*, selective acceptance of the work of diaspora intellectuals, and entry into Western cultural markets—reflect a shift in doctrinal paradigms that the 1992 Constitution refers to as the transition from "Marxist-Leninist ideology" to an "ideological framework based on Marx and Martí."

This policy of "openness" and, especially, market entry has allowed part of the island's cultural camp to separate itself from the state apparatus of political legitimization. This separation is most obvious in music, the visual arts, film, theater, elite literature, and the most academic branches of the social sciences. For at least the past five years, however, intellectual fringe publications, such as the online news source *La Jiribilla* and *Contracorriente* magazine, have joined in the battle of ideas and in the process may have furthered official propaganda against the opposition and exile communities.

The symbolic adjustment of Cuban post-communism in ideological, educational, and cultural policy has reshaped the regime's historical narrative and changed the way political actors, both government and opposition, are represented within a new discourse of official memory that for the most part traces back to the party's Fifth Congress in 1997. The 1997—99 legislation in response to the Helms-Burton Act and the campaigns for the return of Elián González in 1999–2000 and the freeing of the "five heroic prisoners of imperialism" in 2001–2004 identified the enemy as the "Miami anti-Cuban mafia." The government of Fidel Castro uses this epithet to label all exile groups, whether moderate or not, in addition to Cuban American politicians from both parties and the United States government. Since the election of George W. Bush in 2000 and his declaration of a "war on terrorism," the new U.S. administration has been closely identified with this redefined enemy.

Numerous documents reflect the rewriting of official memory that has accompanied this adjustment. Literary examples include General Fabián Escalante Font's *Cuba: la guerra secreta de la CIA* (*Cuba: The CIA's Secret War*) and Jesús Arboleya's *La contrarrevolución cubana* (*The Cuban Counterrevolution*). In the legal sphere, the antidote legislation passed by the National Assembly of People's Power, the 2002 constitutional reforms backing "irrevocable socialism," and prosecution documents from the cases of seventy-five regime opponents in 2003 reflect not only a policy of establishing continuity between the enemies of the past—the "neocolonial bourgeoisie," "Yankee imperialism"—and those of the present— the *grupúsculos* (a pejorative term for small opposition groups), the "Miami anti-Cuban mafia," the George W. Bush administration—but also a detailed accounting of the economic and human toll of hostile U.S. policies.

The late 1990s antidote legislation against the Helms-Burton Act and the domestic opposition clearly intensified the historical narrative of revolutionary nationalism. Examples of its effects include the Claim Brought by the People of Cuba against the Government of the United States for Human Damages, presented in the People's Provincial Tribunal of Havana in May 1999, and the book *Cicatrices en la memoria: terrorismo y desestabilización en Cuba* (*Scars of Memory: Terrorism and Destabilization in Cuba*). In the 1999 claim, Cuba demanded that Washington pay $181 billion in compensation for the 3,478 dead and 2,099 wounded that Havana blames on U.S.-backed sabotage, bombings, and other terrorist acts. In *Cicatrices en la memoria*, eighteen Cuban writers present works of fiction that reenact some of the main military offensives against the Cuban regime attributed to Cuban exiles and the U.S. intelligence services since the 1960s. These include several failed attempts to assassinate Fidel Castro, the public burning in Miami of a painting by the artist Manuel Mendive, the October 1976 terrorist attack on Cubana de Aviación Flight 455, and the dengue fever epidemic that killed 158 residents of the island in 1981 and affected more than 300,000 others.

Following the jailing of seventy-five peaceful and moderate opponents of the regime in spring 2003, legal documents and propaganda and a number of books (such as *Los "disidentes"* [*The "Dissidents"*], by Rosa Miriam Elizalde and Luis Báez, and *El camaján* [*The Snake in the Grass*], by Arleen Rodríguez and Lázaro Barredo) insisted on equating the legal and peaceful opposition with military and subversive elements, thereby erasing all nuances in the opposing camp. The Castro regime identifies all expressions of opposition or direct political criticism—even ones that are peaceful and legal—with its historic enemy, the United States and its goal of destroying Cuban nationhood.

THE PACIFICATION OF MEMORY

Along with the intensification of revolutionary nationalism in the three spheres of symbolic legitimization—ideological policy, education policy, and cultural policy—Cuban post-communism has tolerated some displays of national reconciliation and the pacification of memory. In addition to advancing a cultural policy that promotes classic works of the republican *ancien régime* and diaspora intellectual activity—a policy that coincides with the immigration agenda of the Ministry of Foreign Relations as expressed in the 1993 and 1995 conferences on "nation and emigration"—the Castro government has shown some signs, however timid and symbolic, of seeking to normalize relations with the United States and some sectors of the exile community, as long as the process includes no political conditions.

Among the most significant displays of reconciliation, in symbolic terms, were the tripartite conferences marking the thirtieth and fortieth anniversaries of the Cuban Missile Crisis in 1992 and 2002 and, above all, the March 2001 commemoration of the fortieth anniversary of the Bay of Pigs invasion, all of which were held in Havana. In addition to representatives of the former Soviet Union and a group of distinguished scholars, participants at the first two events included important members of the Kennedy cabinet, among them former Defense Secretary Robert S. McNamara and presidential advisors Arthur M. Schlesinger, Richard Goodwin, and Theodore C. Sorensen. From the point of view of political reconciliation, however, the third conference, on the fortieth anniversary of the Bay of Pigs, was the most productive, for it allowed three veterans of the 2506 Brigade—Alfredo Durán, Luis Tornes, and Roberto Carballo—to meet some of their former military foes—Samuel Rodiles Planas, Ángel Jiménez González, Ramiro Valdés Menéndez, and José Ramón Fernández.

Such encounters are part of the process of pacification of historical memory, in which violence and war between political opponents—the Cuban government on the one hand, and Cuban exiles and the United States on the other—are presented as past scenarios that can be overcome through negotiated management of the conflict. Beyond the short-term political use that the Cuban government makes of these forums to pressure the United States to lift its trade embargo and the Cuban Adjustment Act, the new historical narrative outlined at such events contributes to a gradual normalization of relations between Havana, Miami, and Washington and to overcoming the polarization of the Cold War period.

The Havana restoration project, led by city historian Eusebio Leal, also reflects the shift toward a more flexible historical narrative. With efficient use of resources from the Spanish Agency for International Cooperation; the United Nations Educational, Scientific and Cultural Organization; and various autonomous communities in Spain, the Master Plan for Comprehensive Revitalization of Old Havana, launched in December 1994, has proceeded with architectural and urban conservation and restoration in the historic section of Old Havana, declared a World Heritage site in 1982. In 1997, plans for the Malecón (seafront) and Puerto Carenas expanded the scope of the restoration effort to include not just the historic city center but also buildings, monuments, and public places in the Vedado, el Cerro, and Miramar districts. Sites of key historical interest from the pre-revolutionary, colonial, and republican periods such as the Cristobal Colón Cemetery, the Spanish societies, Beth Shalom synagogue, and monuments to Generals Calixto García and José Miguel Gómez have been included in the restoration efforts.

Since the mid-1990s, the heritage and editorial policies of the Ministries of Culture, Education and Higher Education have joined in acknowledging the republican and emigrant legacies. The island's main intellectual journals, *Gaceta de Cuba, Temas,* and *Unión,* and important cultural institutions such as the National Library, Instituto del Libro, Casa de las Américas, and the Juan Marinello Center have recognized and promoted republican and émigré culture, two aspects of the national tradition that, until recently, were shunned as repositories of bourgeois, neocolonial, and annexationist values. The negative stereotypes that have defined pre-revolutionary Cuba as a "pseudo republic" and the émigré community as the "counterrevolution" since the 1960s are gradually disappearing or weakening their hold over these dimensions of contemporary Cuban culture, which have been less caught up in the battle of ideas.

The works of young Cuban historians also reflect this flexibility. Studies by Rafael Acosta de Arriba, María Antonia Marqués Dolz, Marial Iglesias, Reinaldo Funes Monzote, Ricardo Quiza Moreno, and Duanel Díaz Infante, among others, take an unbiased approach to topics and periods in colonial and republican history considered taboo just a short time ago, such as economic, social, and political development under the Pact of Zanjón (1878–95) or intellectual diversity and legal culture in the republican years (1902–59). This new body of historical work—along with a growing interest in the study of Cuban emigration at institutions such as the University of Havana's Center for Alternative Political Studies, the Juan Marinello Center, or the journal *Temas*—contributes to the pacification of Cuba's historical memory.

Since the early 1990s, new signs of reconciliation with the Cuban diaspora have appeared. These join a tradition of dialogue defended by moderate émigrés since the 1970s. One such sign is the virtual absence of armed opposition groups in the Cuban exile community and a widespread preference for peaceful regime change from within. The idea of a peaceful transition to democracy by a process of national reconciliation has gained support among Cuban exiles since 1992 and has been consolidated in recent years thanks to initiatives in this direction on the part of the regime itself, in its laws and institutions, as well as efforts by the domestic opposition groups such as Concilio Cubano (Cuban Council,

1995), La Patria es de Todos (The Homeland Belongs to All, 1997) and the Varela Project (2002).

In addition to demilitarizing, Cuban intellectuals abroad have led important efforts to improve cultural communications. The Olof Palme Institute seminar called the Bipolarity of Cuban Culture (1994), organized by the Sweden-based novelist René Vásquez Díaz, convened important writers from Cuba and the diaspora. The journal *Encuentro de la cultura cubana,* founded by Jesús Díaz in 1996, has showcased the best works by Cuban and diaspora intellectuals in more than forty issues. Plaza Mayor publishers, directed by Patricia Gutiérrez from San Juan, Puerto Rico, publishes works by authors in Cuba, Europe, Latin America, and the United States. Finally, academic programs such as those run by the Cuban Research Institute at Florida International University and the Bildner Center at the City University of New York promote exchanges with professors and researchers on the island.

U.S. academics have produced an abundance of works on the Cuban Revolution and the social, economic, and political order that this important historical process established in the second half of the twentieth century. Besides the classic studies by Jorge I. Domínguez, Carmelo Mesa-Lago, Louis A. Pérez Jr., and many others, this list includes the works of Marifeli Pérez-Stable, Lisandro Pérez, Jorge F. Pérez-López, J. Damián Fernández, and Alejandro de la Fuente. This scholarly output, which is based on intellectual dialogue with academics on the island and is not intended to serve as part of a discourse of legitimization for either the exile community or the opposition, plays an important role in the pacification of historical memory and national reconciliation among political adversaries.

The first effort—intellectually, at least—to design a specific national reconciliation project is the Task Force on Memory, Truth and Justice led by Marifeli Pérez-Stable, Jorge I. Domínguez, and Pedro A. Freyre. Cuban National Reconciliation (2003), a report produced after a series of meetings among the group's Cuban and non-Cuban members, reviews the ways other countries and regions—Spain, the Southern Cone, South Africa, Central America, and Central and Eastern Europe—have handled issues of justice, truth, memory, and national reconciliation. For the first time ever in studies and debates on Cuba, it proposes a historical accounting of "possible human rights violations by the Cuban government" and "abuses, crimes or atrocities committed by the violent opposition." This double exercise of memory could be an ideal starting point for future Cuban political actors to begin a process of democratic negotiation.

PREMISES FOR TRANSITION

Article 94 of Cuba's 1992 "Martí- and Marxist-Leninist-based" Constitution states that "in case of the absence, illness or death of the President of the Council of State, the First Vice President will substitute him in his duties." Cuba's first vice president is the minister of the armed forces and second secretary of the Cuban Communist Party, Raúl Castro, now interim president. Therefore, Cuba's transition to democracy has begun as a dynastic succession.

It would be difficult for a succession based on the mere substitution of one head of state for another to sustain itself for long in the face of pressure from multiple actors—proponents of reform within the government, the domestic and external opposition, émigrés, the international community, the United States—and the challenges of concentrating power in personal hands in the absence of a leader as unique as Fidel Castro. Even so, all of the possible scenarios for regime change in Cuba—peaceful and negotiated transformation, civil war, social upheaval, U.S. intervention—fall into two categories: succession or democratic transition.

Whatever the path Cuba takes toward democracy, regime change will imply a profound symbolic transformation that will be reflected in the ideology, culture, and memory of political actors and citizens on the island and in the diaspora. Given the Cuban regime's emphasis on these spheres in projecting its legitimacy at home and abroad, the change in ideas, values, and symbols may be traumatic and could hinder or redirect the process of national reconciliation among political actors.

From a symbolic point of view, the transition to democracy in Cuba faces a significant obstacle. The behavior of the four main actors in Cuban politics—the government of Fidel Castro, the opposition, the exile community, and the U.S. government—is based on a logic of confrontation in which the subjects figure as irreconcilable enemies, not loyal adversaries. The historical, ideological, and cultural values that comprise their political identities are grounded in warlike imagery in which one's very existence depends on annihilating the others. The basic premise of a peaceful and negotiated transition to democracy in Cuba must, therefore, renounce violence in both of its historical forms: the subversive violence of the opposition and the repressive violence of the government.

The Cuban political sphere is still restricted enough to obstruct the process of national reconciliation on the cultural front and to block its effects on the pacification of memory. The recognition of civil and cultural diversity on the island and in the diaspora, a process that requires building new political institutions through fair elections and a free and plural society, is another premise of the democratic transition. In the absence of minimal rights of association and expression, culture can serve as a partial bridge toward national reconciliation.

Once the obstacles to the democratic normalization of real pluralism have been overcome, the symbolic problems of Cuban democracy must be faced, taking into account the expectations and demands of established political actors. In this sense, it is not difficult to foresee a restatement of the ideological conflict around the legacies of revolution and exile, the Castro government, and the domestic and external opposition, as contrasting and past dimensions of Cuban history. To minimize the costs of political change, all political actors from Cuba's past must acknowledge the historic legitimacy of opposing groups.

Democracy will imply a break with the past, especially in relations with Miami and Washington. Nationalism, which has been at the sentimental core of all modern Cuban political trends, will not disappear, but it will no longer be the moral monopoly of one group or another. Instead, it will be shared among the different associations, all with the same national legitimacy, which will comprise a new political pluralism. This sharing of the sources of nationalism will make it easier to draw boundaries between state and nation, two entities that the current regime and its symbols and certain exile associations have conflated. It will also allow political actors to develop new strategies that affirm their belonging to a single national heritage encompassing republican, socialist, revolutionary, and émigré elements.

The distinction between state and nation is, at heart, the primary condition for achieving a transition to a democratic regime in Cuba. The range of options for governance possible in a climate of loyal competition can only emerge if all actors accept the equal places in Cuban history of the varying discourses and narratives of the island's past and the present. The political and cultural subjects responsible for these discourses and narratives require, above all, recognition of their legitimacy and acceptance of their right to engage in a civilized dispute for power under conditions of equality and respect.

In any culture that has experienced prolonged civil war, the pacification of memory is never complete. Cuban politics will not be free of conflict in the following decades, nor will the heirs of the two sides end their disputes over their share of the national legacy. The desired goal is to overcome the current polarization through the establishment of democratic standards that guarantee political competition and modulate civil tension. Only in this way will conflicts over heritage give way to a climate of trust where subjective realities can assert themselves without fear of exclusion or annihilation.

TWELVE

Cuba's Future Relations with the United States

WILLIAM M. LEOGRANDE

Since the collapse of the Soviet Union, Cuba's relations with the rest of the world have changed dramatically. The disappearance of the socialist bloc meant that Cuba lost not only its military allies but also its principal trade partners and source of foreign assistance. Since then, Cuba's top foreign policy priority has been to reorient its international economic relations to new trade partners, principally in Europe and Latin America. Cuban troops have come home from Africa, and Havana has abandoned its policy of promoting revolutionary insurgents in Latin America. Fidel Castro still cultivates good relations with other third-world governments, especially those that are skeptical about the benefits of neoliberalism and globalization, such as Hugo Chávez in Venezuela, Luiz Inácio Lula da Silva in Brazil, and Néstor Kirchner in Argentina. But Cuba no longer plays on the world stage the way it did in the 1970s and 1980s, when it sent tens of thousands of troops to Africa.

The one international relationship that changed least as a result of Cuba's diminished place in the new world order was its relationship with the United States. Although pressures have been growing in Washington for a relaxation of U.S. economic sanctions, especially regarding sales of food and medicine and the right of Americans to travel to Cuba, a full normalization of relations between Havana and Washington seemingly remains distant.

The collapse of European communism set in motion significant economic and social changes in Cuba, but little political change. The lesson Fidel Castro took from the experience of the European communist regimes is that attempting political reform in the midst of economic dislocation can prove disastrous. Even after Castro departs from the scene, a Cuban transition to multiparty democracy is uncertain. One can imagine scenarios in which such a transition might take place, but one can also imagine that the regime, rather than rupturing, might continue to gradually evolve and adapt to changing social, economic, and international conditions. China and Vietnam are as likely to be bellwethers for Cuba's future, as are Central and Eastern Europe and the former Soviet Union. How might Cuba's foreign relations, especially its relationship with the United States, be affected by these alternative scenarios?

U.S. RELATIONS WITH FORMER ADVERSARIES

The experience of other cases in which the United States has normalized relations with former adversaries provides some inkling of the issues that are likely to arise in future relations between Cuba and the United States and also the process for addressing them. Two types of examples are relevant: cases in which the adversary state has undergone a leadership succession and evolutionary change but does not experience a regime transition, and cases of regime transition in which the previously hostile regime is replaced by one disposed toward friendly relations with Washington. For the succession scenario, the closest parallels to the Cuban case are China and Vietnam, where gradual changes both in the policies of those regimes and in the international environment led to a process of normalization. For the transition scenario, the closest parallel is Nicaragua, where a pro–United States electoral coalition defeated the Sandinistas in 1990, assuming power after more than a decade of intense bilateral hostility. In all of these cases, the adversary regime embraced a socialist economic model and at least a quasi-Leninist authoritarian political model. All aligned themselves against the United States during the Cold War. Thus, the agenda of bilateral grievances between these regimes and the United States tended to be similar and so, too, the issues that had to be resolved to achieve normalization.

The issues fall into the familiar economic, political, security, and humanitarian categories. Not surprisingly, the specific issues that were center stage vary from case to case, but the issue agenda across cases is, nevertheless, remarkably similar. Economic concerns typically included the elimination of trade sanctions imposed by the United States, U.S. bilateral economic assistance, U.S. policy toward multilateral assistance, and compensation for nationalized U.S. property.

The experiences of Panama after the 1989 U.S. invasion and Nicaragua after the 1990 transition election are a warning not to expect bilateral economic assistance from the U.S. government to carry the burden of financing Cuba's economic recovery. Panama received $395 million in bilateral aid in fiscal year 1990 after the U.S. invasion, but that fell to only $14 million in fiscal year 1995. Nicaragua received almost $300 million in 1990 after the Sandinistas lost the election to the U.S.-backed candidate Violeta Chamorro, but that too fell—to $29 million in fiscal year 1995.

Because socialist governments typically nationalized foreign direct investment (FDI), they often had to resolve property compensation issues with the United States in order to restore normal relations. The rate paid by most other socialist countries on nationalized U.S. property has been significantly less than 100 percent, ranging from a low of 9.7 percent by the Soviet Union to a high of 91 percent by Yugoslavia. Typically, the amounts involved were so small that they posed no real burden. China paid only $80 million and Vietnam $203 million. In both cases, that was less than their assets frozen in the United States, which were freed by normalization. Cuba, in contrast, has only about $100 million in frozen assets, which, as we will see, is tiny in relation to the outstanding claims.

Nicaragua, where it took years to achieve a mutually acceptable framework for resolving property claims, has a special parallel with Cuba. Claims against Nicaragua were not limited to U.S. citizens who lost property. Senator Jesse Helms (R-NC) wrote a law requiring President Chamorro's government to pay compensation to *Nicaraguans* who lost property—if they had become U.S. citizens—before Nicaragua could be eligible for U.S. bilateral aid. This measure vastly expanded the number of claims. A similar provision in the Helms-Burton Act affects Cuba.

The property question proved to be one of the most conflictual issues faced by Chamorro's government. It fractured both her political coalition and the opposition Sandinista party; it provoked land and factory occupations; it spawned gridlock in the judicial and legislative branches of government; it dissuaded business people from reinvesting; and it endangered U.S. economic aid. Almost all of the property claims had to be negotiated and adjudicated on a case-by-case basis, a process that took years. Since Nicaraguan immigrants to the United States continue to achieve citizenship, the number of property claims has grown over time, frustrating efforts to finally settle this nettlesome issue.

The political issues typically on the U.S. agenda with former socialist adversaries have included their human rights practices and their movement toward political liberalization or democracy. In the cases of China and Vietnam, the United States continues to be critical of their human rights performance and their lack of progress toward multiparty electoral democracy. But these issues have been subordinated to other priorities. Commercial interests, combined with Washington's desire to foster strategic cooperation with China in East Asia, led President Bill Clinton to reverse his own policy and grant China permanent normal trade status despite a manifest lack of progress on human rights. Full diplomatic and trade relations with Vietnam resulted from the growth of U.S. business interest in trade, combined with progress on the Prisoners of War–Missing in Action (POW–MIA) issue, around which the most vocal U.S. constituency that opposed normalization was organized.

Even after regime transition in Nicaragua, Washington remained highly critical of Sandinista influence within the armed forces, which it regarded as detrimental to democratic consolidation. President Chamorro, on the other hand, judged that purging the military of Sandinistas would be destabilizing. For most of her presidency, the United States used the leverage afforded by bilateral aid to force her to put Washington's priorities ahead of her own in this sensitive area of civil-military relations. Having played a decisive role in destabilizing the Sandinista government through the covert Contra war and an economic embargo analogous to the embargo against Cuba, U.S. policy makers exhibited the presumptive attitude that they ought to have a major say in shaping post-transition Nicaraguan politics.

The agenda of security issues between Washington and former socialist adversaries has included the foreign policy behavior of the former adversary, as well as the possibility of collaboration on certain security issues in the post–Cold War environment. As mentioned above, security issues have been especially important in the Chinese case, but less so in Vietnam. The lesson from China is that the potential for security cooperation can impel progress toward normalization of relations even in the absence of any noticeable improvement on human rights or political liberalization. In Nicaragua, security cooperation has focused principally on antinarcotics efforts, which is an area of significant mutual interest and potential cooperation with Cuba as well.

Humanitarian issues between the United States and former adversaries have included family contacts and reunification, travel and migration. In the cases of both China and Vietnam, politically powerful émigré constituents within the United States played a pivotal role in delaying the process of normalizing relations. The conservative China Lobby instilled such fear in U.S. politicians that it was able to delay the restoration of normal relations for two decades, until President Richard M. Nixon traveled to China in 1972. For years, the families of U.S. service members captured or missing in Vietnam held enormous domestic political sway. Normalization only became possible under President Clinton when real progress on the highly emotional POW–MIA issue began to be made with increased cooperation on the Vietnamese side.

In all these cases, the process of normalization was relatively long and drawn out, despite the fact that dramatic events—such as Nixon's trip to China in 1972 and the Sandinistas' 1990 electoral defeat in Nicaragua—

sometimes created the popular impression that normalization had been accomplished all at once. In fact, even when there was a clear and virtually irrevocable decision to move toward improved relations, the road often proved to be long and rocky. Agreement tended to be achieved piecemeal, even when undertaken as part of a comprehensive negotiating agenda. From Washington's first gesture toward China—the relaxation of travel restrictions in 1969—it took ten years to achieve full diplomatic relations. Permanent normal trade relations were not established until 2001, almost three decades after Nixon's famous trip. President Jimmy Carter opened discussions with Vietnam in 1977, but diplomatic relations were not restored until 1995. The highly organized and motivated POW–MIA organization was critical to how the process unfolded. President George H. W. Bush was ecstatic when the Sandinistas were voted out of office in 1990, but it was not until the end of Chamorro's presidency in 1996, when issues of property compensation and Sandinista influence in the military were sufficiently resolved, that relations became truly normal.

CUBA AND THE UNITED STATES SINCE THE END OF THE COLD WAR

The hostility between Cuba and the United States has been unrelenting since late 1959, and U.S. economic sanctions have been in place since they were imposed in stages from 1960 to 1962. Nevertheless, almost every U.S. administration has engaged in some dialogue with Cuba regarding specific issues of mutual interest (e.g., international hijacking and migration). Presidents Gerald Ford and Jimmy Carter both embarked on broad negotiations aimed at normalizing relations only to see them breakdown short of that goal.

Since 1996, the basic framework of U.S. policy has been set by the Cuban Liberty and Democratic Solidarity Act (Helms-Burton), which flatly prohibits the reestablishment of normal diplomatic and commercial ties as long as Cuba's one-party socialist system remains in place. Additionally, the Helms-Burton law stipulates in detail how a U.S. president should respond to a Cuban transition. The level of specificity is extraordinary, reflecting the law's original aim to diminish presidential discretion, transferring effective control over U.S. policy toward Cuba into the hands of Congress. Although acknowledging that Cuba has the right to self-determination, "free of interference by the government of any other country," the law defines the goal of U.S. policy as "representative democracy and a market economy." The lifting of U.S. sanctions and the provision of aid is premised on the establishment first of a "transition government" and then of a democratically elected one. Only humanitarian aid can be provided to a transition government; the embargo can be suspended, but not ended until a democratically elected government is in place. A transition government is defined as one that lifts all constraints on political activity, frees all political prisoners, dissolves state security, does not include either Fidel or Raúl Castro, and moves to hold free and internationally supervised elections within eighteen months. Other indicators of a transition government, as specified in the law, are its willingness to extradite fugitives wanted in the United States and return expropriated property to U.S. citizens, including naturalized Cuban Americans.

A democratically elected government is defined as one that results from free elections, has done all the things required of a transition government, has begun to return expropriated property to U.S. citizens, and is "substantially moving toward a market-oriented economic system based on the right to own and enjoy property." That is, a Cuban government, even a freely elected one, that does not embark on a transition to capitalism and does not acknowledge the right of Cuban Americans to regain or be compensated for expropriated property is not, by Washington's definition, democratic and therefore does not meet the conditions for lifting the embargo. Cuba's right to self-determination is confined within these limits if it expects to have normal relations with Washington. Thus is the spirit of the Platt Amendment alive and well in the Cuban Liberty and Democratic Solidarity Act. Imposed on the Cuban Constitution by U.S. occupation forces in 1901, the Platt Amendment limited Cuban sovereignty and laid the cornerstone for U.S. dominance of the island in the first half of the twentieth century.

The terms of Helms-Burton constitute such a straight-jacket for U.S. policy that it is difficult to predict whether it would be honored in the breech. A growing majority in Congress favors relaxing elements of the embargo unilaterally, so it seems likely that significant political change in Cuba would lead to modifications of Helms-Burton's most stringent requirements. But the implicit expectation that a new Cuban government would respond—almost as a matter of course—to U.S. interests and demands, is a harbinger of the potential problems likely to arise in bilateral relations, even in the event of a transition in Cuba to a multiparty democracy.

The Embargo and Compensation

Since the U.S. Central Intelligence Agency (CIA) abandoned direct efforts to overthrow Cuba's government in the 1960s, the economic embargo has been the principal instrument of U.S. policy. Its original intent was to destabilize the Cuban economy and, in concert with the CIA's direct action, set the stage for rebellion. When that aim was abandoned as hopeless, the embargo was retained to serve as an example for other Latin American countries of the price of defying Washington and as a bargaining chip in eventual negotiations for normalization. Finally, after the Soviet collapse, some U.S. policy makers imagined that the embargo might once again tip the balance in favor of Castro's collapse. Over the years, Washington has demanded a variety of concessions from Cuba in exchange for lifting the embargo. During the Cold War, most demands dealt with Cuban foreign policy. They included, at various times, termination of Cuba's military ties with the Soviet Union, an end to support for revolutionary movements in Latin America, and withdrawal of Cuban troops from Africa. Since the end of the Cold War, foreign policy demands have been replaced by the demand that Cuba undergo a democratic transition.

Despite being codified in law by Helms-Burton, the embargo has come under serious political pressure in recent years because the potential for commercial relations with Cuba has piqued congressional interest. The embargo on sales of food and medicine was lifted in 2000 (though restrictions on financing remain), and Congress has voted repeatedly to lift the ban on travel to Cuba, although President George W. Bush has thus far successfully blocked that legislation. The political trend in Congress has been moving against the embargo, and it is conceivable that Congress might eventually vote to lift it unilaterally. During George W. Bush's first term in office, Representative Charles Rangel (D-NY) repeatedly introduced legislation to end enforcement of the embargo, and it lost by smaller margins almost every year.

The issue of compensation for U.S. property nationalized after 1959 is likely to be among the most difficult bilateral issues for Cuba and the United States to resolve. The link between compensation demands and the embargo has always been close; the embargo was initially imposed as punishment for Cuban nationalizations of U.S. property. Since the 1960s, the one consistent U.S. demand in exchange for lifting the embargo has been that Cuba satisfy the compensation claims for expropriated U.S. property. The Helms-Burton law declares that resolving property claims is "an essential condition for the full resumption of economic and diplomatic relations between the United States and Cuba."

The U.S. Foreign Claims Settlement Commission has ratified 5,911 property claims by U.S. corporations and citizens that are worth $1.85 billion. With accumulated interest, the total claim is estimated at $5.6 billion. This total, however, does not include property claims by Cubans who have since become naturalized U.S. citizens and are therefore eligible for compensation under the Helms-Burton law. Since both Bill Clinton and George W. Bush have waived implementation of Title III of Helms-Burton, Cuban Americans have not been able to register formal claims, but in a September 1996 report to Congress, the State Department estimated there could be as many as 200,000 such claims, totaling "tens of billions of dollars."

The Cuban government has long acknowledged the legitimacy of compensation claims by U.S. property owners and has settled similar claims with other governments whose citizens lost property after 1959. In the U.S. case, however, the Cubans have asserted counterclaims based on the damage done to the Cuban economy by the U.S. embargo and the CIA's sabotage campaign. After a U.S. court awarded $67 million in damages to the families of the four Cuban Americans killed in 1996 when Cuban MiGs shot down two Brothers to the Rescue planes, Havana demanded $181 billion in compensation for property damage and for the 3,478 Cubans killed and 2,099 disabled by attacks on the island launched from the United States.

Democracy and Human Rights

The idea that U.S. foreign policy should promote democracy has a long pedigree, but it was eclipsed during most of the Cold War by the realist argument that security and the balance of power were preeminent. When the end of the Cold War made containment irrelevant as an organizing principle for foreign policy, democracy promotion emerged as an alternative, though not to the exclusion of more traditional economic and security interests. The advent of the "war on terrorism" has been occasion for again relegating democracy and human rights to secondary status in certain cases (e.g., Pakistan, Egypt, and other Middle Eastern allies).

In relations with Cuba, human rights emerged as a key U.S. concern during President Carter's initiative to normalize relations. Several thousand Cuban political prisoners were freed as a result of that dialogue. When the Soviet Union collapsed, forcing Cuba to turn inward and abandon its activist foreign policy, the security issues that had been Washington's principal complaint against Havana virtually disappeared. The promotion of democracy rose to replace them. This shift in the U.S. rationale made normalization even more difficult because Washington was now demanding not just an end to objectionable Cuban behavior abroad but to the very character of the socialist state. Not only has the United States demanded a transition to democracy as the price for normalization of relations; since the mid-1990s, Washington has also appropriated several million dollars annually to support opponents of Cuba's socialist regime. In May 2004, President Bush announced that Washington would step up its support for the dissident movement.

The current Cuban government has been utterly unyielding in the face of international criticism regarding human rights. Strict laws criminalize the receipt of aid from the United States by political opponents and have been used to decimate the opposition movement, as witnessed by the spring 2003 arrest and imprisonment of seventy-five dissidents. Yet the cases of China and Vietnam are proof Washington is sometimes willing to normalize relations with former adversaries even in the absence of regime transition if other bilateral interests are sufficiently compelling.

Security Issues, Old and New

Most of Washington's security concerns regarding Cuba disappeared with the end of the Cuban-Soviet military relationship, the withdrawal of Cuban troops from Africa, and Cuba's decision to pursue better state-to-state relations in Latin America rather than support revolutionary movements. There are, however, new security issues that have arisen, many of which are of mutual concern to the two governments, even today, and will continue to be on the bilateral agenda in either a succession or transition scenario. In fact, a transition might well exacerbate these issues since they arise from the limited capacity of the Cuban state to control smuggling of both drugs and people due to the deterioration of the armed forces in the aftermath of the Cold War. According to the U.S. State Department's report, *World Military Expenditures and Arms Transfers, 1999–2000*, the size of Cuba's regular armed forces fell by 80 percent, from 297,000 troops to just 50,000, between 1989 and 1999. Expenditures fell 64 percent (in constant dollars), from $1.73 billion to $630 million, down from 2.9 percent of Gross National Product (GNP) to just 1.9 percent. The severe shortage of petroleum Cuba experienced in the mid-1990s meant that the armed forces rarely trained, and 75 percent of its heavy equipment was moth-balled.

Caribbean routes have been popular with Colombian smugglers in the past. In the late 1980s, some Cuban security officials were corrupted by traffickers into allowing Cuba to be used as a storage site for drugs to be smuggled into the United States on fast boats. More recently, as the Cuban navy's ability to patrol the coastal waters has deteriorated, smugglers have used Cuban waters to escape detection by U.S. law enforcement. As Cuba has opened up to tourism, it has begun to develop an internal drug problem as well.

The issue of migration is the bilateral issue that has been the subject of most cooperation between Cuba and the United States over the past decade. The 1994 rafter crisis led to bilateral agreements that expanded legal migration and inaugurated a U.S. policy of returning migrants to Cuba when they are intercepted in international waters. This has deterred most potential emigrants from setting off across the Florida Straits on homemade rafts, but it has led to the emergence of a people-smuggling business, since illegal migrants are virtually assured permanent resident status under the Cuban Adjustment Act of 1966 if they can reach U.S. soil.

Guantanamo Naval Base is of little security value to the United States but considerable symbolic importance to Cuba. Obtained under the Platt Amendment and ratified by treaty in 1934, U.S. rights to the base "in perpetuity" have long been an affront to Cuban nationalists. After 1959, Castro demanded in vain that U.S. forces return the territory to Cuba. The issue has been on the bilateral agenda ever since, but it has not been high on the agenda. Since the 1960s, the Cubans have settled into routine coexistence with the base and have not protested Washington's decision to use it as a detention facility for Taliban and Al Qaeda prisoners after the Afghanistan war. The Helms-Burton law mentions the return of Guantanamo as one of the concessions Washington should make to a new Cuban government in the event of a transition.

Some analysts have suggested that the base be turned into a joint Caribbean search-and-rescue or weather station. But the ongoing use of the base as a detention facility could complicate such plans. Washington has given no indication of how long it intends to hold the prisoners currently incarcerated at Guantanamo, implying that it could be indefinitely. That might prevent the return of the territory to Cuba and could conceivably become a symbolic rallying point for nationalists in a more open Cuban polity.

Humanitarian Issues: The Cuban American Connection

The forces that historically linked Cuba and the United States so intimately—geography and economics—will be reinforced in the future by the Cuban American community. Arguably, no future aspect of the U.S.-Cuba relationship will be more important. The ties between Cubans and Cuban Americans are already the most extensive of any ties, public or private, between the two countries. A majority of the U.S. residents who travel to Cuba are Cuban Americans. Cuban American travel and remittances have become a major source of hard currency for the island. Cash remittances alone (not counting in-kind aid) have reached nearly $1 billion annually. By comparison, humanitarian assistance from U.S. community and church groups averaged only about $30 million annually during the 1990s, and sales of food and medicine to Cuba were just $165 million in 2002.

Cuban Americans, however, provide far less in remittances on a per capita basis than do immigrants from Mexico, El Salvador, and the Dominican Republic, despite the fact that the Cuban American community is wealthier. The political animosity of many Cuban Americans toward the Castro regime, and U.S. government limits on remittances, are the most likely reasons.

As animosity subsides (which has been occurring gradually even in the absence of political change on the island) and U.S. legal constraints are relaxed, remittances are likely to increase significantly. The passage of time alone is moderating opinion in the Cuban American community as older exiles are replaced by newly arrived immigrants who retain close family ties on the island. Like the infamous China Lobby that intimidated U.S. politicians for decades, the hard-line Cuba Lobby may also prove to be a paper tiger when the moment for normalization finally arrives.

Even the current Cuban government has recognized that relations with the Cuban American community are a key element of future relations between the two countries. In 1994, the government invited more than two hundred exiles to a "Nation and Migration" conference in Havana to begin the process of "normalizing" relations between the island and the diaspora. It was the first significant meeting between the government and the exile community since the 1978 "Dialogue" at the height of President Carter's efforts to improve U.S.-Cuban relations. The agenda was dominated by issues of travel and family contacts. The Cuban government agreed to lift a number of restrictions on travel by exiles, and even offered to allow them to invest in Cuba on the same terms as any foreign investor. The unspoken hope was that easier travel would produce more travel and more external support for family members in Cuba. Several months later, Cuba's then foreign minister, Roberto Robaina, met secretly in Spain with the leaders of three moderate exile opposition groups, two of which maintained explicit ties to dissidents on the island. A second "Nation and Migration" conference was held the following year, and unlike the first conference, invitations were not restricted to those who were generally supportive of the revolution. More than 350 participants came from 34 countries. A third conference was scheduled for April 2003 but was postponed until May 2004 amid the furor caused by Cuba's arrest of seventy-five dissidents. In early 2004, the Cuban government abolished visa requirements for Cubans living abroad to travel to the island, substituting a one-time "entry authorization." Nevertheless, the process of obtaining and renewing Cuban passports, which Cuban Americans are required to use, remains bureaucratic and expensive. By contrast, President Bush's acceptance of the recommendations of his Commission for Assistance to a Free Cuba served to restrict Cuban American ties to their homeland. Family visits were reduced from one per year to one every three years and limited to fourteen days, with a narrower definition of who is counted as family and how much money could be spent per diem. Remittances and gift packages, critical to the standard of living of many ordinary Cubans, were prohibited to senior members of the Cuban Communist Party and government, and their families, which would include tens of thousands of people.

CUBA AND THE UNITED STATES LOOKING FORWARD

Fidel Castro has been such a symbol of the Cuban revolution and its confrontation with the United States that his passing from the political scene, even in the absence of any other significant political change, is nevertheless likely to have a significant impact on U.S.-Cuban relations. It would drain some of the most intense emotion from the Cuban American community's antipathy toward the regime and accelerate the shift toward a more moderate center of political gravity in the community. Castro's passing might accelerate the congressional movement to relax U.S. sanctions as well. In the event of a regime transition to multiparty democracy in Cuba, the pressure in Congress for lifting the embargo would be even stronger, perhaps leading it to supercede the onerous requirements of Helms-Burton. Most presidents would likely support such a change in the law because it would increase their discretion in formulating policy in a fast-changing situation.

Aid and Trade

A successor government in Cuba that retained the one-party socialist system would certainly not be a candidate for U.S. bilateral assistance, but in the event of a regime transition, Washington has already promised to provide financial help. The amount, however, is unpredictable and would depend on such factors as humanitarian need on the island (which, in turn, will be a function of how socially and economically disruptive a transition proves to be), other demands on U.S. international resources (such as the need to rebuild countries like Iraq and Afghanistan), and the U.S. budget deficit. In a 1997 report to Congress, President Clinton promised that Cuba could expect the United States to be the "predominant bilateral provider" of economic assistance but projected only $4 to $8 billion in post-transition external capital flows over six years (including bilateral aid, multilateral loans, FDI, and remittances). Since remittances alone (at their 1997 level) would comprise some $4 billion over six years, Clinton's report implies that Cubans should expect relatively low levels of bilateral U.S. aid. "After this period, the economic transition should be well advanced," the report continues, "and private and commercial flows into Cuba ought to be sufficient to make the economy self-sustaining without significant further external official assistance."

If a transition to multiparty democracy in Cuba is accompanied by further market reforms in the economy, Cuba will need significant external assistance to work its way through this economically disruptive process. Neither the United States nor the international financial institutions (IFIs), however, give out funds unconditionally. The International Monetary Fund (IMF), especially, expects that recipients will follow an IMF-approved model of sound fiscal and monetary policy. This neoliberal model, which has been at the heart of Washington's and the IFIs' policies for the past two decades, has been anathema to Castro and many others in the Cuban leadership. Moreover, its failure to generate significant reductions in poverty elsewhere in Latin America has led to growing skepticism within Latin American public opinion. If a political transition in Cuba is followed by an economic one, domestic economic policy will surely become a matter of intense political debate. Will a new Cuban government simply embrace the "Washington consensus" of neoliberalism? Polls both on the island and among immigrants to the United States indicate that Cuban public opinion solidly supports the social welfare system of free health care and education. Political leaders in a multiparty democracy will face strong pressures to minimize the recessionary effect of economic reforms and maintain the social safety net. If the Cuban state seeks a more gradual economic transition or retains a significant role for the state in the economy, it may find itself in conflict with both Washington and the IFIs over its eligibility for multilateral assistance.

If economic sanctions were lifted, the potential for commercial relations between Cuba and the United States is enormous. Historically, the Cuban economy was closely integrated with the U.S. economy—so much so that it was an issue of contention for Cuban nationalists long before Fidel Castro. Severing that relationship of dependence was one of the goals of the 1959 Revolution. The U.S. embargo, ironically, has become the principal bulwark against resurgent U.S. economic domination of post–Cold War Cuba. During the 1990s, Cuba made considerable progress diversifying its trade partners. Cuba's economic ties with Canada and the European Union have flourished because the U.S. embargo has prevented U.S. businesses from exploiting their natural competitive advantages in Cuba. In the absence of the embargo, there is little doubt that trade with the United States would quickly grow to dwarf trade with every other trade partner; tourists from the United States would vastly outnumber Canadians and Europeans; and investment from U.S. firms (including Cuban American ones) would overwhelm investments from elsewhere. In fact, despite the embargo, the gravitational pull of the U.S. economy is already felt in Cuba. The legalization of the dollar in 1993 accelerated the development of a dual economy in which the dominant currency became the *Yanqui* (Yankee) dollar, not the Cuban peso.

In November 2004, however, in an effort to regain control over Cuba's currency system, the government prohibited domestic transactions in U.S. dollars, and dollars had to be changed to convertible pesos.

Even if Cuba were admitted to preferential trade regimes like the Cotonou Agreement, which allows former European colonies preferential access to EU markets, or an expanded North American Free Trade Agreement (NAFTA), the pull of the U.S. market would be hard to resist. The Dominican Republic, for example, is a Cotonou member, yet about 60 percent of its trade is with the United States. Other Latin American partners like Venezuela and Mexico trade with the Dominican Republic more than any European country does. Similarly, despite NAFTA, less than 2 percent of Mexico's trade is with Canada; less than 5 percent is with the EU. If Cuba were admitted to the Caribbean Basin Initiative (under the Caribbean Basin Trade Partnership Act of 2000), the resulting reduction in tariffs would give U.S. businesses an even greater advantage.

Estimates of trade between the United States and Cuba after the embargo is lifted vary from a low of about $700 million annually to a high of $2.8 billion. The higher figures are more likely accurate since Cuban imports are about $4 billion annually. Before 1959, nearly 80 percent of Cuban trade was with the United States. Even in the face of Cuba's significantly diversified trade relations, it seems more likely that trade with the United States might constitute as much as half of Cuban trade than only 17 percent. Recent studies have focused on the trade potential in the food and travel sectors because the bulk of Cuban imports from the United States in the near future are likely to be food products and because tourism is now the leading sector of the Cuban economy. The American Farm Bureau Federation predicts that sales to Cuba of food and farm inputs alone could approach $1 to $2 billion fairly rapidly, since travel-cost savings for Cuba would be so high when buying bulk grains from the United States instead of elsewhere.

The main constraint on the expansion of U.S.-Cuban trade is not likely to be foreign competition but Cuba's limited ability to pay. Cuba will want to buy far more from the United States than it sells, and its shortage of hard currency will make sustaining a significant trade deficit impossible. Hard-currency earnings will likely increase as a result of the rise in remittances, and Cuba will presumably gain access to loans from international financial institutions. (The United States government has promised to facilitate Cuba's re-entry into the international financial institutions it left after 1959.) But access to significant international credit will require that Cuba resolve its existing hard-currency debt. In 1986, after several restructurings of its $5 billion hard-currency debt (now estimated at $11.2 billion with accumulated interest), Cuba declared a moratorium on payments. Renegotiating this debt is crucial if Cuba hopes to reestablish its international credit and make itself attractive to investors.

Before 1959, Cuba was the top tourist destination in the Caribbean, receiving 18 to 21 percent of all tourists coming to the region. As Castro himself acknowledged when the government began to revitalize the tourist sector in the early 1980s, "the sea, the climate, the sun, the moon, the palm trees . . . are the natural wealth of our country, and we have to take advantage of them." As the principal point of origin for most tourists bound for the Caribbean, the United States is a natural market for Cuban tourism; in the 1950s, 80 percent of the arrivals in Cuba were from the United States. By most estimates, the total number of Americans visiting Cuba annually is now about 150,000 to 200,000, most of whom are Cuban Americans visiting family. Some 30,000 others travel legally under approved licenses, and the rest—somewhere between 20,000 and 50,000—travel illegally. A U.S. International Trade Commission study estimated that if sanctions were lifted, between 100,000 and 350,000 additional U.S. residents would travel to Cuba annually, and these visitors would provide Cuba with between $90 million and $350 million in revenue. Other studies are even more optimistic. One estimated that within five years, 1.4 to 2 million U.S. tourists would travel to Cuba annually. Such a surge in tourism, if the Cuban industry could accommodate it, would almost double the number of international arrivals in Cuba. A proportionate increase in revenue for Cuba would push tourist receipts from $2.6 billion (2000) to more than $5 billion annually.

Such a rapid expansion of the tourism sector holds some danger for Cuba's long-term development. Tourism is not a high valued-added industry, and it fails to exploit Cuba's comparative advantage—a well-educated workforce. A surge in tourism, coming at a time when a more open Cuban economy is eager to import more goods from the United

States and therefore needs hard currency, could lock the Cuban economy into a dependence on tourism rivaling its historic dependence on sugar.

Foreign direct investment from Europe has grown considerably since the 1990s, despite bureaucratic roadblocks in Cuba and the threat of litigation by Cuban Americans under the Helms-Burton law. As of 2000, about $1.7 billion in FDI had been contracted. In the event of a transition that reduced the Cuban government's ideological suspicions about FDI, lifted U.S. prohibitions on investment, and relieved the risk of litigation, FDI from the U.S., especially Cuban Americans, would jump sharply. Even a successor government that retained the one-party socialist system could take steps to make Cuba more investor-friendly, though in that case Washington would be less likely to lift the prohibition on U.S. investment.

Cuba has a clear interest in resolving the issue of property compensation claims, first and foremost because Helms-Burton makes lifting the embargo and providing bilateral assistance contingent on it. Moreover, resolution of the corporate claims would open the way for FDI from the United States, and resolution of the Cuban American claims would probably stimulate FDI from Canada and Europe since it would eliminate the risk of litigation under Title III of Helms-Burton. Finally, reconciliation with the Cuban American community would enlist the help of this politically influential group in increasing bilateral aid to the island, and Cuban Americans could become an invaluable bridge between the two countries, fostering both trade and investment.

On the other hand, a new government in Havana—whether it is a successor government or the product of regime transition—will face serious obstacles on the property issue. It will have to decide whether or not to press Washington to recognize at least some counterclaims for embargo-related damages. It will want to negotiate a reduced rate of compensation, since some U.S. corporations filed claims in Washington for many times the value of the property as declared in Cuba for tax purposes. Lone Star Cement Company, for example, claimed a $24.8 million loss with the Claims Commission for property it valued at just $1.6 million for tax purposes in Cuba. Corporate losses were partially compensated by the U.S. government, which allowed the companies to write them off on their tax returns.

Cuban American claims will be especially problematic, since full recognition of them would be far beyond Cuba's ability to pay. Moreover, such compensation is sure to be unpopular politically. When Helms-Burton was passed, the Cuban government made effective use of its provisions regarding Cuban American property to rally popular sentiment against it. The idea that a huge portion of Cuba's capital stock and national income would be transferred to émigrés living in the United States seems likely to remain unpalatable to many Cubans, even after a transition. It would certainly be unacceptable to any Cuban leadership that succeeds Fidel in the absence of a regime transition.

Even if Cuba accepted in principle the idea of compensation for some Cuban American property, valuing property that was expropriated so long ago is no easy task. Even in cases where titles are clear and undisputed, the original value of most property other than real estate has long since depreciated. In many cases, subsequent investment has improved property or transformed it entirely. Settling on what counts as adequate compensation will be extremely complex. Moreover, Cuba will have a difficult time financing any claims that it agrees to, and it will most likely need to negotiate a long-term payment schedule, as was done in Nicaragua. Cuba's foreign exchange earnings are only about $1.4 billion annually, and it already carries a hard-currency debt of $11.2 billion that will have to be renegotiated before any significant loans will be forthcoming from IFIs. The rate of capital investment in the past decade has been so low that it has not even offset normal depreciation, so Cuba has few resources to spare. No Cuban government, with or without a regime transition, will have the wherewithal to pay significant compensation anytime soon. If some members of Congress were to decide to hold U.S. aid hostage to the issue of compensation—as Senator Helms did to Nicaragua in the 1990s—this issue could cause the first serious crisis in post-transition bilateral relations.

Democracy and Human Rights

Any successor regime that retains Cuba's one-party socialist system is certain to face continuing U.S. scrutiny and criticism on human rights grounds and continuing U.S. efforts to foster multiparty democracy. A successor government might allow for some limited liberalization, but it is likely to continue to regard external support for democracy advocates inside Cuba as subversive.

In the event of a regime transition in Cuba, a new government might be less instinctively hostile to foreign aid programs that promote democracy. But there is a fine line between a foreign policy that advocates human rights and democracy, and one that interferes in the internal affairs of other sovereign states. In President Clinton's 1997 report to Congress on the assistance that the United States and its allies might provide to Cuba during a transition, he went into considerable detail concerning political assistance to "help . . . in building essential democratic institutions" and "to help establish the policy, institutional and legal reforms necessary to stimulate the domestic private sector." The report envisioned U.S. and international aid to the legislature, judiciary, administrative bureaucracy, armed forces, police, and various institutions of civil society. Similar proposals are found in the May 2004 report of the Commission for Assistance to a Free Cuba that was submitted to President Bush.

U.S. government assistance of this sort comes through the Agency for International Development and the National Endowment for Democracy (NED), along with its affiliated institutes. But Washington does not have a good record of providing support to foreign democrats in a nonpartisan way. Which potential recipients are seen as democrats tends to be viewed through the lens of U.S. national interest. In the 1980s, for example, the Republican Institute for International Affairs sent almost half a million dollars to opponents of Costa Rican President Oscar Arias to finance their campaign against his Central American peace plan, which President Ronald Reagan opposed. During the 1990 Nicaraguan election, NED would only provide help to those opposition parties willing to conform to U.S. policy by joining the broad anti-Sandinista coalition cobbled together by the U.S. Embassy. More recently, over three-quarters of a million dollars from NED went into the coffers of opponents of Venezuelan President Hugo Chávez, some of whom were involved in the April 2002 attempted coup. Such examples suggest that political aid from the United States is not divorced from self-interest, and democracy is not always at the top of the policy agenda. It is overly optimistic to think this would be different in the case of post-transition Cuba. Already, rival U.S. organizations have identified their preferred dissidents within Cuba's fractious opposition movement.

One of the remarkable features of the democratic transitions in Central and Eastern Europe has been the resilience of the old communist parties, which reinvented themselves as social democrat and nationalist parties. The successor parties returned to power in Hungary and Bulgaria in 1994, Poland in 1995, and Albania in 1997. In Russia, after being banned in the wake of the attempted coup in 1991, the communists won a third of the seats in the Duma in 1995, making them the largest party. A set of complex causes lies behind the rebound of the deposed communist parties in Europe: (1) the parties' organizational advantages; (2) the availability of natural constituencies such as former party cadres, pensioners, and organized labor; (3) the grievances produced by the transition itself; and (4) the persistence among the population of a "socialist value culture" that favors state involvement in the economy and universal social services such as education and health care. The Cuban Communist Party would be well positioned to make a similar comeback in the aftermath of a transition to multiparty democracy. Its persistent strength might well become a point of significant friction in bilateral relations with the United States, much as the persistence of Sandinista strength in Nicaragua has cast a lingering shadow over relations with Managua.

In all likelihood, Cuban Americans will seek to play a role in transitional politics, and their actions will not be subject to central government control, either by Havana or Washington. While polls indicate that few Cuban Americans would return to live in their homeland, a great many retain an active interest in Cuban politics, and one can easily imagine efforts to mobilize them to support one or another political faction on the island. From the experience of transitional elections in Central and Eastern Europe, we know that a broad spectrum of political parties will emerge, perhaps dozens, and that these will be quickly winnowed down to just a handful of long-term contenders. Resources, especially money, will be a key determinant of which parties thrive and which whither away. The wealth of the Cuban American community, if even a small fraction of it were mobilized, could provide an enormous advantage to recipients on the island. This, in turn, could become a source of resentment. Perhaps the closest European parallel is the East German case, where pre-unification elections were effectively dominated by parties from the West. In the long-term, however, this dominance has sowed seeds of political discontent, as many easterners have come to feel that their society, their values, and their dignity have been trampled by their fellow citizens from the West, who they view as competitive, arrogant, and wealthy. One can imagine the emergence of a similar syndrome in Cuba, in which those who remained on the island come to resent the political influence that money can buy for Cuban Americans in absentia.

An independent poll conducted in 1994 by CID-Gallup found that although two out of three Cubans regarded Cubans abroad as "brothers," a third worried that the return of large numbers of exiles would bring "trouble." A University of Florida poll conducted in 1998–99 among new Cuban immigrants to the United States indicated that Cubans on the island worried that exiles might demand the return of their nationalized property. Needless to say, the property recovery provisions of the 1996 Helms-Burton law exacerbate such fears, which is one of the reasons that the Cuban government focused so much attention on the legislation. The government has also pointed to the racial disparity between the Cuban population as a whole and those who went into exile, most of whom were white. The social stress of the Special Period has noticeably increased racial tensions on the island, in part because so few Afro-Cubans have relatives abroad to bolster their standard of living with remittances.

Drug Trafficking, People-Smuggling, and Terrorism

As noted earlier, the Cuban state's capacity to control its national territory in the face of people smugglers and narcotics traffickers has diminished significantly since the 1990s. In a transition period, the security capacity of the state would be further diminished, at least temporarily. In Europe, post-communist societies routinely experienced a surge in crime when authoritarian controls were lifted. So the danger that Cuba might become a haven for organized crime and a way station for drug smuggling is real.

If a transition were to reduce law enforcement capacity on the island either because of the disruption of those agencies or their preoccupation with the threat of domestic social turmoil, drug traffickers on the island and abroad would have an easier entry. Cuba, after all, is perfectly positioned as a smuggling entrepôt. Cubans have been smuggling goods into the United States in violation of U.S. and Cuban (and before that, Spanish) law for more than two hundred years. During Prohibition, Cuba was one of the main sources of illegal liquor smuggled into the United States, which is how the American mafia first gained a foothold on the island. Smuggling, in turn, has contributed historically to corruption in Cuba, and the 1950s are notorious for the deals struck between U.S. organized crime and the Batista regime. During the transitions in Central and Eastern Europe, the propensity for corruption increased as outgoing officials sought to provide themselves with golden parachutes, and incoming officials were not always able to restrain themselves from taking private advantage of their new public authority. In the worst case, a debilitated Cuban government might find itself confronted with an alliance of international traffickers, domestic traffickers, and corrupt government officials.

The United States, therefore, has an emerging security interest in effective law enforcement agencies and military forces in Cuba, although it will not help to bolster these institutions or collaborate closely with them unless there is a regime transition. Even then, unless the existing Cuban military is demolished in the course of transition (which seems unlikely), residual suspicion is likely to delay the development of close relations between the uniformed services of the two countries. There is already some degree of cooperation between Cuba and the United States on the issue of narcotics trafficking. Both governments see it as a threat, although some conservatives in the United States remain unconvinced that the Cubans are truly interested in cooperation. A successor government would face the same skepticism until efforts at cooperation build mutual confidence. A regime transition, on the other hand, would dispel the mutual suspicions deriving from ideological hostility, but that is no guarantee that this issue will not become a matter of bilateral contention. A surge of drug trafficking through Cuba as a result of diminished state capacity and increased corruption could well lead to acute disillusionment among U.S. policy makers. Some of Washington's sharpest conflicts over the drug war have been with friendly countries like Mexico and Colombia, which Washington did not believe were doing enough to combat drugs. One can imagine that, for a transition government in Cuba, domestic political and economic issues will seem far more important than expending resources to fight drug trafficking.

In the event of a regime transition, the rationale for the Cuban Adjustment Act will disappear, and despite the support the law has in the Cuban American community, one has to assume that Cubans will come to be treated like immigrants from anywhere else. Pressures for migration could rise dramatically in the short term if a transition is economically and socially disruptive, especially if it is violent. In those circumstances, the ability of the Cuban government to control migration could be much reduced, setting the stage for another migration crisis akin to the Mariel boatlift of 1980 and the rafter crisis of 1994. In the long-run, the issue of migration will be a permanent one, as it is in bilateral relations between Mexico and the United States.

If a transitional government in Cuba is unable to control narcotics trafficking and people-smuggling into the United States, then Cuba will also be a potential entry point for terrorists. This danger is exacerbated to the extent that the Cuban economy continues to depend upon an expanding tourism sector that draws heavily on the European market. Terrorists could potentially masquerade as tourists to gain entry to Cuba. The solution to this security problem lies in close intelligence cooperation between the Cuban and U.S. governments, so that the United States can help the Cubans identify potential terrorists as they try to enter Cuba. The current animosity and distrust between Washington and Havana precludes this sort of cooperation, even though Havana has offered to cooperate in the global struggle against terrorism. Such suspicion would probably not be dissipated by a successor government in the absence of a regime transition.

Cuban Americans and U.S. Policy

In the aftermath of a transition, Cuban Americans would surely play a major role both in the formulation of U.S. policy and in the development of commercial relations. Even a successor government in Cuba that left the socialist regime intact would have the same incentives as the current government to continue building better ties with Cuban Americans. Once Fidel Castro has left the scene, such efforts at dialogue may become easier, since many exiles who left in the 1960s harbor a deeply personal animosity toward Castro, who they feel betrayed the Revolution. A diminution of Cuban American hostility toward a successor government would remove one obvious political obstacle to a less hostile U.S. policy.

Nevertheless, in the event of a regime transition in Cuba, the intensity of the Cuban American community's interest will almost surely complicate U.S. policy making, as it did during both the Mariel boatlift and rafter crises. On both those occasions, the desire of Cuban Americans to help their relatives led them to actively oppose U.S. government efforts to control the flow of refugees. If significant social violence were to accompany a transition, one can easily imagine pressure in the community to take unilateral action—such as sailing south to rescue friends and family trying to leave, as happened during Mariel—and to seek U.S. intervention on humanitarian grounds. During the Haitian crisis of the mid-1990s, pressure for humanitarian intervention from the African American community in the United States played an important role in President Clinton's decision to send U.S. troops to Haiti. Such an intervention in Cuba would be an extremely bad foundation for constructive relations. A new Cuban government installed at the point of U.S. bayonets would be tainted from the start by the reassertion of Washington's historic hegemony over the island—the same original sin that doomed successive post-independence governments from 1902 to 1959.

In the event of a transition to multiparty democracy, Cuban Americans will be strong advocates for a generous bilateral assistance program. But they may also be equally strong advocates for conditioning aid on compensation for expropriated property as called for in the Helms-Burton Act. As noted above, that conditionality could severely slow Washington's ability to respond to urgent economic need in Cuba, since sorting out the issue of compensation—even if there were no political resistance on the Cuba side—is likely to be a process lasting years, not months.

When political barriers between the two countries come down, Cuban Americans will be a natural economic bridge, providing the island with much needed foreign investment, managerial skill, and entrée to U.S. markets. Cuban Americans own more than 30,000 enterprises with annual sales of $24 billion, 70 percent of which are located in Florida. Already, remittances from Cuban Americans are an important source of start-up capital for small family businesses, both licensed and unlicensed. In the event of a transition, the Helms-Burton law calls for the president to designate a U.S.-Cuba Council "to ensure coordination between the United States Government and the private sector" to promote trade with Cuba and the creation of a market economy there. No doubt Cuban Americans will play a prominent role. But Cuban American economic resources carry risks as well. If Cuban Americans are perceived by Cubans on the island as carpetbaggers returning to buy up the island's productive assets, thus creating a dominant class of expatriates, they may sow the seeds of instability. One of the fatal weaknesses of the Cuban upper class before 1959 was the common perception that it was too closely tied to the United States, economically and culturally, and hence was an antinationalist force.

THE INESCAPABLE EMBRACE

The scenario of succession without regime transition is predicated on continuity with the past rather than an abrupt rupture from it. Things will not remain static, of course, but currently discernible processes of change will continue to shape the future in ways that are possible to project. The most salient of these processes include: the evolution of attitudes within the Cuban American community and the declining hegemony of the right; the growth of bilateral trade in food and medicine, and the consequent growth of U.S. business interest in commercial opportunities in Cuba; the coalescence of congressional majorities in favor of ending the travel ban and altering other aspects of the embargo; and the continuing need for Cuba to integrate its economy with the world market, which creates an imperative for reducing rather than exacerbating diplomatic hostility.

As these processes create a more favorable environment for improved U.S. relations with a successor government, Cuba could enhance the prospects for rapprochement by working to improve relations with the Cuban American community; cooperating with Washington on issues of mutual interest, such as narcotics, migration, and terrorism; undertaking further economic reforms; and beginning a process of political liberalization. Even then, normalization is likely to be a long and drawn out affair with stops and starts along the way.

A scenario of regime transition is necessarily more speculative because it posits a rupture with the past. Formal normalization is likely to come quickly, assuming that the rigid structures of Helms-Burton can be relaxed. But Washington's (and Miami's) euphoria may create unrealistic expectations for a problem-free future. U.S. aid is likely to be less than Cuba hopes, especially once the drama of transition fades. The property issue will be complex, difficult, and slow to resolve. The migration issue will not disappear, though Cubans are likely to lose their favored legal status. Problems of crime, drug trafficking, people-smuggling, and corruption may get worse before they get better. And the flood of U.S. influence—economic and political—could produce a nationalist backlash.

Someday, the imperative of geography will pull Cuba and the United States back into a close embrace. Will Cuba return to a relationship akin to that which existed before 1959, one of political and economic subordination? Or will Cuba be able to hold on to some degree of independence and autonomy, the hope for which was one of the motivating forces behind the Revolution? Democratically elected governments are often annoying to major powers because their leaders tend to respond to the political demands of their constituents more readily than to the demands of foreign powers, even hegemons. President Chamorro's insistence that peace in Nicaragua required reconciliation with the Sandinistas, not their suppression, was a constant source of tension between her government and Washington. A Cuban government produced by multiparty elections might prove equally aggravating across a range of policy issues. Will Washington be able to tolerate such conflicts with equanimity? The stringent demands of Helms-Burton suggest not.

Will Cuban Americans be a bridge between the two countries or yet another obstacle to the development of normal relations? The reunification of the Cuban family could be an occasion for recrimination and bitterness as well as joy. Cubans, no less than Salvadorans and Guatemalans, must make a conscious decision to seek reconciliation and look ahead toward cooperation rather than backward toward the settling of accounts.

In short, a Cuban political transition would transform U.S.-Cuban relations dramatically, but it will not automatically resolve old problems or avoid new ones. Both Havana and Washington have grown used to their minuet of acrimony, each playing its appointed role. A new relationship could hold the promise of reconciliation and partnership, but it will raise new challenges and conflicts that may surprise and disappoint those who think that the only thing dividing the two countries is Fidel Castro.

Bibliography

Alexander, Jeffrey C., ed. 1998. *Real Civil Societies: Dilemmas of Institutionalization.* London: Sage.

Alvarez Suárez, Mayda. 1996. "Mujer y poder en Cuba." *Temas* 5 (January–March): 4–10.

——— et al. 2000. "Situación de la mujer y la familia en Cuba." Havana: Centro de Estudios de la Mujer, Federación de Mujeres Cubanas.

Andrews, George Reid. 2004. *Afro-Latin America, 1800–2000.* New York: Oxford University Press.

Arato, Andrew. 2000. *Civil Society, Constitution and Legitimacy.* Oxford: Rowman & Littlefield.

Armed Forces and Society. 1997. Volume 25, no. 3 (Spring).

———. 2002. Volume 28, no. 3 (Spring).

Aslund, Anders. 2002. *Building Capitalism: The Transformation of the Former Soviet Bloc.* New York: Cambridge University Press.

Bailey, Stanley R. 2002. "The Race Construct and Public Opinion: Understanding Brazilian Beliefs about Racial Inequality and their Determinants." *American Journal of Sociology* 108, no. 2 (September): 406–39.

Barany, Zoltan. 1997. "Democratic Consolidation and the Military: The Eastern European Experience." *Comparative Politics* 30, no. 1: 21–43.

Bobes, Velia Cecilia, and Rafael Rojas. 2004. *La transición invisible: Sociedad y cambio político en Cuba.* Mexico City: Océano.

Burki, Shahid Javed, and Daniel P. Erikson, eds. 2005. *Transforming Socialist Economies: Lessons for Cuba and Beyond.* New York: Palgrave Macmillan.

Campuzano, Luisa. 1996. "Ser cubanas y no morir en el intento." *Temas* 5 (January–March): 4–10.

Carlson, Elwood, and Megumi Omori. 1998. "Fertility Regulation in a Declining State Socialist Economy: Bulgaria, 1976–1995." *International Family Planning Perspectives* 24, no. 4 (December): 184–87.

Carothers, Thomas. 2002. "The End of the Transition Paradigm." *Journal of Democracy* 3, no. 1 (January): 5–21.

Centro de Investigaciones Psicológicas y Sociológicas. 2001. *Familia y cambios socioeconómicos a las puertas del nuevo milenio*. Departamento de Estudios sobre Familia.

Chomsky, Aviva, Barry Carr, and Pamela Maria Smorkaloff, eds. 2004. *The Cuba Reader: History, Culture, and Politics*. Durham, NC: Duke University Press.

City of Havana Provincial People's Court. 1999. "The People of Cuba vs. the Government of the United States of America for Human Damages." http://www.cuba.cu/gobierno/documentos/1999/ing/d310599i.html.

Clemente Díaz, Tirso, and Olga Mesa Castillo. 2001. "El concepto de matrimonio en el código de familia de Cuba: Breve análisis desde el derecho romano." *Temas de derecho de Familia*. Edited by Olga Mesa Castillo. Havana: Editorial Félix Varela.

Comisión de Ayuda a una Cuba Libre. 2004. "Breve resumen: Reporte de la Comisión de Ayuda a una Cuba Libre presentado al presidente." Washington, DC: U.S. Department of State. http://usinfo.state.gov/espanol/cuba/04050605.htm.

Comité Central de Estadísticas and Oficina Nacional de Estadísticas. 2002. *Anuario estadístico de Cuba 1989–2001*. Havana.

Commission for Assistance to a Free Cuba. 2004. *Report to the President*. Washington, DC: U.S. Department of State. http://www.state.gov/p/wha/rt/cuba/commission/2004.

———. 2006. *Report to the President*. Washington, DC: U.S. Department of State. http://www.cafc.gov/cafc/rpt/2006/c18232.htm.

Constitución de Cuba. 1994. México: FCE/UNAM.

De Ferranti, David et al. 2004. *Latin America: Breaking with History?* Washington, DC: World Bank.

De la Fuente, Alejandro. 2001. *A Nation for All: Race, Inequality, and Politics in Twentieth-Century Cuba*. Chapel Hill: University of North Carolina Press.

Degtiar L. 2002. "The Transformation Process and the Status of Women (Based on the Example of Central and Eastern Europe)." *Russian Social Science Review* 43, no. 4 (July–August): 48–60.

Diamint, Rut. 2003. "The Military." *Constructing Democratic Governance in Latin America*. 2nd ed. Baltimore: Johns Hopkins University Press.

Diamint, Rut., ed. 1999. *Control civil y fuerzas armadas en las nuevas democracias latinoamericanas*. Buenos Aires: Universidad Torcuato Di Tella.

———. 2001. *Democracia y seguridad en América Latina*. Buenos Aires: Universidad Torcuato Di Tella.

Diamond, Larry Jay. 2002. "Thinking about Hybrid Regimes." *Journal of Democracy* 13, no. 2 (April): 21–35.

Domínguez, Jorge. 1989. "International and National Aspects of the Catholic Church in Cuba." *Cuban Studies* 19: 43–60.

————. 2003. *A Constitution for Cuba's Political Transition: The Utility of Retaining (and Amending) the 1992 Constitution.* Miami: Institute for Cuban and Cuban–American Studies, University of Miami.

Domínguez, Jorge, and Michael Shifter, eds. 2003. *Constructing Democratic Governance: Latin America and the Caribbean in the 1990s.* Baltimore: Johns Hopkins University Press.

Domínguez, María I., and María Elena Ferrer Buch. 1996. *Jóvenes cubanos: Expectativa en los 90.* Havana: Pinos Nuevos.

Espina Prieto, Mayra Paula. 2001. "The Effects of the Reform on Cuba's Social Structure: An Overview." *Socialism and Democracy* 15, no. 1 (Spring–Summer).

Evenson, Debra. 1994. *Revolution in the Balance: Law and Society in Contemporary Cuba.* Boulder, CO: Westview.

————. 2003. *Law and Society in Contemporary Cuba.* 2nd ed. The Hague: Kluwer Law International.

Eyal, Gil, Iván Szelényi, and Eleonor Townsley. 1998. *Making Capitalism without Capitalists. The New Ruling Elites in Eastern Europe.* New York: Verso.

Farer, Tom, ed. 1999. *Transnational Crime in the Americas: An Inter-America Dialogue Book.* New York: Routledge.

Federación de Mujeres Cubanas. 2002. *II Seminario Nacional de Evaluación. Plan de Acción Nacional de Seguimiento a la Conferencia de Beijing.* Havana.

Fernandes, Sujatha. 2003. "Fear of a Black Nation: Local Rappers, Transnational Crossings, and State Power in Contemporary Cuba." *Anthropological Quarterly* 76, no. 4 (Fall): 575–608.

Fernández, Damián J. 2000. *Cuba and the Politics of Passion.* Austin: University of Texas Press.

Fernández, Nadine T. 1996. "The Color of Love: Young Interracial Couples in Cuba." *Latin American Perspectives* 23, no. 1 (Winter): 99–117.

Fernández Retamar, Roberto, et al. 2003. *Cicatrices de la memoria: Terrorismo y desestabilización en Cuba.* Mexico City: Océano.

Gal, Susan, and Gail Kligman. 2000. *The Politics of Gender after Socialism: A Comparative-Historical Essay.* Princeton: Princeton University Press.

García, María Cristina. 1996. *Havana USA: Cuban Exiles and Cuban Americans in South Florida, 1959–1994.* Berkeley: University of California Press.

Ghai, Dharam, ed. 2000. *Social Development and Public Policy.* Geneva: UNRISD.

Githens, Marianne. 1996. "Reproductive Rights and the Struggle with Change in Eastern Europe." In *Abortion Politics: Public Policy in Cross-Cultural Perspective.* Edited by Marianne Githens and Dorothy McBride-Stetson. New York: Routledge.

Gotkowitz, Laura, and Richard Turits. 1988. "Socialist Morality, Sexual Preference, Family, and State Intervention in Cuba." *Socialism and Democracy* 6 (Spring–Summer).

Grenier, Guillermo J., and Lisandro Pérez. 2003. *The Legacy of Exile: Cubans in the United States.* Boston: Allyn & Bacon.

Gros, Daniel, and Marc Suhrcke. 2000. *Ten Years After: What Is Special about Transition Countries?* Working Paper No. 56. European Bank for Reconstruction and Development.

Grupo de Trabajo Memoria, Justicia y Verdad. 2003. *Cuba: La reconciliación nacional.* Miami: Latin American and Caribbean Center, Florida International University.

Horowitz, Irving Louis, and Jaime Suchlicki, eds. 2003. *Cuban Communism.* 11th ed. New Brunswick, NJ: Transaction.

Htun, Mala. 2003. *Sex and the State: Abortion, Divorce, and the Family under Latin American Dictatorships and Democracies.* New York: Cambridge University Press.

————. 2004. "From 'Racial Democracy' to Affirmative Action: Changing State Policy on Race in Brazil." *Latin American Research Review* 39, no. 1 (February): 60–89.

Hunter, Wendy. 1997. "Continuity or Change? Civil-Military Relations in Democratic Argentina, Chile, and Peru." *Political Science Quarterly* 112, no. 3: 453–75.

Huntington, Samuel P. 1991. *The Third Wave: Democratization in the Late Twentieth Century.* Norman: University of Oklahoma Press.

International Institute for Strategic Studies. 2002. *The Military Balance, 2002–2003.* London.

International Monetary Fund. 2001. "Transition Economies: How Much Progress?" *IMF Staff Papers* 48. Washington, DC.

Karatnycky, Adrian, Alexander J. Motyl, and Amanda Schnetzer, eds. 2001. *Nations in Transit 2001: Civil Society, Democracy and Markets in East Central Europe and the Newly Independent States.* New Brunswick, NJ: Transaction.

————. 2002. *Nations in Transit 2002: Civil Society, Democracy, and Markets in East Central Europe and the Newly Independent States.* New Brunswick, NJ: Transaction.

————. 2003. *Nations in Transit 2003: Democratization in East Central Europe and Eurasia.* New Brunswick, NJ: Transaction.

————. 2004. *Nations in Transit 2004: Democratization in East Central Europe and Eurasia.* New Brunswick, NJ: Transaction.

Kornbluh, Peter. 2000. "Cuba, Counternarcotics, and Collaboration: A Security Issue in U.S.-Cuban Relations." Cuba Briefing Paper No. 24. Washington, DC: Georgetown University.

Kotkin, Stephen. 2001. *Armageddon Averted: The Soviet Collapse, 1970–2000.* New York: Oxford University Press.

Linz, Juan J. 2000. *Totalitarian and Authoritarian Regimes.* Boulder, CO: Lynne Rienner.

Luciak, Ilja. 2000. "Gender Equality and Democratization in Cuba: Report to the European Union." Contract CA/B7–6110/2000/02. European Commission.

Masud-Piloto, Felix Roberto. 1996. *From Welcomed Exiles to Illegal Immigrants: Cuban Migration to the United States, 1959–1995*. Lanham, MD: Rowman & Littlefield.

McAdams, A. James. 1993. *Germany Divided: From the Wall to Reunification*. Princeton: Princeton University Press.

Mesa Castillo, Olga. 2001. "Adulterio y aborto: Tratamiento jurídico en Cuba." In *Temas de Derecho de Familia*. Edited by Olga Mesa Castillo. Havana: Félix Varela.

Mesa Castillo, Olga, Osvaldo M. Álvarez Torres, and Luis L. Palenzuela Páez. 2001. "Fundamentación de la necesidad de implementar en Cuba el derecho procesal de familia." In *Temas de Derecho de Familia*. Edited by Olga Mesa Castillo. Havana: Félix Varela.

Mesa-Lago, Carmelo. 2002. *Growing Economic and Social Disparities in Cuba: Impact and Recommendations for Change*. Miami: Institute for Cuban and Cuban American Studies, University of Miami.

Molyneux, Maxine. 1985. "Family Reform in Socialist States: The Hidden Agenda." *Feminist Review* 21 (Winter): 47–64.

Morley, Morris, and Chris McGillion. 2002. *Unfinished Business: America and Cuba after the Cold War, 1989–2001*. Cambridge: Cambridge University Press.

Nazarri, Muriel. 1983. "The 'Woman Question' in Cuba: An Analysis of Material Constraints on its Solution." *Signs: Journal of Women and Culture in Society* 9, no. 2 (Winter): 246–63.

Nelson, C. Richard, and Kenneth Weisbrode, eds. 1997. *Reversing Relations with Former Adversaries: U.S. Foreign Policy after the Cold War*. Gainesville: University of Florida Press.

Nesporova, Alena. 2002. "Unemployment in Transition Economies." *Economic Survey of Europe 2002*. Geneva: United Nations European Economic Commission. 75–91.

Núñez Sarmiento, Marta. 2001. "Cuban Strategies for Women's Employment in the 1990s: A Case Study of Professional Women." *Socialism and Democracy* 15, no. 1 (Spring–Summer): 41–64.

Patallo Sánchez, Laura. 2003. *Establishing the Rule of Law in Cuba*. Miami: Institute for Cuban and Cuban-American Studies, University of Miami.

———. 2003. *The Role of the Judiciary in a Post-Castro Cuba: Recommendations for Change*. Miami: Institute for Cuban and Cuban-American Studies, University of Miami.

Pérez, Lisandro. 1992. "Cuban Miami." In *Miami Now! Immigration, Ethnicity, and Social Change*. Edited by Guillermo J. Grenier and Alex Stepick III. Gainesville: University Press of Florida.

Pérez Firmat, Gustavo. 1994. *Life on the Hyphen: The Cuban-American Way.* Austin: University of Texas Press.

Pérez Sarduy, Pedro, and Jean Stubbs, eds. 2000. *Afro-Cuban Voices: On Race and Identity in Contemporary Cuba.* Gainesville: University Press of Florida.

Pérez-Stable, Marifeli. 1999. *The Cuban Revolution: Origins, Course, and Legacy.* 2nd ed. New York: Oxford University Press.

Poyo, Gerald E. 1989. *"With All, and for the Good of All": The Emergence of Popular Nationalism in the Cuban Communities of the United States, 1848–1898.* Durham: Duke University Press.

Preston, Julia, and Samuel Dillon. 2004. *Opening Mexico: The Making of a Democracy.* New York: Farrar, Straus and Giroux.

Pridham, George, and Attila Agh, eds. 2001. *Prospects for Democratic Consolidation in East-Central Europe.* New York: Manchester University Press.

República de Cuba. 1976. *Código de Familia.* Gobierno Revolucionario, República Socialista de Cuba. Bucaramanja: Ediciones Laher.

———. 1997. *Plan de Acción Nacional de Seguimiento a la Conferencia de Beijing.* Havana. Photocopy.

Sanders, Ed, and Patrick Long. 2002. *Economic Benefits to the United States from Lifting the Ban on Travel to Cuba.* Washington, DC: Cuba Policy Foundation. http://www.cubafoundation.org/CPF%20Cuba%20Travel%20Study.htm.

Schedler, Andreas, and Javier Santiso, eds. 1999. *Tiempo y democracia.* Caracas, Venezuela: Nueva Sociedad.

Schwartz, Herman. 2000. *The Struggle for Constitutional Justice in Post-Communist Europe.* Chicago: University of Chicago Press.

Sen, Amartya. 2000. *Development as Freedom.* New York: Anchor Books.

Smith, Lois, and Alfred Padula. 1996. *Sex and Revolution: Women in Socialist Cuba.* New York: Oxford University Press.

Smith, Peter H. 2005. *Democracy in Latin America: Political Change in Comparative Perspective.* New York: Oxford University Press.

Smith, Wayne S., and Esteban Morales Domínguez, eds. 1988. *Subject to Solution: Problems in Cuban-U.S. Relations.* Boulder, CO: Lynne Rienner.

Stepan, Alfred. 1988. *Rethinking Military Politics: Brazil and the Southern Cone.* Princeton: Princeton University Press.

Stiglitz, Joseph E. 2001. *Globalization and Its Discontents.* New York: Norton.

Stone, Elizabeth, ed. 1981. *Women and the Cuban Revolution: Speeches and Documents by Fidel Castro, Vilma Espín and Others.* New York: Pathfinder.

Stoner, K. Lynn. 1991. *From the House to the Streets: The Cuban Women's Movement for Legal Reform, 1898–1940.* Durham: Duke University Press.

Svejnar, Jan. 2002. "Transition Economies: Performance and Challenges." *Journal of Economic Perspectives* 16, no. 1: 3–28.

Tellez, Edward. 2004. *Race in Another America: The Significance of Skin Color in Brazil.* Princeton: Princeton University Press.

Torres, María de los Angeles. 1999. *In the Land of Mirrors: Cuban Exile Politics in the United States.* Ann Arbor: University of Michigan Press.

Transparency International. 2005. *Global Corruption Report 2005.* London: Pluto.

Travieso-Díaz, Matías. 1997. *The Laws and Legal System of a Free-Market Cuba.* Westport, CT: Quorum Books.

Tribunal Provincial Popular de Ciudad de La Habana. 1999. "Demanda del pueblo de Cuba al gobierno de los Estados Unidos por daños humanos." *Granma* 3 (Noviembre): http://www.granma.cubaweb.cu/secciones/verdad/a018htm.

Tulchin, Joseph S., Lilian Bobea, Mayra P. Espina Prieto, and Rafael Hernández, eds. 2005. *Changes in Cuban Society Since the Nineties.* Washington, DC: Woodrow Wilson Center for International Scholars.

United Nations Development Program. 2002. *Human Development Report 2002.* Oxford: Oxford University Press.

———. 2004. *Democracy in Latin America: Towards a Citizens' Democracy.* Buenos Aires: Aguilar, Altea, Taurus, Alfaguara.

United States Agency for International Development. 1997. "Support for a Democratic Transition in Cuba." ["Apoyo para una transición democrática en Cuba"] Washington, DC: USAID.

United States International Trade Commission. 2001. *The Economic Impact of U.S. Sanctions with Respect to Cuba.* Publication 3398. Washington, DC.

Walker, Phyllis. 2002. "National Security." In *Cuba: A Country Study.* Edited by Rex A. Hudson. Area Handbook Series. Washington, DC: U.S. Government Printing Office.

Whitehead, Laurence. 2002. *Democratization: Theory and Experience.* Oxford: Oxford University Press.

Wolchik, Sharon. 1979. "The Status of Women in a Socialist Order: Czechoslovakia, 1948–1978." *Slavic Review* 38, no. 4 (December): 583–602.

World Bank. 1996. *From Plan to Market: World Development Report 1996.* New York: Oxford University Press.

———. 2002. *Transition: The First Ten Years—Analysis and Lessons for Eastern Europe and the Former Soviet Union.* Washington, DC: International Bank for Reconstruction and Development/World Bank.

———. 2003. *World Development Report 2003.* New York: Oxford University Press.

Contributors

GUSTAVO ARNAVAT is a Director and Senior Legal Counsel for the Latin America market region of the private bank division of one of the largest financial institutions in the world. Based in New York, he focuses primarily on capital markets, investment management, and commercial banking issues. He has also acquired extensive corporate finance, joint venture, and mergers and acquisitions experience throughout Latin America both as a lawyer and a banker. He has been an observer of Cuban legal and economic issues for many years and is a frequent contributor on such issues as a member of the Association for the Study of the Cuban Economy.

JORGE I. DOMÍNGUEZ is the Antonio Madero Professor of Mexican and Latin American Politics and Economics and Vice Provost for International Affairs at Harvard University. He is co-editor and chapter author of *The Cuban Economy at the Start of the Twenty-First Century* (Harvard University Press, 2004) and *Mexico's Pivotal Democratic Election: Candidates, Voters, and the Presidential Campaign of 2000* (Stanford University Press, 2004). He is also a past president of the Latin American Studies Association.

DANIEL P. ERIKSON is Senior Associate for U.S. Policy and Director of Caribbean programs at the Inter-American Dialogue in Washington, DC, where his work focuses on U.S. foreign policy challenges in the Western Hemisphere. He is co-editor of *Transforming Socialist Economies: Lessons for Cuba and Beyond* (Palgrave Macmillan, 2005).

DAMIÁN J. FERNÁNDEZ is Director of the Cuban Research Institute and Professor of International Relations at Florida International University (FIU) in Miami. He is Vice Provost of FIU's Biscayne Bay campus and the principal investigator of the National Science Foundation–funded project on Civic and

Place Engagement in Latino Neighborhoods in Transition. He is the author of *Cuba and the Politics of Passion* (University of Texas Press, 2000), the co-editor of *Cuba, the Elusive Nation: Reinterpretations of National Identity* (University Press of Florida, 2000), and the editor of *Cuba Transnational* (University Press of Florida, 2005).

ALEJANDRO DE LA FUENTE is Associate Professor of Latin American and Caribbean History at the University of Pittsburgh. He is the author of *A Nation for All: Race, Inequality, and Politics in Twentieth-Century Cuba* (University of North Carolina Press, 2001), which has been published in Spanish as *Una nación para todos: raza, desigualdad y política en Cuba, 1900–2000* (Editorial Colibrí, 2001), and editor of "Su único derecho: los esclavos y la ley" ["Their Only Right: Slaves and the Law"], which appeared in *Debate y Perspectivas* 4 (Fundación Mapfre-Tavera, 2004).

MALA HTUN is Associate Professor of Political Science at the New School for Social Research. She is the author of *Sex and the State: Abortion, Divorce, and the Family under Latin American Dictatorships and Democracies* (Cambridge University Press, 2003). Her current research focuses on the political representation of women and ethnic and racial minorities in Latin America and worldwide.

WILLIAM M. LEOGRANDE is Dean of the School of Public Affairs at American University in Washington, DC. He has written widely in the field of Latin American politics and United States foreign policy, with a particular emphasis on Central America and Cuba. Most recently, he is the author of *Our Own Backyard: The United States in Central America, 1977–1992* (University of North Carolina Press, 1998).

CARMELO MESA-LAGO is Distinguished Service Professor Emeritus of Economics and Latin American Studies at the University of Pittsburgh. Former President of the Latin American Studies Association and founder of the journal *Cuban Studies*, he is the author of 74 books and 240 articles and chapters, among them *Market, Socialist and Mixed Economies: Economic Policy and Performance—Chile, Costa Rica and Cuba* (Johns Hopkins University Press, 2000) and *Cuba's Aborted Reform: Socioeconomic Effects, International Comparisons and Transition Policies*, with Jorge F. Pérez-López (University Press of Florida, 2005).

LISANDRO PÉREZ is Professor of Sociology at Florida International University (FIU). His research and publications have focused primarily on the Cuban presence in the United States. He is the coauthor of *The Legacy of Exile: Cubans in the United States* (Allyn & Bacon, 2003). From 1999 to 2004, he served as the editor of the journal *Cuban Studies*. For twelve years, he was the Director of FIU's Cuban Research Institute, which he founded in 1991.

JORGE F. PÉREZ-LÓPEZ is an international economist who has conducted research and written on many aspects of the Cuban economy, including national income accounting, energy issues, and foreign trade and investment. His most recent book, coauthored with José Alvarez, is *Reinventing the Cuban Sugar Agroindustry* (Lexington Books, 2005).

MARIFELI PÉREZ-STABLE is Vice President for Democratic Governance at the Inter-American Dialogue in Washington, DC, and Professor of Sociology at Florida International University in Miami. She is an editorial contributor for the *Miami Herald;* her column on Latin American topics, which *Tiempos del Mundo* subsequently translates and publishes, appears every other Thursday. She is the author of *The Cuban Revolution: Origins, Course, and Legacy* (Oxford University Press, 2nd edition, 1999); a Spanish-language edition has been published by Editorial Colibrí (1998). She chaired the Task Force on Memory, Truth, and Justice, which issued the report *Cuban National Reconciliation* in April 2003 (http://memoria.fiu.edu).

RAFAEL ROJAS is an editorial board member and former Codirector (2002–2006) of the magazine *Encuentro de la Cultura Cubana* and Professor and Investigator at the Centro de Investigación y Docencia Económicas in Mexico City. His most recent books include *La transición invisible: sociedad y cambio político en Cuba* (Océano, 2004) and *Fernando Ortiz: el diálogo de las culturas* (Fondo de Cultura Económica, 2005).

Index

Marifeli Pérez-Stable

is professor of sociology and anthropology at Florida International University and vice president for democratic governance at Inter-American Dialogue. She is author and editor of a number of books, including *The Cuban Revolution: Origins, Course, and Legacy.*